GW01507660

Nature, Action and the Future

Climate change is the great challenge of modern politics. In this volume, leading political theorists and historians investigate how the history of political ideas can help us make sense of it. The contributors add a historical perspective to contemporary debates in political theory. They also show that the history of political thought offers new directions for thinking about the environment today. By situating the relationship between humans and nature within a wider history of ideas, the essays provide alternative ways of thinking about the most intractable problems of environmental politics: the status of science in modern democracies, problems of collective action and the challenges of fatalism.

This volume will create new avenues of research for scholars and students in political theory and the history of political thought. It is essential reading for undergraduate students interested in environmental challenges: both those in politics seeking a historical perspective and those in history who want to link their studies to the present.

KATRINA FORRESTER is Assistant Professor of Government and Social Studies at Harvard University.

SOPHIE SMITH is Associate Professor of Political Theory at the University of Oxford.

Nature, Action and the Future

Political Thought and the Environment

Edited by

Katrina Forrester
Harvard University

Sophie Smith
University of Oxford

CAMBRIDGE
UNIVERSITY PRESS

CAMBRIDGE
UNIVERSITY PRESS

University Printing House, Cambridge CB2 8BS, United Kingdom

One Liberty Plaza, 20th Floor, New York, NY 10006, USA

477 Williamstown Road, Port Melbourne, VIC 3207, Australia

314–321, 3rd Floor, Plot 3, Splendor Forum, Jasola District Centre,
New Delhi – 110025, India

79 Anson Road, #06–04/06, Singapore 079906

Cambridge University Press is part of the University of Cambridge.

It furthers the University's mission by disseminating knowledge in the pursuit of
education, learning, and research at the highest international levels of excellence.

www.cambridge.org
Information on this title: www.cambridge.org/9781107199286
DOI: 10.1017/9781108185509

© Cambridge University Press 2018

First published 2018

Printed in the United Kingdom by Clays, St Ives plc

A catalogue record for this publication is available from the British Library.

ISBN 978-1-107-19928-6 Hardback

Cambridge University Press has no responsibility for the persistence or accuracy
of URLs for external or third-party internet websites referred to in this publication
and does not guarantee that any content on such websites is, or will remain,
accurate or appropriate.

For our mothers,
Lisa Appignanesi and Cindy Smith

Contents

List of Figures   *page* ix
List of Contributors   x
Acknowledgements   xi

1   History, Theory and the Environment   1
KATRINA FORRESTER AND SOPHIE SMITH

Part I   Time, Nature and the Land   21

2   Is There Any Place for Environmental Thinking in
Early Modern European Political Thought?   23
ANNABEL BRETT

3   'Sustainability', Resources and the Destiny of States
in German Cameralist Thought   43
PAUL WARDE

4   Abundance and Scarcity in Geological Time, 1784–1844   70
FREDRIK ALBRITTON JONSSON

5   Slack   94
MALCOLM BULL

Part II   Science, Agency and the Future   113

6   The Nature of Fear and the Fear of Nature from Hobbes
to the Hydrogen Bomb   115
DEBORAH R. COEN

7   Between Frankfurt and Vienna: Two Traditions of Political
Ecology   133
JOHN O'NEILL AND THOMAS UEBEL

8   Uncertainty, Action and Politics: The Problem of Negligibility   157
    MELISSA LANE

9   What Kind of Problem Is Negligibility? A Response to
    Melissa Lane   180
    RICHARD TUCK

10 Optimism, Pessimism and Fatalism   202
    DAVID RUNCIMAN

    Afterword: Climate Change in the Light of the Past   221
    QUENTIN SKINNER

    Index   231

Figures

4.1 Thomas Sopwith, "The small Forest of Dean model." *page* 71

Contributors

ANNABEL BRETT Gonville and Caius College, University of Cambridge

MALCOLM BULL The Ruskin School of Art, University of Oxford

DEBORAH R. COEN Yale University

KATRINA FORRESTER Harvard University

FREDRIK ALBRITTON JONSSON The University of Chicago

MELISSA LANE Princeton University

JOHN O´NEILL The University of Manchester

DAVID RUNCIMAN Trinity Hall, University of Cambridge

QUENTIN SKINNER Queen Mary University of London

SOPHIE SMITH University College, University of Oxford

RICHARD TUCK Harvard University

THOMAS UEBEL The University of Manchester

PAUL WARDE Pembroke College, University of Cambridge

Acknowledgements

We would like to thank the individuals and the institutions that helped us with this book. The essays were first delivered as papers at the Philomathia Conference on Political Thought and the Environment in May 2012 at the University of Cambridge's Faculty of History and Trinity Hall. For supporting that event, we are grateful above all to the Philomathia Foundation, particularly Wilfred Chung, without whom it would not have been possible, as well as to the Arts and Humanities Research Council, the Faculty of History's Graduate Training Fund, the George Macaulay Treveleyan Fund and to Trinity Hall.

For their guidance then and since, we are indebted to Annabel Brett and David Runciman, who helped to turn an idea into reality. Our further thanks are due to Duncan Bell, Christopher Brooke, Joel Isaac, Emma Jones, Duncan Kelly, Quentin Skinner and Greg Zucker for their help and advice, and to Dominic O'Mahony, who assisted in all kinds of ways in the lead-up to and during the conference itself. We are especially grateful to Jane Bennett, Simon Caney, Sarah Fine, Vincent Geoghegan, Bob Goodin and John Roemer for participating in the conference and for their parts in making it such a stimulating two days. Caroline Diepeveen provided the index and Alice Spawls designed the image we used on the cover; we owe them both a debt of gratitude. Thanks also to Jamie Martin and Amia Srinivasan for their support in this, as in everything. It is a pleasure, finally, to be able to thank our contributors for their patience and for such an excellent set of papers, and to John Haslam, Laura Blake and two anonymous reviewers at Cambridge University Press for their enthusiasm and feedback.

1 History, Theory and the Environment

Katrina Forrester and Sophie Smith *

Climate change is the great challenge of modern politics. Much of its difficulty lies in its novelty: nothing quite like it has ever happened before. Though it seems certain that things will get bad, no one yet knows exactly how bad, and in which ways. Unprecedented global inequality, mass migration, instability, war and total social breakdown all seem possible. Without a historical precedent, climate change campaigners say, we must act now to avoid the worst.

Yet climate change can also be made to look familiar. Worries about dramatic changes in the natural world are certainly not new, and neither is the fear of natural disasters. Ancient earthquakes, biblical floods, millenarian visions of the end of days: there have always been ideas of an uncertain, unknowable 'Nature' capable of destroying cities and hastening the onset of the apocalypse. The more recent history of environmental politics is likewise filled with prophecies of doom – predictions of nuclear winters and population bombs that have not, so far, been proven right. Though such analogies are generally strained, they have been put to effective political use in dismissing and downplaying the importance of climate change.

There may be no straightforward historical analogy for climate change. But this does not mean that history cannot help. Contemporary environmental discourse is largely a product of the growth of environmental politics since the Second World War. But many of the concerns that now belong to 'environmental', 'ecological' or 'green' political thought have longer lineages, which sometimes have little to do with 'environmental' ways of thinking. Ideas that today are central to environmental politics in general and to climate change in particular – about resource use, collective action or expertise – often have their origins in debates that are not exclusively ecological or environmental but part of the broader history of social, political and economic thought.

* The authors would like to thank Emma Jones, Jamie Martin, David Runciman, Quentin Skinner and Amia Srinivasan for their feedback on this chapter.

1

This book is about how that history can be used to help make sense of current environmental dilemmas. It both traces the history of political thinking about environmental problems and charts the history of specific ideas that are central to the politics of the particular environmental predicament that is climate change. It works in two temporal registers, addressing problems that have become important to politics only very recently, while also examining the deep roots of the ideas and assumptions that frame discussion of these problems today.

In this introductory chapter, we lay out some of the ways that the history of political thought can contribute to existing histories of environmental ideas on the one hand, and to current debates in environmental political theory on the other. Environmental history has flourished as a field in the last decades.[1] There is a vast literature that charts how the natural world has shaped, enabled and been moulded by the development of modern politics, political economy and culture, and there are now both regional and global histories of the environment and environmental histories of most parts of the globe.[2] Environmental historians

---

[1] For classic surveys of the field, see S. P. Hays, *Explorations in Environmental History* (Pittsburgh: University of Pittsburgh Press, 1998); C. Merchant, *American Environmental History: An Introduction* (New York: Columbia University Press, 2007); J. R. McNeill, 'Observations on the Nature and Culture of Environmental History', *History and Theory* 42 (2003), 5–43; J. D. Hughes, *What Is Environmental History?* (Malden, MA: Polity Press, 2006). For climate history, see D. Chakrabarty, 'The Climate of History: Four Theses', *Critical Inquiry* 35 (2009), 197–222.

[2] Influential regional studies include D. Worster, *Dust Bowl: The Southern Plains in the 1930s* (New York: Oxford University Press, 1979), 3–8; W. Cronon, *Changes in the Land: Indians, Colonists, and the Ecology of New England* (New York: Hill and Wang, 1983), 19–20, 75–79, 165–170; W. Cronon, *Nature's Metropolis: Chicago and the Great West* (New York: W. W. Norton, 1991); D. Arnold and R. Guha (eds), *Nature, Culture and Imperialism: Essays on the Environmental History of South Asia* (Oxford: Oxford University Press, 1996); J. McCann, *Maize and Grace: Africa's Encounter with a New World Crop, 1500–2000* (Cambridge, MA: Harvard University Press, 2005); J. Tropp, *Natures of Colonial Change: Environmental Relations in the Making of the Transkei* (Athens: Ohio University Press, 2006); D. Blackbourn, *The Conquest of Nature: Water, Landscape, and the Making of Modern Germany* (New York: W. W. Norton, 2006); J. Weaver, *The Great Land Rush and the Making of the Modern World, 1650–1900* (Montreal: McGill-Queen's University Press, 2003). On scale in environmental history, see R. White, 'The Nationalization of Nature', *Journal of American History* 86 (1999), 976–986; S. Amrith, *Crossing the Bay of Bengal: The Furies of Nature and the Fortunes of Migrants* (Cambridge, MA: Harvard University Press, 2013). For surveys of and new directions in global environmental history, see J. R. McNeill, *Something New under the Sun: An Environmental History of the Twentieth-Century World* (New York: W. W. Norton, 2000); P. Sutter, 'What Can U.S. Environmental Historians Learn from Non-U.S. Environmental Historiography?' *Environmental History* 8 (2003), 109–129. A. Hornborg, J. R. McNeill and J. Martinez-Alier (eds.), *Rethinking Environmental History: World-System History and Global Environmental Change* (Lanham, MD: Altamira, 2007); E. Burke III and K. Pomeranz (eds.), *Environment and World History* (Berkeley: University of California Press, 2009); J. D. Hughes, *An Environmental History of the World* (London: Routledge, 2009); I. G. Simmons, *Global Environmental History* (Chicago: University of Chicago Press, 2008). For classic and more recent histories of the climate, see E. Le Roy Ladurie, *Times of Feast, Times of Famine: A History of Climate since the Year 1000* (Garden

have tended to treat the study of environmental thought as part of their broader efforts to understand the ways that humans relate to and are shaped by the land; related histories of environmental ideas have tended to focus on ideas of ecology or nature.[3] As such, their engagement with political theory as a distinctive field of inquiry has often been limited.[4] By contrast, ethicists and political theorists preoccupied by environmental problems rarely engage directly with the history of those problems. Only recently have intellectual histories begun to be written that bring together political theory with the history of environmental ideas.[5] In what follows, we suggest how this project might continue.

The first section of this introduction looks at how environmental ideas are currently understood in history and theory. The second section introduces the approach taken in this book, which tries to place environmental ideas into a wider political, economic and philosophical context. We do so by identifying a number of themes that not only are key to environmental and climate politics today, but also have been central problems for much of the history of political thought: concerns about nature, economics, scientific knowledge, political action and the future.

I

The ideas that dominate environmental discourse today are the product of the dramatic rise of environmental politics in the twentieth century. 'Environment' is an old term that acquired its modern meaning in the

---

City, NY: Doubleday, 1971); G. Parker, *Global Crisis: War, Climate Change and Catastrophe in the Seventeenth Century* (New Haven: Yale University Press, 2013).

[3] R. F. Nash, *Wilderness and the American Mind* (New Haven: Yale University Press, 1967); C. Glacken, *Traces on the Rhodian Shore: Nature and Culture in Western Thought from Ancient Times to the End of the Eighteenth Century* (Berkeley: University of California Press, 1967); S. L. Flader, *Thinking Like a Mountain: Aldo Leopold and the Evolution of an Ecological Attitude toward Deer, Wolves and Forests* (Columbia: University of Missouri Press, 1974). D. Worster, *Nature's Economy: A History of Ecological Ideas* (San Francisco: Sierra Club Books, 1977) and C. Merchant, *Reinventing Eden: The Fate of Nature in Western Culture* (London and New York: Routledge, 2003).

[4] On the place of theory in general within environmental history, see D. Worster, 'Appendix: Doing Environmental History', in D. Worster (ed.), *The Ends of the Earth: Perspectives on Modern Environmental History* (Cambridge: Cambridge University Press, 1988), 289–307; J. Donald Hughes, 'Three Dimensions of Environmental History', *Environment and History* 14 (2008), 319–330.

[5] D. Winch, 'Thinking Green, Nineteenth-Century Style: John Stuart Mill and John Ruskin', in M. Bevir and F. Trentmann (eds.), *Markets in Historical Contexts: Ideas and Politics in the Modern World* (Cambridge: Cambridge University Press, 2004), 105–128; M. Lane, *Eco-Republic: What the Ancients Can Teach Us about Ethics, Virtue, and Sustainable Living* (Princeton: Princeton University Press, 2011); E. Rothschild, 'Introduction to Forum: The Idea of Sustainability', *Modern Intellectual History* 8 (2011), 147–151; F. A. Jonsson, *Enlightenment's Frontier: The Scottish Highlands and the Origins of Environmentalism* (New Haven: Yale University Press, 2013); J. Purdy, *After Nature: A Politics for the Anthropocene* (Cambridge, MA: Harvard University Press, 2015).

1940s, when it came to be used to 'describe the human interface with the planet and nature and all its life-sustaining processes'.[6] But the explosion of environmental politics – at the level of both social movements and government – was in large part a postwar phenomenon. In those years, concern with the environment in both Western Europe and the United States grew steadily, reaching a new height in the 1960s and early 1970s.[7] An era in which the relationship of politics and nature had been characterized by ideas of conservation gave way to one underpinned by new holistic understandings of an interdependent nature, and the environment as a complex system to be protected and regulated.[8] The publication of Rachel Carson's *Silent Spring* in 1962 and the celebration of Earth Day in 1970 have long been understood as symbols of this new environmental consciousness, which itself underpinned local and international campaigns – around issues of pollution, pesticide abuse and resource exploitation – that issued in a new wave of environmental law-making and internationalist mobilization. The 1972 United Nations Stockholm Conference on the Human Environment marked the beginning of a period in which global environmental diplomacy had some success – most notably with chlorofluorocarbon (CFC) reduction and the protection of the ozone layer in the 1980s and 1990s.[9]

Even as environmental politics in general was met with increasing enthusiasm, the objects of its concern were changing. The 1972 Club

[6] Chapter 3 in this volume; L. Robin, S. Sorlin and P. Warde, *The Future of Nature: Documents of Global Change* (New Haven: Yale University Press, 2013). For a pioneering use of 'environment' as a historical category, see the 1966 amendment to Fernand Braudel's *The Mediterranean and the Mediterranean World in the Age of Philip II*, 'Has the Climate Changed since the Sixteenth Century?', in F. Braudel, *The Mediterranean and the Mediterranean World in the Age of Philip II* (Berkeley: University of California Press, 1995), vol. I, 267–275.
[7] For environmental politics in the United States, see N. M. Maher, *Nature's New Deal: The Civil Conservation Corps and the Roots of the American Environmental Movement* (Oxford: Oxford University Press, 2008); A. Rome, '"Give Earth a Chance": The Environmental Movement and the Sixties', *The Journal of American History* 90 (2003), 525–554; in Europe, see C. Rootes (ed.), *Environmental Protest in Western Europe* (Oxford: Oxford University Press, 2003); S. Milder, 'Thinking Globally, Acting (Trans-) Locally: Petra Kelly and the Transnational Roots of West German Green Politics', *Central European History* 43 (2010), 301–326; H. Nehrin, 'Genealogies of the Ecological Moment: Planning, Complexity and the Emergence of the "Environment" as Politics in West Germany, 1949–1982', in S. Solin and P. Warde (eds.), *Nature's End: History and the Environment* (London: Palgrave Macmillan, 2009), 115–138; and for a survey of 'global' environmentalism, see J. McCormick, *Reclaiming Paradise: The Global Environmental Movement* (Bloomington: Indiana University Press, 1991).
[8] S. P. Hays, *A History of Environmental Politics since 1945* (Pittsburgh: University of Pittsburgh Press, 2000).
[9] J. R. McNeill, 'The Environment, Environmentalism, and International Society in the Long 1970s', in N. Ferguson, C. S. Maier, E. Manela and D. J. Sargent (eds.), *The Shock of the Global: The 1970s in Perspective* (Cambridge, MA: Harvard University Press, 2010), 263–278.

of Rome report *The Limits to Growth* marked a high point of anxieties about global overpopulation, but the neo-Malthusianism that had been a key feature of the new environmentalism faded from view by the decade's end.[10] Worries about resource depletion became widespread following the famines and spiralling oil prices in the 1970s. The perceived energy crises in turn confirmed the belief that the postwar nation-state was suffering a crisis of legitimacy; the lasting consequences of that decade were mistrust in government, environmental deregulation and a further enabling of anti-statist strains of environmentalism.[11] When in the 1980s the radical, ecological politics of the previous decade was domesticated and fears of apocalyptic catastrophe waned (or were channelled into renewed anxieties about nuclear war), the language and paradigms of contemporary environmentalism were born. The idea of 'sustainability', for instance – a word that came into use in the 1970s – was enshrined by the report of the UN's Brundtland Commission, *Our Common Future*, in 1987.[12] Global warming became an object to be studied by the new 'global change' research community, and the idea of the 'Anthropocene' – a new era in which humans were the agents of geological change – was first proposed.[13] Climate change became the new disaster to be feared.

---

[10] D. H. Meadows, D. L. Meadows, J. Randers and W. W. Behrens III, *The Limits to Growth: A Report for the Club of Rome's Project on the Predicament of Mankind* (New York: Universe Books, 1972). See also the second report to the Club of Rome two years later, M. Mesarovic and E. Pestel, *Mankind at the Turning Point: The Second Report to the Club of Rome* (New York: E. P Dutton, 1974). For the 'limits to growth' debate, see F. Sandbach, 'The Rise and Fall of the Limits to Growth Debate', *Social Studies of Science* 8 (1978), 495–520; M. Schoijet, 'Limits to Growth and the Rise of Catastrophism', *Environmental History* 4 (1999), 515–530. For international population politics and neo-Malthusianism, see A. Bashford, *Global Population: History, Geopolitics and Life on Earth* (New York: Columbia University Press, 2014); A. Bashford and J. Chaplin, *The New Worlds of Thomas Malthus: Rereading the Principle of Population* (Princeton: Princeton University Press, 2016), and its American incarnation, T. Robertson, *Global Population Growth and the Birth of American Environmentalism* (New Brunswick, NJ: Rutgers University Press, 2012).

[11] Ferguson et al., *The Shock of the Global*; M. Jacobs, *Panic at the Pump: The Energy Crisis and the Transformation of American Politics in the 1970s* (New York: Hill & Wang, 2016); J. M. Turner, '"The Specter of Environmentalism": Wilderness, Environmental Politics and the Evolution of the New Right', *Journal of American History* 96 (2009), 123–149.

[12] P. Warde, 'The Invention of Sustainability', *Modern Intellectual History* 8 (2011), 153–170; The World Commission on Environment and Development, *Our Common Future* (Oxford: Oxford University Press, 1987). For a critical view of the Brundtland report, see P. Anker, 'The Economic Fix: The Norwegian Approach to Climate Change' (unpublished paper presented at Workshop on Historicizing Climate Change, Princeton, May 2014).

[13] Robin et al, *The Future of Nature*, 4–5; S. L. Lewis and M. A Maslin, 'Defining the Anthropocene', *Nature* 519 (2015), 171–180; W. Steffen, J. Grinevald, P. Crutzen and J. McNeill, 'The Anthropocene: Conceptual and Historical Perspectives', *Philosophical*

These transformations in environmental politics since the 1960s led to a corresponding increase in academic interest in environmental problems. Environmental history became a flourishing field. Its proponents tracked the role of nature in shaping human history, examined the blurred lines between nature and culture and explored how those categories were weaponized in imperial contexts.[14] Gradually, many other historians – of science, economics or culture – came to take on board the insights of this new history.[15] The intellectual histories that came out of this period of transformation tended, like the environmental politics which prompted them, to use an ecological lens. They drew on what became a familiar and canonical tradition of thinkers – first and foremost Henry David Thoreau and Ralph Waldo Emerson – and historicized the conservationist and ecological strands of twentieth-century thought.[16] Though environmental historians certainly challenged the idea at the heart of much popular environmentalism – that 'nature' and 'wilderness' are normative goods that stand apart from humanity – such ideas (in their newly historicized forms) still stood at the centre of histories of environmental ideas, which

Transaction of the Royal Society A 369 (2011), 842–867; J. McNeill and P. Engelke, *The Great Acceleration: An Environmental History of the Anthropocene since 1945* (Cambridge, MA: Harvard University Press, 2016).

[14] D. Arnold, *The Problem of Nature: Environment, Culture and European Expansion* (Oxford: Blackwell, 1996); R. Drayton, *Nature's Government: Science, Imperial Britain and the 'Improvement' of the World* (New Haven: Yale University Press, 2000); P. Anker, *Imperial Ecology: Environmental Order in the British Empire, 1895–1945* (Cambridge, MA: Harvard University Press, 2002); A. Crosby, *Ecological Imperialism: The Biological Expansion of Europe, 900–1900* (Cambridge: Cambridge University Press, 2004); W. Beinart and L. Hughes, *Environment and Empire* (Oxford: Oxford University Press, 2007); J. R. McNeill, *Mosquito Empires: Ecology and War in the Greater Caribbean 1620–1914* (Cambridge: Cambridge University Press, 2010); R. White, *Railroaded: The Transcontinentals and the Making of Modern America* (New York: W.W. Norton, 2011). For a helpful recent discussion of two distinctive approaches within US environmental history, see J. Specht, 'Finding Its Way: Thoughts on Environmental History', www.processhistory.org/finding-its-way-thoughts-on-environmental-history (accessed 20 July 2016). For the foundational texts for a different interdisciplinary approach to climate history, see R. I. Rotberg and T. K. Rabb (eds.), *Climate and History: Studies in Interdisciplinary History* (Princeton: Princeton University Press, 1981), and T. M. L. Wigley, M. J. Ingram and G. Farmer (eds.), *Climate and History: Studies in Past Climates and Their Impact on Man* (Cambridge: Cambridge University Press, 1981).

[15] For recent examples, see G. Cushman, *Guano and the Opening of the Pacific World* (Cambridge: Cambridge University Press, 2013); C. F. Jones, *Routes of Power: Energy and Modern America* (Cambridge, MA: Harvard University Press, 2014); A. Malm, *Fossil Capital: The Rise of Steam Power and the Roots of Global Warming* (London: Verso, 2016); T. Mitchell, *Carbon Democracy: Political Power in the Age of Oil* (London: Verso, 2011).

[16] L. Marx, *The Machine in the Garden: Technology and the Pastoral Ideal in America* (Oxford: Oxford University Press, 1964); Worster, *Nature's Economy*; C. Merchant, *Ecological Revolutions: Nature, Gender and Science in New England* (Chapel Hill: University of North Carolina Press, 1989).

described the development of an ethos, a way of ethically relating to nature and appreciating the environment.[17] Such narratives serve an aspirational purpose in environmental debates, where ecological ideas are invoked in models for a better ethical life. As such, they show more about how the history of ideas can be used in contemporary political argument than they do about the history of environmental political thought.

While it is likely that those concerned with ecology and the environment today care about climate change, the new politics of climate change does not necessarily require an 'environmental' or 'ecological' perspective of the kind these narratives provide. Climate change is not only an ecological issue. Debates about the intrinsic value of nature or the appropriate ethical relationship to it go only so far to answering the question of what is to be done in the face of our changing climate. Indeed, tying it exclusively to ecological concerns misses that climate and environmental politics in general, are – and will no doubt continue to be – a central part of modern politics. An exclusively ecological perspective masks the kinds of political puzzles climate change poses and the ways that it exacerbates existing problems within modern political systems. Climate change shapes considerations of social and distributive justice, and is intimately tied to questions about the fate of modern capitalism. It illuminates the dangers of the short-term thinking characteristic of democratic rulers who have their eye on the next election rather than the long-term future. It brings into sharp relief the conflict of interests between states, citizens and other non-governmental and supra-national organizations and associations. It aggravates ongoing problems of how to redress the legacies of colonialism and empire and it exacerbates global inequalities and injustices, and existing distributional conflicts.[18] And it highlights the many prevailing – and today quickly worsening – tensions between experts and citizens, politics and markets, and the conflicts between democracies, technocracies and autocracies.

In an era where environmental politics are now inextricably bound not to ecology but to climate change, new resources that bridge the gap

---

[17] For the classic critique of this tendency, see W. Cronon, 'The Trouble with Wilderness; or, Getting Back to the Wrong Nature', in W. Cronon (ed.), *Uncommon Ground: Rethinking the Human Place in Nature* (New York: W. W. Norton, 1995), 69–90.

[18] Examples of the vast literature on environmental justice, racism and anti-imperialism include A. H. Deming and L. E. Savoy (eds.), *The Colors of Nature: Culture, Identity, and the Natural World* (Minneapolis, MN: Milkweed Editions, 2011); R. Nixon, *Slow Violence and the Environmentalism of the Poor* (Cambridge, MA: Harvard University Press, 2011); L. Westra and B. Lawson (eds.), *Faces of Environmental Racism: Confronting Issues of Global Justice* (Lanham, MD: Rowman & Littlefield, 2001).

between histories of ecological ideas and these complex political problems are needed. For political theorists and philosophers, dealing with environmental issues has increasingly involved addressing these problems. Since the 1970s social and political theorists, much like historians, have turned to the host of issues we now group as environmental.[19] Then, deep ecologists and radical environmentalists called for a total revaluation of the relationship between the human and non-human world.[20] A new field of environmental ethics, which examined questions about animal rights and whether the earth and nature has intrinsic value, attempted to decentre the place of humans in modern moral and political thought.[21] Others went beyond the ecological, extending conventional philosophical ideas to address the new environmental politics.[22] Responding to concerns with overpopulation and world famine, Anglo-American analytical philosophers developed theories of 'global' and

[19] For surveys of environmental political theory, see the special issue of *Contemporary Political Theory* (2009), essays by M. Saward, A. Dobson, S. MacGregor and D. Torgerson; M. Humphrey, 'Green Political Theory', in D. Bell (ed.), *Ethics and World Politics* (Oxford: Oxford University Press, 2010), 181–199. Key contributions to environmental political theory include A. Dobson, *Green Political Thought: An Introduction* (London: Harper Collins, 1990); R. Eckersley, *Environmentalism and Political Theory: Towards an Ecocentric Approach* (Albany: State University of New York Press, 1992); R. Goodin, *Green Political Theory* (Cambridge: Cambridge University Press, 1992); J. Barry, *Environment and Social Theory* (London: Routledge, 1999); A. de-Shalit, *The Environment: Between Theory and Practice* (Oxford: Oxford University Press, 2000). For the question of whether political theory should deal with climate change as an isolated issue or as part of a theory of justice, see S. Caney, 'Just Emissions', *Philosophy & Public Affairs* 40 (2012), 255–300.

[20] A. Naess, 'The Shallow and the Deep, Long-Range Ecology Movement: A Summary', *Inquiry: An Interdisciplinary Journal of Philosophy* 16 (1973), 95–100; B. Devall and G. Sessions, *Deep Ecology: Living as If Nature Mattered* (Salt Lake City: Gibbs Smith, 1985); J. Baird Callicott, *In Defense of the Land Ethic* (Albany: State University of New York Press, 1989); B. Devall, 'Deep Ecology and Radical Environmentalism', *Society and Natural Resources* 4 (1991), 247–258; J. Davis (ed.), *The Earth First, Reader: Ten Years of Radical Environmentalism* (Salt Lake City: Gibbs Smith, 1991). For a survey, see B. Devall, 'The Deep, Long-Range Ecology Movement: 1960–2000: A Review', *Ethics and the Environment* 6 (2001), 18–41. For the eco-feminist extension of deep ecology, see G. Gaard (ed.), *Ecofeminism: Women, Animals, Nature* (Philadelphia: Temple University Press, 1993); M. Mellor, *Feminism and Ecology* (New York: New York University Press, 1997); and for the eco-Marxist extension, see J. O'Connor, 'Introduction', *Capitalism, Nature, Socialism* 1 (1988), 1–38; J. B. Foster, *Marx's Ecology: Materialism and Nature* (New York: Monthly Review Press, 2000); P. Burkett, *Marxism and Ecological Economics: Toward a Red and Green Political Economy* (Leiden: Brill, 2006).

[21] P. Singer, *Animal Liberation: A New Ethic for Our Treatment of Animals* (New York: Harper Collins, 1975); S. R. L. Clarke, *The Moral Status of Animals* (Oxford: Oxford University Press, 1977); M. E. Zimmerman, J. Baird Callicott, G. Sessions, K. J. Warren and J. Clark (eds.), *Environmental Philosophy: From Animal Rights to Radical Ecology* (Upper Saddle River, NJ: Prentice Hall, 1993).

[22] A. Dobson and R. Eckersley (eds.), *Political Theory and the Ecological Challenge* (Cambridge: Cambridge University Press, 2006).

'intergenerational' justice to ask whether and what obligations are owed to individuals far away, and to future generations, in a world of declining or limited resources. Economists and philosophers became increasingly concerned with how to manage ecological threats, like resource depletion, that occurred over long periods of time into the future.[23] By the 1980s, social theorists like Ulrich Beck and Anthony Giddens described this novel iteration of modernity – in which the threat of ecological disaster had forced all to look at the future through a managerial framework of risk, costs and benefits – as a new 'risk society'.[24]

Since then, environmental political theory has largely gone in two directions. On the one hand, it has furthered the decentring of the human world begun by earlier environmentalists and, by building on a tradition in the sociology of science – as environmental historians have also done – has sought to endow nature and non-humans with agency.[25] On the other, it has tended to downplay the agency or intrinsic value of nature, instead showing how existing theories of distributive, intergenerational and global justice developed in the 1970s can be 'greened', and how theories of deliberative democracy and ecological citizenship can be combined.[26]

Contemporary political theorists therefore already take environmental issues seriously. Though some focus on ecological concerns alone, many recognize the importance of treating ecological problems as part of moral, political and economic thought more broadly. Many theories of distributive justice and citizenship, and accounts of ethical life now address the

---

[23] R. I. Sikora and B. Barry (eds.), *Obligations to Future Generations* (Philadelphia: Temple University Press, 1978); D. MacLean and P. G. Brown (eds.), *Energy and the Future* (Totowa, NJ: Rowman and Littlefield, 1983).

[24] U. Beck, *Risk Society: Towards a New Modernity* (London: Sage, 1992); U. Beck, *Ecological Politics in an Age of Risk* (London: Polity Press, 1995); A. Giddens, *Modernity and Self-Identity: Self and Society in the Late Modern Age* (Stanford: Stanford University Press, 1991).

[25] B. Latour, *We Have Never Been Modern*, trans. C. Porter (Cambridge, MA: Harvard University Press, 1993); J. Bennett, *Vibrant Matter: A Political Ecology of Things* (Durham, NC: Duke University Press, 2010); L. Nash, 'The Agency of Nature or the Nature of Agency', *Environmental History* 10 (2005), 67–69; T. Mitchell, *Rule of Experts: Egypt, Techno-Politics, Modernity* (Berkeley: University of California Press, 2002), esp. ch. 1, 'Can the Mosquito Speak?'. Cf. C. Palmer, 'Does Nature Matter? The Place of the Nonhuman in the Ethics of Climate Change', in D. G. Arnold (ed.), *The Ethics of Global Climate Change* (Cambridge: Cambridge University Press, 2011), 272–291.

[26] S. Caney, 'Global Distributive Justice and the Environment', in R. Tinnevelt and G. Verschraegen (eds.), *Between Cosmopolitan Ideals and State Sovereignty: Studies on Global Justice* (London: Palgrave, 2006), 51–63; A. Dobson, *Justice and the Environment* (Oxford: Oxford University Press, 1998); A. Dobson and D. Bell (eds.), *Environmental Citizenship* (Cambridge, MA: MIT Press, 2006); M. I. Humphrey, *Ecological Politics and Democratic Theory: The Challenge to the Deliberative Ideal* (London: Routledge, 2007).

peculiar challenges of environmental problems, as well as the associated problems of cooperation, burden distribution and managing the future.[27] However, where political theorists look to history, they often rely on the same aspirational, ecological tradition of thought constructed in the first decades of the new environmental politics, and rarely connect their ideas to the history of political thought more broadly understood.[28] This makes it difficult to see beyond contemporary approaches to environmental problems, or to locate their intellectual roots. Addressing the climate threat requires answers to political problems – of coordination, political action, representation, distributive justice, the management of population and resources, even perhaps that of imagining the end of the world. These are deep-rooted problems of modern politics, which themselves have histories. We are unlikely to find solutions to them by simply looking at old ways of talking about nature in the history of ecological ideas alone.

This book begins the work of integrating historical treatments of these problems in political theory and contemporary politics into the history of environmental ideas. It offers some historical perspectives on contemporary environmental political thought, and brings the perspective of political theory to the history of environmental ideas. The aim is for a history of political thought that presents environmental questions as more than just problems of value and nature; one that does not take environmental issues as peripheral, but places them in the context of the political problems we routinely take as central – problems of states, markets, democracy and political action. Historians of political thought are used to thinking about problems often understood as environmental: in debates about land, settlement and empire, about what nature has been used to justify, and how its normative limits have been conceived.[29]

---

[27] For the now vast field of intergenerational justice and climate ethics, see A. Gosseries and L. H. Meyer (eds.), *Intergenerational Justice* (Oxford: Oxford University Press, 2009); S. M. Gardiner, S. Caney, D. Jamieson and H. Shue (eds.), *Climate Ethics: Essential Readings* (Oxford: Oxford University Press, 2010); I. González-Ricoy and A. Gosseries (eds.), *Institutions for Future Generations* (Oxford: Oxford University Press, 2016).

[28] For a recent survey of the use of the 'canon' by political theorists interested in environmental issues, see H. Wilson, 'Environmental Political Theory and the History of Western Political Theory', in T. Gabrielson, C. Hall, J. M. Meyer and D. Schlosberg (eds.), *The Oxford Handbook of Environmental Political Theory* (Oxford: Oxford University Press, 2016), 19–33.

[29] A. Brett, *Changes of State: Nature and the Limits of the City in Early Modern Natural Law* (Princeton: Princeton University Press, 2011); D. Armitage, *Foundations of Modern International Thought* (Cambridge: Cambridge University Press, 2013); A. Fitzmaurice, *Sovereignty, Property and Empire 1500–2000* (Cambridge: Cambridge University Press, 2014); S. Muthu (ed.), *Empire and Modern Political Thought* (Cambridge: Cambridge University Press, 2012); A. Pagden, *Lords of All the World: Ideologies of Empire in Spain, Britain and France c. 1500–c. 1800* (New Haven: Yale University Press, 1995).

They are also used to thinking about the political issues that exacerbate and shape environmental politics: the clash between democracy and experts, and the politics of knowledge more broadly understood.

Most pertinently, perhaps, historians of political thought have long been preoccupied with the institution most challenged by climate change, and potentially most responsible for addressing it – the modern state. Environmental problems do not respect state borders; the political world is divided in a way the natural world is not. Where the latter is made up of interconnected eco-systems, the former remains governed by states, even where globalization and international organizations threaten their sovereignty. States may well have to adapt significantly if they are to deal with climate change. The history of political thought is directly engaged with the question of the adaptability of the idea of the state: it has tracked how it has been adapted over time, and has also demonstrated how some ideas about the state might be peculiarly adaptable.[30] Many chapters in this book build on this engagement to trace how the modern state came to relate to nature as it now does, and how it might handle the crisis of climate change in the future. This is just one way that this book illuminates how past thinkers have treated problems that are now central to environmental politics but are not themselves exclusively 'environmental'. In doing so, it goes beyond how present political thinkers make use of the past and also offers a history of how thinkers in the past imagined the future.

II

The chapters in this volume approach a number of interrelated themes raised by contemporary environmental politics and climate change, including the relationship between nature and the land, the politics of scientific and economic knowledge, our obligations to one another across time, and problems of political action under conditions of uncertainty. They take two broad approaches to the task of rethinking the history of environmental political thought. Those in the first part treat the problem that conventionally lies at its core: the use of nature and of natural resources, and the political and economic relations of humans to the land. The chapters in the second part address a constellation of ideas that

---

[30] For example, Q. Skinner, 'The State', in T. Ball, J. Farr and R. L. Hanson (eds.), *Political Innovation and Conceptual Change* (Cambridge: Cambridge University Press, 1989), 90–131; D. Runciman, *Pluralism and the Personality of the State* (Cambridge: Cambridge University Press, 1997); R. Tuck, *The Sleeping Sovereign: The Invention of Modern Democracy* (Cambridge: Cambridge University Press, 2016); I. Katznelson, *Fear Itself: The New Deal and the Origins of Our Time* (New York: W. W. Norton, 2014).

are more explicitly connected to the particular environmental predicament that is climate change.

The first part of this book, then, focuses on how past thinkers have conceived of the relationship between human beings and the natural world and how they drew the boundaries of those categories. For many contemporary environmentalists – save those who accept an instrumental view of the natural world in the name of social justice across nations and between generations – a concern with the 'environment' signals a way of caring for the natural world in a non-instrumental sense. Nature here has an intrinsic value, and humans are its custodians. They subscribe to what William Cronon has called the view of 'Nature as Eden', and to a history of environmental ideas – the lessons of environmental history notwithstanding – where 'nature' demands protection. So too do they view industrialization as responsible for corrupting a relationship between humans and nature that was once based on care and reciprocity rather than economistic exploitation.[31]

The chapters here take a different view of the historical relation of humans and nature, and proceed chronologically, showing how ideas about this relationship have unfolded since the early modern period. Taken separately, each treats a distinct set of debates about the relationship between politics and the land; taken together, they provide an account of the historical origins and development of (as well as alternatives to) dominant modern ideas about economic growth, the use and exhaustion of resources, and the role of politics in how that growth and use came to be managed. In doing so, they also address two sets of ideas that are fundamental to thinking about environmental problems today, and which every chapter in this volume makes central: ideas about the future, and about expertise.

Annabel Brett's chapter opens the volume by challenging the view of early modernity as the period when a sharp break emerged between a commitment to the care and cultivation of nature on the one hand, and the development of ideas about its control and domination on the other. She examines the ways that some early modern thinkers transformed their political categories to try and bring both animals and the land into relationships with humans that went beyond that of property and use. Early modern ideas about the natural world were not limited to an ethic of care, even if respect for 'Nature' was central to many strands of that period's political thought. Brett suggests new directions for the study of the 'environment' in early modern thought: we should look to early

---

[31] This story is often told by deep ecologists; see note 20.

modernity, she argues, not for the origins of our thinking about the category of the 'environment' but for their ways of discussing communities as situated spatially and temporally. These debates have implications for the development of modern ideas about obligations both to non-human animals and to future generations. Contemporary accounts of what present generations owe to the future tend to be abstract and cosmopolitan: obligations, for many theorists of intergenerational justice, are seen to stretch across space and time in equal measure. Brett shows that some early modern thinkers concerned about the future and their descendants appealed instead to the idea of the *patria* – the homeland, or fatherland – in a way that emphasized the connection of particular human communities to particular territories. In such cases, the future was understood in terms of the past: care for the land, for the very soil, was an act of respect for our common parent, the *patria*. These authors did not argue that present generations must look to the future, but that all generations must look to their situated past. In contradistinction to much contemporary global environmental ethics, they rejected the claim that thinking about communities over time could be done in abstraction from thinking about the place and space in which those communities were found.

Paul Warde's chapter addresses similar themes in seventeenth- and eighteenth-century Germany. It too debunks a set of received ideas about the relationship of humans to the natural world: that sustainability is a pre-industrial idea, corrupted by industrialism and only recently revived. In place of this history, Warde traces the development of ideas of sustainability in early modern arguments about forestry and resource management. He charts its transformation from an idea associated with state-controlled access to, and distribution of, resources, to the name for a new kind of political expertise and engineering, focused on innovation, resource growth and durability. With claims about this new knowledge in hand, the state came to conceive of itself as responsible for providing and maintaining resources and coordinating that provision over both time and space. This change was implicated in and effected by a significant shift in the nature of political knowledge in general, and in particular the development of new forms of expertise – neither removed from nor reducible to knowledge about the land. In an age where expert knowledge is often understood as in tension with local knowledge, such ideas provide alternatives to modern notions of expertise. Negotiating the tension between theories of land management and the knowledge of specific plots was a central part of debates about state intervention in the management of natural resources. Where modern experts are so often detached from the nature they assess, the first early modern advocates of sustainability argued for the importance of deep local knowledge, and the participation of those who had such knowledge in decision-making.

It is not just defenders of local knowledge and expertise who tend to occupy opposing sides in contemporary political debate (environmental or otherwise). When it comes to addressing the tensions between economic growth and resource depletion, debate is similarly polarized: on one side stands the pro-growth lobby of cornucopian, technological optimists who believe in the adaptability of capitalism; on the other, environmental groups, characterized by a fatalistic, often apocalyptic, pessimism about the resilience of the ideal of growth. Though the idea of economic growth as a basis for political legitimacy in modern states gained ground only after the Second World War, the widespread challenges to that idea have met with little success.[32] Today, the language of sustainability is used flexibly. The idea of sustainable growth is used as a modifier to capitalism, to capture alternatives to the often-perceived need for unlimited growth; it is also used to respond to crises of growth, as a way in to thinking about easing decline. Yet as Warde shows, where contemporary ideas of sustainability arose in response to the critique of growth-led politics and its corresponding crisis of values in the 1970s, the idea of conserving and managing resources has not always been crisis-driven, nor tied to liberal capitalism. Sustainability emerged in early modern Germany as a new form of political knowledge, one aimed at securing the ends of the state, which were, increasingly, industrial ends. That is to say, worries about sustainability arose in tandem with industrialization, not simply because of its crisis.

The idea that a state gains its democratic legitimacy through economic growth may be new (and it might yet be fleeting) but ideas of economic development, expansion and cornucopia have roots in the earlier history of economic thought. Contemporary arguments that markets can overcome environmental pressures through engineering fixes or the decoupling of economic development from its material basis have precursors in the eighteenth century. Like Warde, in Chapter 4 Fredrik Albritton Jonsson charts a series of arguments about growth, the development of expert knowledge and the governance of resources, focusing in particular on the conflict between ideologies of growth and cornucopianism, and of exhaustion and depletion. He shows that there is a long history of thinking about long-term growth before the twentieth century. By charting how eighteenth- and early nineteenth-century thinkers developed different timescales for understanding the 'economy of nature'

[32] C. S. Maier, 'The Two Postwar Eras and the Conditions for Stability in Twentieth-Century Western Europe', *American Historical Review* 86 (1981), 327–352.

and debated how humans could intervene, master and manage these long-term natural cycles (as well as what kind of political regimes these interventions would require), he shows that it was in these debates that concerns about future generations, geological time and the physical limits to growth first entered political economy – and that it was here, too, that modern cornucopianism has its origins.

These chapters contribute to a history of ideas of exploitation of resources on the one hand, and conservation on the other. Malcolm Bull's chapter straddles these, and also contributes to a different history – of non-use, idleness and decadence. Growth was not always the first aim of politics; economic decline was not always the worst thing that could happen. Bull's chapter concludes this part of the book by moving the story into the twentieth century. He examines alternatives to cornucopianism and growth in arguments about the non-use of resources and the idea of slack, by exploring American theories of the firm, and the management of nature and businesses. Where Warde and Jonsson focused on the development of ideas about the duty of states to manage resources, Bull here turns to how ideas about resource management transform conceptions of both politics and future timescales. He shows how ideas about non-use (of both labour and natural resources) connect to those about economic decline and political inertia, which in turn provide a basis for understanding inaction as a means for renewal, change and long-term durability. These ideas, Bull suggests, might actually be fruitful ways to think about the future in the context of climate change.

The chapters in the second part continue to address the fundamental themes of the first: each treats problems of time and the future, and each has something to say about the crucial problem of expertise. But while in the first part the focus was on the development of new forms of political and economic knowledge, in the second it is on the predictive claims of scientists and economic experts and their relationship to democratic politics. Thinking about nature and its resources also involves thinking about natural knowledge and its relationship with political knowledge – put another way, the relationship between science and politics. When it comes to climate change, and environmental problems more broadly, scientific knowledge is just as important as economic knowledge – it is, after all, science that proves the climate is changing, and on which predictions about the future are based.[33]

---

[33] N. Oreskes, 'The Scientific Consensus on Climate Change: How Do We Know We're Not Wrong?', in J. F. C. DiMento and P. Doughman (eds.), *Climate Change: What It Means for Us, Our Children, and Our Grandchildren* (Cambridge, MA: MIT Press, 2007), 65–100.

In modern democratic states, science has a difficult status.[34] For many, it is best understood as the motor of progress and development. But it is also seen as a tool for the manipulation of citizens and a pretext for policies that consolidate state power. In an age where demagogic politics is on the rise and the legitimacy of expertise is under threat, science has an ambiguous position. With many forms of knowledge now more technical than ever, it has long been easy to see experts as above the political fray, but today the idea that scientific experts, like other experts with technical knowledge, are outside politics is under increasing pressure. The argument that democratic citizens should be sceptical of science relies on a variety of claims: that science props up the order that rules, exploits and dominates them, for example. Or, relatedly, that because scientific knowledge is alienated from most ordinary citizens – the prerogative of experts, outsourced by the intellectual and political division of labour characteristic of representative democracies – it is, as such, illegitimate.[35]

Climate science occupies a distinctive place in these arguments. It is at once political in the same sense that all science is, but it also explicitly provides the grounds and the tools for political arguments in ways that other forms of science often do not. The particularly science-dependent character of the politics of climate change exacerbates existing tensions between the rule of experts and the place of citizens: for those sceptical of expertise in general, the predictions of climate science are not to be trusted. Much contemporary environmentalism shares this democratic scepticism. Some worry that the reliance on science risks a kind of deference which stands in conflict with the anti-elitist, grassroots ethic that animates the environmental movement. Others see science as simultaneously whistleblower and culprit, revealing climate change on the one hand, but producing technologies that exacerbate it on the other. Both views contribute to the same paradox: modern environmentalism is both anti-scientistic and sceptical of expertise, and yet wholly reliant on science for its claims about how climate change will shape the future.

Deborah Coen's chapter looks to a period before citizens were alienated from the production of scientific knowledge. By charting the development of a science of natural disasters in late nineteenth- and early twentieth-century America, she shows that modern views of scientific

---

[34] For a recent account of the relationship between science and democracy in the United States in particular, see A. Jewett, *Science, Democracy, and the American University: From the Civil War to the Cold War* (Cambridge: Cambridge University Press, 2014).

[35] A. Roberts, *The Logic of Discipline: Global Capitalism and the Architecture of Government* (Oxford: Oxford University Press, 2009).

expertise – which often claim to be 'beyond politics', which circumvent democratic processes and which equate knowledge with control – do not, as is sometimes suggested, originate in either seventeenth-century political philosophy or eighteenth- and nineteenth-century disaster science, but are far more recent developments. Despite claims to the contrary, Thomas Hobbes was neither the founder of modern ideas of state-controlled science nor the first to make the familiar modern claim that there could be a predictive natural science that stands above politics. He did not rely on scientific expertise to predict the future, but suggested that a more predictable future relied upon a sovereign informed but unconstrained by expert opinion. Neither, Coen shows, was nineteenth-century seismology the source for science as a tool of prediction and social control. Rather, attempts to understand and predict disasters in that period were both democratic and pluralist, grounded in common, public experiences and reliant upon local knowledge which was to be respected as a distinctive and scientifically valuable way of seeing and perceiving the world. Only since the 1870s, and in particular since the Cold War, has scientific expertise been detached from common experience. The story of the emergence of disaster science in the nineteenth century makes clear that science has not always been in conflict with democracy; nor has it always been a technical realm, far removed from the political practices of citizens.

John O'Neill and Thomas Uebel begin their chapter with an acknowledgement of the opposition between scientific expertise and democratic politics that Coen historicizes, and look for a way of reconciling the two. They point to a specific problem within environmental politics: the clash between its science-scepticism and its science-dependence. Where Coen, by tracing the history of how knowledge-claims about environmental predictions were reached, recovers an alternative vision of the relationship between scientific expertise and democracy in which science was not oriented to control, O'Neill and Uebel look to the Vienna Circle and the Frankfurt School to trace two different perspectives from which prevailing views of science as control can be challenged. The first – common among environmentalists today – condemns scientific expertise as necessarily part of a technocratic reactionary politics; the second – and their preferred – allows for a science-dependent politics of a kind that can underpin a radical, democratic environmentalism. This second perspective offers new ground for resisting scepticism about the rule of experts (a scepticism presented powerfully by Friedrich Hayek, whose challenge to expertise appears more than once in these chapters) and a compelling way forward for democrats and socialists who are also environmentalists. Environmentalists, they suggest, do not need to be trapped by the science dependence of climate politics and their science scepticism, but can look to radical views of science like that provided by Otto Neurath instead.

From reconciling democratic deliberation and scientific expertise, and the status of science within democracies, Melissa Lane and Richard Tuck move on to consider the prospects for individual and collective political action under conditions of uncertainty, scientific and otherwise. Problems of political action in the context of climate change are particularly acute, partly because of its global nature. Collective action problems are most pronounced at the international level: climate science provides reasons for urgent action to cut carbon emissions, but so long as many states do nothing to curb emissions, it is easy to find good reasons to do nothing at all. At the level of government, climate change has thus far met with inaction – or, at least, with inaction relative to the scale of action that climate scientists recommend. The same problem applies at an individual level: why give up meat, or fly less, if no one else is? Is it rational to sit by and wait until others act or are there good grounds for thinking that we should do something ourselves regardless?

Motivating individual and collective political action is made all the more difficult because of two further issues particular to climate change: the timeframe that action on climate change requires and the uncertainty involved in any decision to act. Trusting climate science does not only entail squaring respect for expert knowledge with democracy; it also demands that both individuals and governments learn to think differently about the future. This inaction is often self-reinforcing: democratic governments are plagued by short-termism. Because the full effects of climate change will not be felt for many years, or many decades, and because the short-term costs of taking action on climate change will be felt immediately, politicians in power have so far chosen to do very little. When it comes to choosing between threat of disaster later or the costs of acting now, governments choose to avoid the latter. And so climate change is a particularly serious problem for democratic states: unable to think beyond the next election, democratic leaders may not act until it is too late. Comforted by the thought of adaptation, they waste time and risk disaster. At the non-governmental level, many groups advocating action do so in the name of an uncertain future. Waiting for the point at which adaptation makes sense, they argue, will spell disaster. The kind of open-ended uncertainties presented by climate change can justify all kinds of political action (as well as total inaction).

Lane and Tuck's chapters deal with the broader problem of political action in the face of climate change by focusing on the technical issue of 'negligibility': the idea that one individual's contribution to reducing emissions is negligible – so much so that it does not effect any outcome that one might care about. Lane and Tuck provide contrasting views on the issue of negligibility and the importance of individual action in the face of collective inaction. Even if we trust in science, expert knowledge might not tell us how to act. Even if it does, why should we act if others do not? Lane shows how perspectives from the history of political thought regarding the nature of politics can help us to overturn the assumptions of contemporary rational choice theory and moral philosophy to provide an account of the kind of individual action that may well be necessary for combatting climate change. In his response to Lane, Tuck focuses not on the importance of unilateral individual action but on the rationality of collective action, and draws from a tradition of pre-twentieth-century economic thought that reaches back to David Hume and Adam Smith. Lane's and Tuck's chapters thus both deal with problems of political action that are particularly acute in the case of climate change (Tuck's solutions – contra Lane's call for individual action – are collective enforcement mechanisms and refraining from individual action, the latter of which has something in common with Bull's account of idleness). Concerns with these technical philosophical problems, which impose idealized conditions from economic theory onto political action in general, are recent. On one view, the history of political thought provides contemporary accounts of political action with a broader vision of ethical and responsible agency in the face of uncertainty and the future – a vision of precisely the kind that is crucial in the context of climate change. On the other, the history of political thought shows just how intractable these problems of collective action are, and casts doubt on the possibility of addressing climate change at all.

David Runciman's chapter, which closes the second part, begins with the observation that it is the themes of the previous chapters combined – trust in science and expertise, and collective action problems – that makes environmental politics so fatalistic. He distinguishes between the different kinds of fatalism that bolster not only environmental resignation, but also climate scepticism. Bringing together preoccupations from across the volume – on cornucopianism, expertise, disaster, passivity and activity – Runciman shows that framing current debate as one between technological optimists and fatalistic pessimists is too simple. The technological optimists and climate sceptics who champion growth politics can be fatalists too. But fatalism should not be the framework for thinking about the limitations or the possibilities of human agency in the context of democratic politics, scientific prediction and an uncertain future. To deal with the problems of modern environmental politics, overcoming fatalism will be crucial.

Taken together, as Quentin Skinner shows in his Afterword, the essays in the two parts show the variety of ways in which the history of political thought can help make sense of problems in environmental politics in general and climate politics in particular. They reveal how the ideas that are at the crux of all environmental politics – about the use, exploitation and non-use of resources – have developed since the early modern period. But they also show that the answers to the questions raised in contemporary environmental politics – about the status of science or problems of agency – may well be found in traditions that are not primarily (or not only) concerned with the use and abuse of natural resources. Thinking seriously about modern environmental politics also requires thinking about the future, and about the kinds of expertise and knowledge (whether scientific, economic or political) we rely on when we act with a view to the future.

The themes addressed in this book are not the only themes addressed in contemporary environmental politics, nor are they the only areas in which the history of political thought can provide insight. Much is left untouched by the chapters here – for instance, international politics does not feature centrally, and neither do the problems of imperialism, colonialism, and of the responsibility for historical, structural and racial injustice, that are so bound up with climate change and its differing consequences for the global North and South. But we hope that the chapters here point towards how the history of environmental political thought, as conceived in this volume, could contribute to the debates about these problems, as well as to the ongoing debates about the Anthropocene, and about what climate change means for the future of capitalism, the politics of inequality and distributive and intergenerational justice. That is to say, this book aims simply to make a start on the very large task of showing how the history of political thought can be used to address environmental problems in a way that goes beyond the ecological tradition.

Part I

Time, Nature and the Land

2 Is There Any Place for Environmental Thinking in Early Modern European Political Thought?

Annabel Brett *

This chapter advisedly has only an interrogative for a title. It does no more than explore the contours of what is nevertheless an interesting and rewarding question, which can be rephrased as follows: Do the ways in which political philosophers in early modern Europe think of human agency and of human political structures allow an idea of co-existence or cooperation with the natural world and with non-human beings such that the latter can be included within political relations, even of a very broad kind, and such that there is some political limit on what human beings can do to them? To rephrase in this way is necessary in view of the fact that early modern thought has no equivalent term or concept of 'the environment'. More than that, however, it is also suggestive of the ways in which early modern categories and concerns might resonate with certain strands, at least, of modern environmental and ecological thinking. For the purposes of this chapter I take 'early modern' to refer to the period 1500–1700, and I draw upon examples from across Europe. They serve to illustrate the sophistication and seriousness with which thinkers of that time considered the relationship between the human and the non-human, a subject that, for them, was not at the margins but at the very foundations of their understanding of the political.[1]

At first glance, the idea that early modern political thought might constitute an environmental political thought – in however mediated a

---

* This chapter was first presented at the conference which was the occasion for the present volume, and subsequently at the colloquium 'Politics, nature and the imagination in the thought of Sir Francis Bacon' held at Berkeley, California, in March 2014. I am grateful to participants at both events for their thought-provoking responses, and especially to my commentator at Berkeley, Diego Pirillo. I would also like to thank John Robertson and Sophie Smith for helpful comments on the first draft.
[1] I have argued this case in *Changes of State: Nature and the Limits of the City in Early Modern Natural Law* (Princeton: Princeton University Press, 2011), ch. 2, 'Constructing Human Agency'.

24   *Annabel Brett*

fashion – seems implausible. These centuries are not generally known for ecological sensitivity. Indeed, numerous studies of different aspects of the period suggest quite the reverse, with technological change, the development of early modern capitalism and colonial activity – all related – being associated with control of nature rather than respect for its operation or agency. This judgement extends to the intellectual history of the period as well. Carolyn Merchant's work of 1980, *The Death of Nature: Women, Ecology and the Scientific Revolution*, tells a story in which an ancient, 'Gaia'-like conception of the earth as mother, flourishing anew in various Renaissance forms including the alchemy of Robert Fludd and the chemistry of Paracelsus, was replaced by a mechanistic science of nature the ultimate aim of which was domination, as opposed to respect. Francis Bacon (1561–1626) and Thomas Hobbes (1588–1679), as political as well as natural philosophers, are particular culprits here.[2] This book has been strongly contested for the gendered reading of early modern texts, especially those of Francis Bacon, involved in its thesis of death and domination.[3] Nevertheless, for all that critics are right to point out Bacon's insistence that in order to command nature, we must obey her, the 'trials' of nature in the *New Atlantis* seem to belie any courtliness that Merchant is accused of having misconstrued as rape.[4] And in general, it is not hard to find, in early modern philosophy, examples both of language (although the role of metaphor is precisely one of the things at issue) and of substantive philosophical conclusions (to the extent that these can be divorced from each other) which seem at odds with any kind of ecological perspective. Two key foundational texts, the biblical Book of Genesis and Aristotle's *Politics*, do indeed see human nature as related to all other nature, but that is in the sense of giving

---

[2] C. Merchant, *The Death of Nature: Women, Ecology and the Scientific Revolution* (San Francisco: Harper and Row, 1980). The story is less black-and-white than the main title may suggest: Merchant acknowledges that the transition she charts is not so clear, because alchemy continued decisively to inform early modern science, and conversely modern environmentalism has a technical and managerial dimension that is indebted to modern science. She also appreciates that, while Arcadian and Edenic visions of human beings at peace in a natural world are important for her story, they are not unambivalent in their implications for relations either with nature or with women.

[3] For the debate, see K. Park, 'Women, Gender and Utopia: The Death of Nature and the Historiography of Early Modern Science', *Isis* 97 (2006), 487–495; B. Vickers, 'Francis Bacon, Feminist Historiography and the Dominion of Nature', *Journal of the History of Ideas* 69 (2008), 117–141, and the contributions by Park and Merchant in the same volume. Park develops her own analysis of the female figure of nature in the early modern period in id., 'Nature in Person: Medieval and Renaissance Allegories and Emblems', in L. Daston and K. Park (eds.), *The Moral Authority of Nature* (Chicago: University of Chicago Press, 2004), 50–73.

[4] F. Bacon, *New Atlantis*, in B. Vickers (ed.), *Francis Bacon: The Major Works* (Oxford: Oxford University Press, 2002), 457–488, esp. 482.

humans dominion over it or making humans the *telos* of all other natures.[5] The world and all its creatures are for the purposes of man, as the most excellent of the creatures.

Despite this apparent intellectual-cultural consensus, however, one does not have to look far to find the converse, either. If Descartes's anti-Aristotelianism gives us the animal-machine, it also gives us the rejection of Aristotle's human-centric teleology, his idea that all things were made for man. If Hobbes mechanized nature, he also mechanized human nature.[6] More broadly, a range of early modern authors, drawing on multiple strands of ancient philosophy and literature, discuss the capabilities, including speech and wisdom, of animals, sometimes deliberately inverting the traditional order of human superiority.[7] To some extent, certainly, this was a classical *topos*, a moral rhetoric designed to stimulate human reflections on their own failings, and not intended to have concrete consequences for human treatment of animals beyond the avoidance of cruelty as another moral failing. Nevertheless, the integration of animals into the lives and thoughts of early modern human beings, reflected in literature as well as philosophy, goes deeper than this.[8] The culture is marked by a sense of the proximity of the animal, and of the natural more generally; 'being human' is neither comfortable nor taken for granted.

In this contribution, I want to move away from the moral dimensions of this sensibility, which have been explored by others, to ask whether it finds a place in specifically political discourse. That distinction cannot be entirely clear-cut, given that much (although not all) of early modern political thought is premised upon a continuity between the moral and the political. Nevertheless, political relationships in early modern thought – relations of citizenship, of subjection, of rule – do not reduce to moral relationships, and this is the sense of the question as framed. I shall confine myself to three key political notions: society (or community), *dominium* (I use the Latin term for its semantic capaciousness: besides the literal English translation 'dominion', it can mean mastery, lordship, or ownership/property), and native land or fatherland (in the Latin, *patria*).

---

[5] Genesis I:26; Aristotle, *The Politics*, book I, ch. 8.

[6] T. Hobbes, *Leviathan*, ed. R. Tuck (Cambridge: Cambridge University Press, 1996), part I, 'Of Man'.

[7] See R. W. Serjeantson, 'The Passions and Animal Language, 1540–1700', *Journal of the History of Ideas* 62 (2001), 425–444.

[8] See, among an increasing number of studies, E. Fudge, *Brutal Reasoning: Animals, Rationality and Humanity in Early Modern England* (Ithaca, NY, and London: Cornell University Press, 2006).

I begin with a generalization, which is that political thought in the sixteenth and seventeenth centuries is centrally concerned with relations between human beings, not between human beings and anything else. This is the central space of the political. Of course, early modern political thought works in multiple idioms or languages, and not all of them conceive that space in the same way; the differences will become important as we go along. But, generally speaking, thinkers in this period see human beings as a particular kind of animal, capable of doing what no other animals – let alone plants or rocks – can do: that is (in Aristotelian terms which are not universally shared but which, *mutatis mutandis*, will do for the broad point), living in *communities* or *societies* rather than, for example, herds or flocks. Human beings *associate*; they do not just *congregate*. We need to add a qualification here, which is that early modern authors inherited from Aristotle a notion of degrees of 'politicality', with some animals, particularly bees, being really quite political; and the beehive was more generally a familiar and vivid model for correct political functioning.[9] But, even on the strongest assumption, bee politicality is only *analogous to* human politicality, not *shared with* humans. Bees can be political with other bees, but not with human beings, and by the same token no bee, or any other animal, is political in the same way that human beings are. Conversely, it is universally accepted that humans can live animal-like lives, but this is precisely a mark of their lack of civilization or true politicality. Thus, one of the distinguishing dynamics of early modern political thought is to construct the space of the political against the proximity of the animal and of the natural to which I alluded above.

There are complex reasons for this exclusion of animals (and a fortiori other natural entities) from political society. Some of them have to do with what we might call this 'horizontal' dynamic of association. Either implicitly or explicitly, society – *societas* in Latin – implies, beyond simply 'fellowship', a shared purpose: being associates, allies, partners, in some enterprise. There is a teleology to association; people in society with each other get something from it that they do not get outside it. There is some shared concept of a good involved. In the case of political society, this good involves security and a certain degree of material advantage, but beyond that it also involves a mutual public space and a mutual public life. Thus, the shared concept is of a *shared good*. But animals, lacking reason, cannot properly conceive their own good,

---

[9] Aristotle, *Politics*, book I, ch. 1. J.-L. Labarrière, *Langage, Vie Politique et Mouvement des Animaux* (Paris: Vrin, 2004); B. Wilson, *The Hive: The Honeybee and Us* (London: John Murray, 2004), ch. 3, 'Politics'.

let alone a shared good; nor can they engage in discursive means–end reasoning about how it might be achieved; nor, lacking speech, can they communicate this conception, which they don't have, to others. In its voluntarist modulation, belonging to society also involves an act of will, again normally construed as the corollary of the possession of reason and of a perception of the good that animals don't have. Thus, animals, lacking the necessary form of agency, cannot *join* associations. Nor can they share the costs of political association: they cannot obey the laws that regulate it, nor can they undertake any obligation to it, or to other members. In sum, then, they cannot be *part* of it, because they cannot be *partners*. 'It' is not just a living together in the same space, but a mutual bond, a nexus. This is vividly illustrated by the early seventeenth-century political scientist and jurist Johannes Althusius, who explicitly introduces *symbiosis* (his term) as the basis of all human relations. But he moves immediately to supplement this basic 'living together' with a stronger notion of association. *Symbiosis* is 'con-living', not just 'co-living', and con-living requires some kind of bond that transforms mere symbionts into a community.[10]

Mutuality has a further dimension, another key marker of political society in most idioms: freedom. Here is where the 'horizontal' dynamic of association meets the 'vertical' dynamic of *dominium*, understood principally in terms of property but also more broadly in terms of other rights of use and disposal. Those who are mutually part of a civil society may not be equal in all or even in most respects, but they are equal in not being slaves of anyone else. A citizen is subject to the law, whoever or whatever makes that law, and not to the orders of a master. He is not property; rather, he *has* property, or he shares in common property. Juridical status – having some kind of *suum*, something that is one's own – is thus a critically important dimension of early modern citizenship, and justice, the virtue that gives to each his own, is a key political virtue.[11] Here we need to add another complication to the story, however. At the intersection of citizenship and property lies the family. This is an association that is not strictly political, in the sense that it is not a space of independent agents associating on terms of

---

[10] J. Althusius, *Politica methodice digesta*, ed. and tr. C.J. Friedrich (Cambridge, MA: Harvard University Press, 1932), ch. 1, n. 2, 15, and see Brett, *Changes of State*, 128–129, 213–221.

[11] This language is perhaps most prominent in, though not exclusive to, the republican idiom analyzed in Q. Skinner, *Liberty before Liberalism* (Cambridge: Cambridge University Press, 1997). For an analysis that challenges the ubiquity of this 'Roman' understanding of justice, see E. Nelson, *The Greek Tradition in Republican Thought* (Cambridge: Cambridge University Press, 2004).

mutual equality. The wife is a dependent of her husband, and the children are dependents of both parents. Yet, these individuals are not slaves, even if they are not citizens, and the household is involved in political society through the involvement of the head of household. Again, property, especially landed property, is held in families as well as by individuals, and thus property-based citizenship is a function of family and not merely of having the requisite conditions on agency.[12] To this extent, women and children also participate in the political sphere, even if not equally with men. But animals (and a fortiori other natural entities) are excluded from this sphere. They have nothing of their own; they have no juridical status, nor can they suffer violation of right (injury, *iniuria*). They are purely the objects rather than the subjects of *dominium*.

I think that most versions of early modern political thought articulate this kind of space: early modern natural law, early modern republicanism, early modern political Aristotelianism, the sixteenth-century English discourse of commonwealth, 'Ancient Constitutionalism' – but also legal absolutism and divine right absolutism, for neither of these wants to eliminate the civic sphere even while insisting that the prince is above the law. Hobbes is a partial outlier, as I shall discuss later, reformulating as he does the animal/human, slave/citizen, family/commonwealth and indeed the natural/juridical divide per se. Patriarchal thought is much more of an outlier, for, in contrast to the complicated inter-relation between the political and the familial which most early modern political thought delineates, it collapses the distinction between political and household relationships. So too, perhaps, is the discourse we know as 'reason of state', with its emphasis on the passionate rather than rational nature of man, its recognition of discontinuity between the moral and the political, its a-juridicality. On a Foucauldian reading, this discourse radically alters both the individual human being and the political community as subjects of law and right, refiguring both of these into the object of governmental techniques.[13] It thereby changes the relation of both to the animal and to the natural world more generally. The people (*populus*) is naturalized into the population, with the result that the distinction between managing nature and governing humans becomes blurred.

---

[12] For my appreciation of the sophisticated interplay between family and politics in early modern political thought I am indebted to A. Becker, 'Gender and Political Thought in Northern Italy and France, c. 1420–c. 1578', unpublished PhD thesis, Cambridge University, 2010. For property, see J. Brewer and S. Staves (eds.), *Early Modern Conceptions of Property* (London: Routledge, 1996), esp. parts I–III.

[13] M. Foucault, *Security, Territory, Population: Lectures at the Collège de France 1977–1978*, tr. G. Burchell (Basingstoke: Palgrave Macmillan, 2007).

Indeed, we may lose the 'human' entirely.[14] Now, getting rid of the 'human' *as opposed to the animal*, or to the natural, might be precisely what we want to do as modern environmental and ecological thinkers. But what I want to explore in this chapter, and what I think the early moderns are fruitful for exploring, is how one might begin to do this while keeping hold of key political notions such as society, justice and law, to articulate a genuinely shared, and genuinely political, space. In any case, and as Foucault himself admits, the fully naturalized conception is not yet in evidence in the sixteenth or seventeenth centuries. On his understanding, this is a function of the continuing centripetal pull of the juridical model of sovereignty, with politics not yet liberated into economics as it would be in the eighteenth century. I would say, however, that it is also a function of the continuing centripetal pull of 'society', still forcefully present in this discourse even if it is differently defined.[15]

As a general point, then, this emphasis on human community or society as the mark of the political tends to push all other kinds of beings into non-political space and hence to close off the possibility of political relations between them and humans. Relations instead become the non-political relationship of property or use. However, the case of the slave precisely shows the ambivalence here: is the slave part of the political or not? The slave is not a citizen, but he (or she) lives alongside citizens, is integrated in their lives, one might say. As we have already seen with Althusius, this living alongside is not enough to constitute a genuinely political relationship. Thus, the way in which early modern thinkers conceived of limits on the use of slaves was not to rethink the primacy of community but to refer instead to a wider community: a 'society of the human race', governed by natural law and right (*ius naturale*: the Latin term *ius* can mean either 'law' or 'right', and sometimes implies both at the same time). Slaves can belong to this community, can be in a broader political relationship to other human beings, and their treatment can be limited by natural law even if they are 'nothing' in civil law. The important point here for our purposes is that this belonging does not require any action on the part of the member, no *joining*: it belongs by nature. Given this, the question

---

[14] Thus, one of the major authors of this discourse, the Flemish humanist Justus Lipsius, describes *Imperium* or sovereignty as 'that rod of Circes, that tameth *both men and beasts*' (emphasis added): J. Lipsius, *Politica* (1589), tr. John Stradling as *Six Bookes of Politickes* (London, 1594), book II, ch. 1.

[15] Thus Lipsius argues (ibid.) that civil society consists in *Imperium* and *Commercium*, commerce or 'Traffique' being a distinctively human form of exchange. Likewise it is still present in Francis Bacon, otherwise much indebted to this new humanist discourse, whose Machiavellian ideal of civic greatness is about a citizenry and not just about the life forces of a population. See M. Peltonen, *Classical Humanism and Republicanism in English Political Thought, 1570–1640* (Cambridge: Cambridge University Press, 1995), ch. 4.

arises whether there is any sense in which this community can be extended, even in a very broad sense, to natures other than human.

The most fruitful place for this kind of question is the legal discussion surrounding the Roman jurist Ulpian's assertion, in the first title of the Digest 'On justice and right' (D. 1.1.1.3), that *ius naturale* is 'what nature taught all animals': it is not peculiar, *proprium*, to human beings, but common, *commune*, to both humans and other animals. Ulpian mentions as belonging to it 'the union of male and female, which we call marriage' and the 'procreation and rearing of children', and 'we see' that all animals, even wild ones, are versed in this *ius naturale*. One strand of humanist jurisprudence saw this, quite simply, as a mistake.[16] *Ius* demands the kind of other-regarding behaviour, the kind of community that only human beings, as rational creatures, are capable of. Other jurists were more sympathetic to the idea that animal agency could be lawful, or that we could talk of right in respect of them. Thus the French humanist lawyer Jacques Cujas (1522–1590) held that animals have been taught *ius naturale*, and follow it equally as do humans, in such things as rearing their young. But all the same, he explicitly ruled out any 'community of right' between animals and humans: there is no shared juridical space, and thus no space for justice or injustice between human beings and animals. From a different direction, the Dutch humanist Hugo Grotius (1583–1645) recognized a right (or at least the rightfulness) of self-preservation in all animals, human or otherwise.[17] However, he placed this right of pursuing one's own good explicitly prior to any recognition of the other's good, and thus prior to any justice 'properly so-called' and to the natural society that depends upon it. This requires reason, which animals don't have. Grotius did accord them a glimmering of regard for others, for example in the way that they care for their young, but held that this faint sense is not enough for justice or for natural society.[18] Since Grotius sees particular political societies as a development from within universal human natural society, the right that both human beings and animals share is explicitly pre-political, even in the

---

[16] The best discussion of the debate is in M. Scattola, *Das Naturrecht vor dem Naturrecht. Zur Geschichte des «ius naturae» im 16. Jahrhundert* (Tübingen: Niemeyer, 1999), 161–178; see also Brett, *Changes of State*, ch. 3.

[17] H. Grotius, *Commentary on the Law of Prize and Booty*, ed. M. van Ittersum (Indianapolis: Liberty Fund, 2006), ch. 2, 21–23. This feature of Grotius's argument is highlighted especially by Richard Tuck, in several studies. See id., 'The Modern Theory of Natural Law', in A. R. D. Pagden (ed.), *The Languages of Political Theory in Early Modern Europe* (Cambridge: Cambridge University Press, 1985); more recently, *The Rights of War and Peace: Political Thought and the International Order from Grotius to Kant* (Oxford: Oxford University Press, 1999), ch. 3.

[18] Grotius, *Commentary on the Law of Prize and Booty*, 25–28.

broadest sense. Likewise Thomas Hobbes, at least in *De cive* (*On the citizen*, 1642), places animals and humans in the same juridical space when he says that a man will kill an animal with the same right that an animal kills a man.[19] But this space is the 'condition of nature', which Hobbes famously equates with a condition of war, in which again there is no justice, or at least no justice in effect.[20] It is characterized by the right of self-preservation generating a *ius in omnia* or 'right to all things', and is the antithesis of political space.

Not all early modern philosophical jurisprudence negotiated the divide in the same way, however. One of the most thoughtful and innovative of all was Alberico Gentili, Regius Professor of Civil Law in late sixteenth-century Oxford, who has been associated with Grotius and Hobbes in positing a natural right of self-preservation.[21] In a deliberately controversial early essay published in 1584, he certainly begins by offering a version of this argument. The opponent he conjures up for himself takes a very humanist line in thinking of the sphere of right purely in terms of human community. On this line of reasoning, even the actions of *human* individuals which relate only to themselves, and not to others, are excluded from this space. In consequence, given that it is only this kind of action that human beings share with animals, animals too must be excluded from right.[22] Gentili counters the argument by moving all such self-regarding behaviours *into* the sphere of right, both for human beings and for animals, making his argument turn on the right of self-defence that was universally taken as a key natural right for human beings. The imaginary opponent then plays the community card directly: 'Right (they say) exists where there is community. But for us together with the animals there is no community, and therefore no right for us together with animals.' To this Gentili replies that he has, precisely, defined natural *ius* on grounds other than community.[23]

---

[19] T. Hobbes, *De cive*, ed. and tr. R. Tuck and M. Silverthorne (Cambridge: Cambridge University Press, 1998).

[20] Hobbes, *Leviathan*, ch. 13.   [21] Tuck, *Rights of War and Peace*, ch. 2.

[22] A. Gentili, *Lectionum et epistolarum, quae at ius civile pertinent, Liber Tertius* (Oxford, 1584), cap. I, p. 2: 'if those things that are common between us and animals, ought to be included in the term "right", then it will also be right to acquire food, and sleep, and run, and rest, and all other things of that sort.' My renewed thanks to Diego Pirillo, who suggested to me a possible association between Gentili's thought on animals and that of Giordano Bruno, another Italian in England whom we know to have had connections with Gentili.

[23] It is worth noting, however, that in his subsequent, and deliberately more humanist work *On embassies* (1585), Gentili sides instead with the humanists in defining right through community: A. Gentili, *De legationibus libri III*, edition of 1594 (New York and Oxford: Carnegie Endowment for International Peace, 1924), vol. II (translation), ch. 7 (*ius, quod nihil nisi communio, et foedus est*).

Thus, the community argument does not push animals out of juridical space altogether. It places them in the sphere of natural right in which human beings also exist, even though human beings (differently from animals) exist in other spaces of right (the law of nations and civil law) as well. The question is, however, can that space of natural right be understood as in any sense a *political* space, in early modern terms? If there is no involvement of others at all in this kind of right, it is hard to see how we might read it as a political phenomenon. Gentili offers another argument, however, which centres not directly on right but on the violation of right, *iniuria*. The opponent argues that animals don't have rights because they are not capable of *iniuria*: force against them is against their nature, but it is not against their right, and therefore self-defence is not, for them, a right. Gentili responds that there are two senses of *iniuria*. The first, and central, sense is that of a deliberate violation, which requires a mind (*animus*) and is peculiar to human beings. Gentili characterizes it as a kind of contumely or contempt of right. But in a second sense, we can say that everything that happens without right, *sine iure*, happens by *iniuria* as a kind of un-right or non-right, and animals as well as humans are capable of this. His example is that of a cuckoo not rearing its own young. The cuckoo cannot be charged with *iniuria* in the first sense; but it does sin against natural *ius*. Thus, the argument from *iniuria* does not serve to exclude animals from any kind of right.

Gentili did not tackle head-on what this means for human behaviour towards animals. Given that human beings, unlike cuckoos, are capable of *iniuria* with contumely, the question is whether human beings can ever violate the right of animals in such a way. Does *contumely* require community? The argument carries the possibility that it doesn't, and that we can violate the rights of animals in this way. I take it that, for Gentili, the action of a human being killing a deer that was needed for food would not constitute any kind of contumely, although I think it would still be 'without right' in the sense that the human's right is for self-preservation, and not directly for the killing of the deer. But if the human killed the deer just for fun, Gentili's argument does allow for this to be construed as a violation of right in a human, contumelious way, and thus for human beings to be in political relations with animals, at least in the broadest sense. There is support for this interpretation in Gentili's later work, *On the law of war* (1598). Here Gentili addresses the treatment of captives in war, and, interestingly, parallels the treatment of slaves and of animals, both equally without any rights against their captors either under civil law or under the law of nations. The implication is that they are both confined to the sphere of natural right in the same way. His initial point is that 'kindness stretches further than justice', and his example is the Athenians, who allowed their animals rest, pasture and even burial after 'the long labours of life'. The argument takes a more legal turn, however, when he invokes 'the law of God', i.e. Deuteronomy: 'Thou shalt not muzzle a threshing ox.' Gentili concludes by saying simply that God willed that we should be *humani* to all things. The obvious translation of *humani* here would be 'humane'. But does that quite capture the force of what he is saying? A more risky, but more interesting and still justifiable translation would be that God willed us to be *human* to all things.[24]

If we now turn to Catholic scholastic natural law discourse, here too, just as in the more conventional humanist jurisprudence, we find the argument from capacity for *iniuria* doing important work in denying rights to animals. In the scholastic tradition it is inflected by their distinctive understanding of *dominium*, the focal meaning of which is *dominium* over one's own actions as a result of reason and will.[25] Only humans have this, and therefore only humans are capable of *dominium* over anyone or anything else. This is how the scholastics understood God's words in Genesis I:26, here in the Authorised Version: 'And God said, let us make man in our image, and after our own likeness; And let him have dominion over the birds of the air, and the fish of the sea, and over the earth, and every living thing that moveth upon it.' The dominion that man has over the earth and its creatures is a consequence of the dominion he has over himself, itself a consequence of the reason and will by which he is made in God's image and likeness. Sixteenth- and seventeenth-century scholastics inherited Thomas Aquinas's understanding of this original *dominium* as granted for the sake of use, and most of them also accepted his argument that animals are incapable of use just as they are incapable of *dominium*. Given that, increasingly, scholastic juridical philosophers of the period conceived a broad equivalence between *dominium* and right, at least in the sense of signalling a capacity for *iniuria*, the consequence was to push animals, again, out of the sphere of right entirely: to make them purely used rather than users. An extreme example is the Jesuit Luis de Molina (1535–1600) in his massive treatise *On justice and right*, remarking that animals are incapable

---

[24] A. Gentili, *De jure belli libri tres*, 2 vols. (Oxford: Clarendon Press, 1933), book III, ch. 9.

[25] See A. Brett, *Liberty, Right and Nature: Individual Rights in Later Scholastic Thought* (Cambridge: Cambridge University Press, 1997), chs. 1 and 4; id., *Changes of State*, 21–23, 38–47; B. Tierney, 'Dominion of Self and Natural Rights before Locke and After', in V. Mäkinen and P. Korkmann (eds.), *Transformations in Medieval and Early Modern Rights Discourse* (Dordrecht: Springer, 2006), 173–203.

of suffering *iniuria* and that therefore no more wrong is done to an animal in killing it than in snapping a twig off a tree.[26]

This does not mean that scholastic philosophers offered no rights to animals at all. Like Gentili, some were prepared to see them as possessing not right in the sense of *dominium*, but right in a different sense, a right to the activities and goods required for the flourishing of their particular nature.[27] This might have no implications at all for the rightfulness of human treatment of them; it might simply mean that they were behaving in a naturally rightful manner in running away, for example, but not that any wrong was done to them in capturing them. The Jesuit Juan de Salas (1553–1612), however, argued for such rights within an Aristotelian teleology wherein plants are made for animals and animals made for man: 'one should concede to animals – yes, and even to inanimates – right in the sense of what is rightful, or a kind of faculty of doing something, the use of which it would be an injustice to interfere with. For they demand, as if by their own proper right, the things that are naturally due and proportioned to them, so that they may exist in a good state, and be preserved, and serve the uses of men for whose conveniences they were brought forth.'[28] In this conception, then, justice and rights can exist within a user–used relationship; indeed, it is precisely this God-given relationship, at least in part, which argues for the right. And this is a right that it is 'injustice' to interfere with, thus arguing that the centrally political virtue of justice is not confined to relationships between human beings nor to relations between equals. Compare, in the fraught context of the English civil wars, Antony Ascham's passionate plea for the rightfulness of self-preservation: 'Man were of all living creatures most miserable, if he might not during this life have that measure which God would not have an Oxe defrauded of. Thus hath every dunghill Flye a right to live, and to remain insectile, which besides existence hath sence, and may not justly be deprived of that its chiefest felicity, unlesse it be importunate to a nobler Creature.'[29]

---

[26] L. de Molina, *De iustitia et iure* (Mainz, 1614), tract. II, disp. 3, n. 6. I have not seen the twig analogy in any other scholastic writer, and do not think that it is representative of a general sensibility; nevertheless, the position that it is not possible to violate the right of an animal is absolutely standard.

[27] This conception is rather similar, I think, to Martha Nussbaum's Aristotelian capability-right, which she herself applies to animals: id., *Frontiers of Justice: Disability, Nationality, Species Membership* (Cambridge, MA: Belknap Press, 2006).

[28] J. de Salas, *Tractatus de legibus* (Barcelona, 1611), tract. 13, disp. 2, sect. 2, fol. 35. Salas was in other contexts a friend to animal agency, combatting Aquinas's idea that they are incapable of use. However, he still excluded them from all *dominium* or right in things.

[29] A. Ascham, *Of the Confusions and Revolutions of Governments* (London, 1649), 12.

Finally on animals, and in the same context, I turn to the work of Thomas Hobbes, a philosopher who is always fruitful for thinking with on the animal/human divide. In one aspect, his work involves a variation of the *iniuria* argument, although understood very differently and in direct opposition to the conception of human agency that lies behind the scholastic version of the argument. For Hobbes, animals do not have reason, but they are perfectly capable of prudential behaviour based upon experience, often much more capable than human beings. Likewise, they are just as capable as human beings of appetites and aversions towards particular desired or feared objects, and thus equally capable of acts of will, understood as acts that deliberate them upon a particular course of action.[30] However, Hobbes argues, they don't have speech with which to signal their will to another, nor can they accept a sign of a will from someone else; it is therefore impossible to make covenants with them, that is, mutually to agree upon a limitation of rightful possibilities of action.[31] As a result, although they may have right (as we saw earlier), they will nevertheless be outside any sphere of *iniuria*: an animal cannot violate the right of a human being, since it cannot transfer or give up any of its right in that person's favour. Neither can a human being violate the right of an animal, for exactly the same reason.

But the matter is more complicated than that. In the case of human beings Hobbes allows that speech is not a necessary condition of covenant. In chapter 20 of *Leviathan* (1651), Hobbes discusses the relationship of dominion that a parent acquires over a child and a victor over the vanquished. Here he politicizes the relationship by arguing that, like all subjection, it requires an act of will or covenant on the part of the one who is to be subject. It is not simply a function of the natural act of generation, nor of sheer force. But Hobbes explicitly allows that there can be other signs of the will than speech, as the case of very young children clearly demands. Consent can even, perhaps, be supposed just from the natural operation of the will, if that is the way we interpret Hobbes's continuing argument that irresistible power yields dominion: we cannot but assent to its sway over us.[32] If that is so, however, and politics is radically naturalized in this way, then why cannot a dog that obeys its master be supposed to have consented, and thus be in a 'Commonwealth by Acquisition' with its master? Some light is shed on

---

[30] Hobbes, *Leviathan*, chs. 4–6; see further Brett, *Changes of State*, 57–60.

[31] Ibid., ch. 14, 97. For the importance of speech to Hobbes's political thought, see P. Pettit, *Made with Words* (Princeton: Princeton University Press, 2008).

[32] See K. Hoekstra, 'The de facto Turn in Hobbes's Political Philosophy', in L. Foisneau and T. Sorell (eds.), *Leviathan after 350 Years* (Oxford: Oxford University Press, 2005), 33–73.

farmed animals by a passage in *The Questions concerning liberty, necessity, and chance* (1656), in which Hobbes argues against the proposition that human beings naturally have dominion over animals as a function of their superior nature.[33] Oxen and sheep, Hobbes says, don't obey us any otherwise than they would any other predatory animal of superior force, a wolf or a lion, say. Any such dominion is purely based on superior force – *if* the dominion we have over such animals can be called dominion, 'which properly it cannot'. Why not? The answer seems to lie in the teleology of obedience, which is protection.[34] We are not 'protecting' the sheep that we farm, and so the sheep cannot be presumed to have consented, because no one can consent to their own destruction. Nevertheless, the case of sheep and oxen doesn't seem to include dogs, cats or horses that we keep not to kill, but for other purposes. In the case of humans, protection does not exclude a relationship of use (the servant in *Leviathan* ch. 20 gives the master the *use* of his life and liberty, at his pleasure); nor does it involve any obligation not to kill the subject. Thus, again, it's hard to see why a dog, for example, couldn't be in a political relationship with its master, or any other animals that we might protect for any reason.

I want to turn now from relations with animals to relations with non-animate nature. I shall focus on the land, as the central object of early modern attention in this respect, although increasingly sea, rivers, forests and even air figure too. Here, the strong conditions on agency required for political community mean that conceptions of the land as an agent and partner in such community in some sense are very hard to find, although it is not the case that there is absolute silence. One example that I know of is the mid-sixteenth-century Spanish jurist Fernando Vázquez de Menchaca, in his deliberately provocative *Illustrious controversies* of 1564.[35] Here Vázquez alters the standard juridico-political account of community-formation by incorporating an Ovidian perspective in which man was originally at peace, along with the animals, in an untouched natural world. Humans, animals, earth and seas were then free in the sense of being at large, unbounded. But with the decline of the ages man turned to tyranny, and the important point is that the tyranny is both over the land and over his fellow men, intertwined with each other. The traditional vices that in the republican

---

[33] T. Hobbes, *The Questions Concerning Liberty, Necessity, and Chance* (London, 1656), 141–142.

[34] Hobbes, *Leviathan*, ch. 21, 153: 'The end of Obedience is Protection; which, wheresoever a man seeth, either in his own, or in anothers Sword, Nature applyeth his obedience to it, and his endeavour to maintaine it.'

[35] For a full analysis, see Brett, *Liberty, Right and Nature*, ch. 5.

tradition destroy human community and open the door to tyranny – ambition, avarice, self-love – also destroyed the natural symbiosis between human beings and their environment: it caused them to put boundary-stones on the land and to chop down the trees in order to set sail over the oceans, which God had set in place as natural divisions. And those same vices caused them to oppress and to tyrannize over the weak among their own kind. Thus, the political corruption of our relations with nature, and the political corruption of our relations with human beings, go hand in hand. This is not merely a metaphorical usage of a 'suffering earth' trope, but genuinely serves to place land, sea, animals and humans in the same, original natural space of freedom. It is clear that this is a lost world, and not a possible political model for human lives in the present; and yet it does serve as a point of critique on the contemporary dynamic of utility, artifice and servitude, and to valorize the pockets of original liberty that remain.

Thus, an agentic conception of the land is not a conceptual impossibility within early modern political thought, and I am sure there other examples unknown to me. It is true nonetheless that human relations with the land and with other constituents of the natural environment are overwhelmingly figured in terms of *dominium*. This relationship certainly involves moral considerations: it is understood as *use*, not *abuse*, and the idea of using something rightly appeals to a broader conception of the ends of human life, and of the role of the land in achieving those ends. This is very commonly linked with an appeal to God's purposes, based on the same text of Genesis we looked at in the context of animals. The virtues of husbandry, industry and improvement transform the land in accordance with the divine plan for mankind. Walter Blith's *The English improver improved* of 1652 makes God 'the Originall, and first Husbandman', who made man 'to Husbandise the fruits of the Earth, and dresse, and keepe them for the use of the whole Creation'.[36] More famously, John Locke in the fifth chapter of his *Second Treatise of Government*, first published in 1688, argues that the earth was given to man for his benefit, and therefore to the 'industrious and the rational' who would cultivate it and make it fruitful.[37] An emblem of George Wither, dating from 1635, depicts a man planting a tree with the motto *Posteritati* ('For posterity').

---

[36] W. Blith, *The English Improver Improved* (London, 1652), ch. 1, 3. See P. Warde, 'The Idea of Improvement, c. 1520–1700', in R. Hoyle (ed.), *Custom, Improvement and the Landscape in Early Modern Britain* (Farnham-Burlington: Ashgate, 2011), 127–148.

[37] J. Locke, *Two Treatises of Government*, ed. P. Laslett (Cambridge: Cambridge University Press, 1988), Second Treatise, ch. 5, 'Of Property'. It ought to be acknowledged, however, that this text can be read as far more ambivalent from an ecological point of view, especially in a colonial context: the premium on agriculture and permanent

The associated poem, lamenting the contemporary despoiling of the woodlands, shows that the general good that is part of this ethic of cultivation could extend to future generations: 'For, if they thinke their *Children* shall succeed; Or, can believe, that they begot their Heires; They could not, surely, doe so foule a Deed, As to deface the *Land*, which should be theirs.'[38] The centrality of family to the early modern understanding of landed property is here exploited to produce a more general ethic of environmental responsibility.

Although this *dominium* over the land is not in itself a political relationship, then, its political implications were never far away. Blith's *English improver* stresses throughout the benefit to the commonwealth of such improvement. But that benefit is modulated through the key institution of property, which transforms a relationship with the land into a relationship with other people. Early modern thinkers argued fiercely over the best form of property in the land and its relationship to the best state of the commonwealth. Book I of Thomas More's *Utopia* of 1516 stresses the social and political evils resulting from private enclosure of the commons, generating poverty and violence, with the suggestion of consequent animal/human inversion between the sheep and the hanged men. Famously, in Utopia 'nothing is private', and a virtuous citizenry fruitfully cultivates the land for the common benefit of all.[39] In the middle years of the seventeenth century, Gerrard Winstanley and the 'Diggers' argued for the right of every man to work the commons for himself, rather than to work private land as hired labour. Private property he associates with sin and the distortion of God's original

---

livestock farming implied in its values tends to invalidate other, less intensive uses of the land, let alone the idea that the land might not be there to be used at all. There was nothing exceptional in this basic attitude of Locke's, even if the theorizing is distinctive: wilderness areas held no appeal to early modern sensibilities, and lives lived through hunting or through nomadic pastoralism were generally seen as inferior rather than viewed sympathetically as accommodations between humans and natural environment. Locke's theory of property has generated a vast commentary literature: for a detailed consideration that includes the colonial perspective, see J. Tully, *An Approach to Political Theory: Locke in Contexts* (Cambridge: Cambridge University Press, 1993), section II.

[38] G. Wither, *A collection of Emblemes Ancient and Moderne* (London, 1635), 35.

[39] T. More, *Utopia*, ed. and tr. G. M. Logan and R. M. Adams (Cambridge: Cambridge University Press, 1989). The English 'commonwealth' tradition and republican thought more generally are particularly marked by the idea that healthy political relationships are mediated through healthy arrangements for the distribution of land, which in turn fosters the other virtues (courage, independence) needed for the maintenance of the political community. Thus, Francis Bacon in his essay 'Of the True Greatness of Kingdoms and Estates' praises the English system of yeoman farming for yielding the manly fighters the commonwealth needs: Bacon, *Major Works*, 397–403. The classic of this approach is James Harrington, *The Commonwealth of Oceana*, ed. J. G. A. Pocock (Cambridge: Cambridge University Press, 1992).

creation of mankind.[40] But others saw the dynamic between human relations with the land and human relations with other human beings very differently. So, for example, Luis de Molina establishes an unusually close link between the necessity to divide land into private properties and the necessity to establish political structures. If the land remains in common, it will be abandoned and uncultivated, with consequent poverty and neediness. On his account this leads directly to fighting, rebellion and tyrannical oppression, a picture of economic disintegration generating political disorder and decay.[41]

The indirectly political relationship with the land that goes through *dominium*, however, cuts against another distinctive aspect of early modern political thought, which is a function of its associative dimension. In this perspective, as we have seen, political society or community is fundamentally defined inter-personally, as a relationship between human beings that creates an association rather than a mere local gathering. The corollary of this is that political space is *not* defined spatially or geographically, despite appearances to the contrary. For all that physical place (situation, location) is in the background to community, community itself is not essentially something situated. A range of early modern authors argued, in consequence, that a political society can change place without change of identity. This idea was inherited from the same classical tradition that provided so much of their language of politics. Aristotle had insisted that a political community is not defined by its walls,[42] and the Romans had distinguished between the *urbs* – the built city, spatially situated – and the *civitas* – the political community. Thus the Romans, conquering the city of Capua, decided that it should be 'inhabited as an *urbs*': they destroyed the *civitas*, the political structure of magistrates and laws, but left the *urbs*, the built city, intact.[43] Contrariwise, conquering Carthage, they destroyed the *urbs*, but kept the *civitas*: that is, they decided to leave Carthage free, with its own laws and magistrates, but they imposed a change of site for the *urbs*, forcing it to be moved inland, away from the sea. That is, it made no difference to the political community where Carthage was.[44]

---

[40] On Winstanley, see T. Kenyon, *Utopian Communism and Political Thought in Early Modern England* (London: Pinter Publishers, 1989), part III.

[41] Molina, *De iustitia et iure*, tract. 2, disp. 20, n. 5. See further A. Brett, 'Molina on Law and Power', in A. Aichele and M. Kaufmann (eds.), *A Companion to Luis de Molina* (Leiden: Brill, 2014).

[42] Aristotle, *Politics*, book III, ch. 3.

[43] The story occurs in Livy's *History of Rome*, book 26, 16.

[44] The reference is to the Roman consul Censorinus's speech in Appian's *History of Rome: The Punic Wars*, 89: 'we offer you whatever place you choose to take, and when you have taken in, you shall live under your own laws ... We consider you to be Carthage, not the ground or buildings where you live.'

In this way of thinking, the city as the political community is discon-
nected from the place in which it is situated. This generates the question
of how, if at all, human beings can relate *politically* to the place that they
are in. To answer this question, I think we have to step outside the
vocabularies that we have been looking at so far and turn instead to the
language of *patria* – the land of one's fathers, the place where one was
born, one's native land. This is a rich seam of discourse that has been
gaining more attention lately, primarily in filling out the story about
human community and its duties. However, we can also look at it as a
discourse that links human community fundamentally to a particular
place, with ties of duty, loyalty, affection and honour. Here again, familial
virtues and feelings are moved up to a political level as a supplement to
the more strictly juridico-political language of citizenship and
commonwealth. We find this, for example, in the *De republica* ('On the
commonwealth') of the early seventeenth-century German Aristotelian
political scientist Henning Arnisaeus, who argues against dual citizenship, beginning with a reference to Cicero's assertion in his own *De
republica* that the *patria* is the more ancient parent, and more is owed to
it than to our actual parents. Nature, Arnisaeus says, *planted* us in our
patria or commonwealth. Against the Stoic claim that the whole world is
the *patria* of the wise, he argues that 'the native soil entices to itself the
minds of all with a quiet sweetness'; the Stoics must first overturn nature
before they can eradicate this affection. 'We live beneath the sky, as a
common place, but that does not mean that each thing is not attracted by
its own proper place, as Aristotle teaches.'[45]

In Arnisaeus's hands, this argument from *patria* is an argument for the
commonwealth rather than for any more local form of citizenship; the
built environment of the *urbs* is not, for him, a political thing in the strict
sense. Alberico Gentili, by contrast, appeals to *patria* to attack the very
distinction between the *civitas* and the *urbs* that was inherited from the
classical tradition. Here we are in his *Wars of the Romans* of 1599, and in
book I, which is the attack of the Italian accuser against the Roman wars
as exercises in sheer brutality and the merciless pursuit of empire.
Discussing the razing of Carthage consonantly, or so the Romans said,
with preserving the city and its freedom, the Italian exclaims: 'What point
in repeating the speech of the Roman consul, the minister of this crime?
With this speech he strove to render acceptable to the deceived Cartha-
ginians the ruin of their native land' – *patria* – 'and the building of a new
urbs . . . Go, Romans, go to the speech of Camillus' – this is in Livy – 'the

---

[45] H. Arnisaeus, *De republica* (Frankfurt, 1615), book I, ch. 5, sections 7 and 8.

speech that once upon a time kept you in the ruins of your *urbs*, in the rubble and the ashes, and which will show you how base and nefarious is that sophistical distinction of yours between an *urbs* and a *civitas* . . . Is the soil of one's native land to that extent nothing? Nothing the earth, that we call mother? And the region to which our eyes have become accustomed? And the sky, under which we were born, and raised? What of Carthage's location, its farmland, its sea . . .?'[46] Gentili's argument here represents the conceptual possibility of opening political community to include a particular situation, a region, with its natural features and its characteristic *views* – 'the region to which our eyes have become accustomed' – shaping the way we see. The ancient language of mother earth, which Carolyn Merchant found dead or dominated in the political and scientific thought of the seventeenth century, is here incorporated within an innovative critique of the classical *civitas* that eschews its equally classical Arcadian alternative. Instead, Carthage's location becomes part of how its citizens *are*, and thus part of their political community.

I do not want to suggest that *patria* is an unproblematic way to think of the political agency of the land from a present point of view. Modern environmental thought stresses the interconnectedness of different ecosystems, and the consequent need for global action and global eco-citizenship. We might well view Arnisaeus's deliberate anti-cosmopolitanism with some suspicion as an early form of state patriotism that could have threatening implications for the environment even while it sentimentally celebrates it. And yet current environmental political thought as well as activism has a strong local dimension too, and here Gentili's stress on the aesthetic element of situated citizenship appears much more attractive. Either way, a consideration of the role of the natural environment in political life prompted these early modern authors to stretch the inherited categories of politics in suggestive ways. Likewise, the essentially theological narrative of *dominium* over the earth and its creatures had the potential, as we have seen, not merely to underwrite but also to challenge established understandings and practices of hierarchy, both between human beings themselves and between human beings and animals, and between human beings and the natural world more generally. Finally, the serious and sustained analysis of the agency of animals, which characterizes early modern philosophy as a whole, led some authors to rethink the related notions of justice, rights

---

[46] A. Gentili, *De armis romanis*, tr. D. Lupher as *The Wars of the Romans* (Oxford: Oxford University Press, 2011), 70–73. That this is Gentili's own opinion is clear from his *De iure belli* of 1598, in which this Roman distinction between *civitas* and *urbs* is lambasted as a flagrant example of verbal fraud.

and the reach of the community in which they operate – sometimes denying the need for community altogether; sometimes challenging the idea that justice can exist only within a community of equals. In all these ways, early modern European political thought poses questions that are still relevant to us: how *are* we to relate to beings that don't relate to each other, or to us, in exactly the same way as we relate to each other; and what are the legal and political consequences of that?

3   'Sustainability', Resources and the Destiny of States in German Cameralist Thought

Paul Warde

It might easily be assumed that societies that were clearly dependent on the bounty of the earth for food, fodder, raw materials and fuel would be acutely aware of the necessity of what we call 'sustainability' and of the possibility of exhausting those resources and hence undermining the conditions that make society possible. One could move swiftly on, as some green thinking has, to argue that modern environmental ills and anxieties are a product of 'industrialism'. In industrialism an ethic of sustainability becomes replaced by a set of attitudes, spanning the full range of the traditional political spectrum, that anticipates the possibility of, for all intents and purposes, endless economic growth without serious consideration being given to the finitude of resources or the limited capacity of the earth to act as a sink for pollutants.[1] Of course, many optimists about growth have acknowledged the existence of environmental problems, but have argued that these would be resolved by technological advances (and thus the growth process could be considered both the cause and solution of such problems).[2] In the optimists' account, an environmental politics is really a matter of the allocation of 'services', usually conceived of in terms of leisure preferences, to a population who, with the benefits of higher incomes, view nature as another good to be consumed and are prepared to bear the cost (through paying or campaigning) of preserving it. Many environmentalists would argue that it is precisely the commodification of nature that has arisen with industrialism, and the illusory substitutability of nature and consumer goods, that puts sustainability at risk.

Yet this 'green' critique, so intuitively reasonable, of a world that has lost touch with the material and ecological underpinnings that sustain it, is not true: at least in terms of the history of *political* discourse. Ensuring

---

[1] A. Dobson, *Green Political Thought* (London: Routledge, 1990), 29–33.
[2] For an exemplar of the very extensive debates in this issue, see P. Sabin, *The Bet: Paul Ehrlich, Julian Simon, and Our Gamble over the Earth's Future* (New Haven, CT: Yale University Press, 2013).

the fertility of a field certainly did matter to people in pre-industrial societies the world over. We have plenty of evidence of the many agricultural and ritual practices in place to ensure this, or to minimize the risk of harvest failure. But until a surprisingly late date, the fertility of a *nation*'s soils was not a cause for discussion. I have argued that, with a very few exceptions, this emerged as a theme only after the middle of the eighteenth century, the reason being that before this time, learned discourse in Europe did not by and large recognize that there was anything in the soil that you could permanently exhaust. Hence 'unsustainability' could be only a localized problem, manifest on the scale of a village at most, and was susceptible to local remedies. Far from being forgotten, concerns about sustainability actually tended to *rise* with industrialization.[3]

Nevertheless, the Enlightenment did not lack *political thought* about natural resources, and this chapter will seek to trace that thought without the assumption of familiarity. The discussion will focus on Germany, as emblematic of although not identical to a wider European trend. Rulers were highly aware that the distribution of landed resources did influence the wealth and success of states, even if they had a very different idea of environmental risk to us. Equally, during the Enlightenment the 'natural sciences' saw themselves as advancing rapidly and providing information essential to the more effective management of the polity – a significant claim in terms of their institutionalization and idea of what kind of person (or expert) was needed to govern well. Hence new scientific knowledge was potentially new political knowledge too, with implications for discussions about the best form of government. In this chapter I will argue that over the early modern period we see a shift in the role of government in resource management: from arbitrator among competing claims, seeking to secure order, where resource 'sustainability' (as we might call it) was more a question of access and rights, to one concerned with growth and innovation where the durability of the resource became a serious issue to be resolved by expert knowledge. In turn, there was a related shift in political discourse away from arguments that stressed government as a guarantor of fundamental *needs*, towards one where action was justified because it would bring greater 'happiness' or allow 'flourishing'. This is analogous to what we would call growth, although the term was not used and the age lacked definitive metrics of what increased with the improvements anticipated and aimed for.

The dominant line of reasoning across the eighteenth century was that the earth was, by and large, under-exploited; that industry and

---

[3] P. Warde, 'The Invention of Sustainability', *Modern Intellectual History* 8 (2011), 153–170.

population provided a stimulus to more productive management of the land; and that evidence of poor usage by ordinary folk was so manifest that coercion was justified in supplying those same people with their needs and securing their happiness. Governors, and thinkers about government, thus saw themselves as facing two challenges in regard to resources in Enlightenment Germany. One was distributional, to provide desirable (from the point of view of the ruler) and just (in responding to the claims of subjects) allocations both in terms of the entitlements of households, and among different industries, regions and localities. The second was to *improve* yields from the land and stimulate manufactures, often from levels that were considered seriously below par. Writers on these themes did not argue that resources were fixed, but recognized that soils were variably productive. In hindsight one can perhaps see this as a shift from emphasizing the first task according to a kind of 'law of the minimum',[4] justifying the political order by ensuring fair allocations, to one more preoccupied with general improvement, an endlessly receding (or advancing, depending on your point of view) horizon of greater happiness. We should not, however, dramatize this shift too hyperbolically as a fundamental change between a Renaissance and an Enlightened state. Efforts to innovate and disseminate knowledge about resources were already present in the fifteenth century.[5]

The current German translation of 'sustainability', *Nachhaltigkeit*, is often attributed to the German forester and mining official Hans Carl von Carlowitz's work *Silvicultura oeconomica*, published in 1713, and sits squarely in the era under consideration. There is always a danger in expecting to find coherence and tractability in ideas – mythologizing – and this is perhaps especially apparent in the case of talking about the history of 'the environment' where there has been a tendency to explain sweeps of history through telling stories of wisdom lost or gained (harmony with nature, or the progress of technology). In English

---

[4] I take this from the theories of nineteenth-century soil science articulated by Carl Sprengel and Justus von Liebig, that soil fertility is limited by the state of the nutrient in shortest supply, no matter how much other nutrients are available.

[5] L. Sporhan and W. Von Stromer, 'Die Nadelholz-Saat in den Nürnberger Reichswäldern zwischen 1469 und 1600', *Zeitschrift für Agrargeschichte und Agrarsoziologie* 17 (1969), 79–109, 79; K. Appuhn, *A Forest on the Sea: Environmental Expertise in Renaissance Venice* (Baltimore: Johns Hopkins University Press, 2009); J. Buis, *Historia forestis. Nederlandse bosgeschiedenis* (Utrecht: HES, 1985), 18; J. Buis, 'Über Entwicklungs- und Verbreitungslinien der Forstwissenschaft und der Baumzucht in Nordwest Europa 1400–1800', in S. Cavaciocchi (ed.), *L'uomo e la foresta* (Florence: Le Monnier, 1995), 723–734; P. Warde, 'Fear of Wood Shortage and the Reality of the Woodland in Europe, c. 1450–1850', *History Workshop Journal* 62 (2006), 28–57; K. Mantel, *Forstgeschichte des 16. Jahrhunderts unter dem Einfluß der Forstordnungen und Noe Meurers* (Hamburg: Paul Parey, 1980).

'sustainability' is a neologism of the 1970s. Does that mean that the underlying idea had really been lurking all this time, untranslated or neglected, only then to come into its own?[6] Certainly some foresters and forestry literature have claimed this early provenance for the concept, not so much sustainability *avant le mot* as one hidden in plain sight.[7] The uptake of *Nachhaltigkeit* was influential in the 'scientific forestry' (*Forstwissenschaft*) of Enlightenment Germany, and translated as 'sustained yield theory' in English in the nineteenth century, it is the ancestor of our modern usage.[8] However, while the preoccupations of forestry have a necessary connection with the ground from which trees grow, this was not necessarily framed in terms of a wider ecology (itself a late nineteenth-century concept that was only popularized and seriously applied even by natural scientists some decades after being coined by Ernst Haeckel in 1866).[9] Contrariwise, in some recent accounts, rather than being a saviour that introduced sustainable management and future-thinking in a world rapaciously consuming its wood supplies, German scientific forestry (*Forstwissenschaft*) was the original form of misguided central planning, trampling roughshod over local knowledge and ecological variation with its geometry, projections and academic expertise.[10] Yet just as visions of sustainability have not been singular, either over time or at any one time, neither have theories or practices of

[6] L. Robin, S. Sörlin and P. Warde, *The Future of Nature: Documents of Global Change* (New Haven, CT: Yale University Press, 2013); P. Warde, 'The Environment', in P. Coates, D. Moon and P. Warde (eds.), *Local Places, Global Processes: Histories of Environmental Change in Britain and Beyond* (Oxford: Windgather Press, 2016), 32–46; U. Grober, *Die Entdeckung der Nachhaltigkeit. Kulturgeschichte eines Begriffes* (Munich: Kunstmann, 2010), esp. 105–125.

[7] In fact he did not use the word *Nachhaltigkeit*, but he wrote that woodland management should be *nach haltende*, which we might translate as the contemporary English word 'sustained', which derives from the Latin *sustenare*. H. C. von Carlowitz, *Sylvicultura oeconomica oder haußwirthliche Nachricht und naturmäßige Anweisung zur Wilden Baum-Zucht* (Leipzig, 1713), 68; Warde in Robin, Sörlin and Warde, *Future of Nature*; K. Hasel and E. Schwartz, *Forstgeschichte. Ein Grundriss für Studium und Praxis*, 3rd ed., (Remagen: Kessel, 2006); Sächsische Carlowitz-Gesellschaft (ed.), *Die Erfindung der Nachhaltigkeit. Leben, Werk und Wirkung des Hans Carl von Carlowitz* (Munich: oekom verlag, 2013).

[8] This occurs more often in the adjectival form *nach haltig*, as for example in the widely disseminated textbook of Moser. W. G. Moser, *Grundsätze der Forst-Oeconomie* (Frankfurt and Leipzig: Brönner, 1757), 31, 78, 83, 113, 148, 163.

[9] S. E. Kingsland, *The Evolution of American Ecology 1890–2000* (Baltimore: Johns Hopkins University Press, 2005), 68–69; L. K. Nyhart, *The Rise of the Biological Perspective in Germany* (Chicago: University of Chicago Press, 2009); R. P. McIntosh, *The Background of Ecology: Concept and Theory* (Cambridge: Cambridge University Press, 1985), 2–3, 23, 28–39; E. Haeckel, *Allgemeine Anatomie der Organismen: Kritische Grundzüge der mechanischen Wissenschaft von den entwickelten Formen der Organismen* (Berlin: Georg Reimer, 1866).

[10] J. C. Scott, *Seeing like a State: How Certain Schemes to Improve the Human Condition Have Failed* (New Haven, CT: Yale University Press, 1998). This is dependent for its

professional forestry. Before too glibly attributing much later twentieth-century attitudes and interventions in the landscape to Enlightenment forebears (whom twentieth-century foresters, and their historians, have for the most part never read), we must think carefully about how they may or may not be connected, and be aware of contingency in both the history of ideas and how practice is shaped by a range of contextual factors.

This chapter will return to Carlowitz's context and the emergence of *Nachhaltigkeit*, in part to give a more accurate account of the thinking of the time. It will also argue that political thought about and schemes for managing resources can be understood only in relation to ideas about the fundamental purposes of government, whether articulated by administrators, savants or claimants on the state's services. It was these purposes that in the end were to be sustained.

I.   Cameralism: The Ethic of Activist Government

Writing about early modern German government is frequently termed 'cameralism', derived from the German *Kammer*, for chancellery or treasury. 'Cameralist' thought encompassed a wide variety of views, and has been defined both narrowly and broadly by Enlightenment writers and in the subsequent historiography. Indeed, both the contemporary literature and more especially subsequent writing about it can feel like rather dismal and convoluted debates about definition, demarcation and genre that shed little light on the substantive *content* of how these writers thought states should be administered or the sources from which they drew their ideas.[11] Rather than defining cameralism as a very particular approach to government unique to a moment of time, it might be more accurate to gloss it as a label that contemporary authors found useful to identify themselves with, and later historians found helpful to describe a set of texts that appealed above all to the transformatory powers of central authorities as the means to social betterment (even if this could very occasionally mean de-regulation). As a genre cameralist

---

discussion of forestry on H. E. Lowood, 'The Calculating Forester: Quantification, Cameral Science and the Emergence of Scientific Forestry Management in Germany', in T. Frängsmyr, T. L Heilbronn and R. E. Rider (eds.), *The Quantifying Spirit in the 18th Century* (Oxford: Oxford University Press, 1990), 315–342; and C. Maser, *The Redesigned Forest* (San Pedro, CA: R&E Miles, 1988).

[11] Keith Tribe notes that the form of many books, and the preoccupation with definition and repeated exposition, probably arises from their origin as lectures. K. Tribe, *Governing Economy: The Reformation of German Economic Discourse 1750–1840* (Cambridge: Cambridge University Press, 1988), 17.

works were preoccupied with the art of administration, as distinct from the tradition of writing about political acumen on the part of rulers (*Staats-klugheit*).[12] At the time, writers often made three major distinctions. *Camer-wissenschaft* was the most directly preoccupied with the management of the prince's assets or sources of income, the older *Polizeiwissenschaft* sought to regulate or steer the behaviour of the population, usually through prohibitions on activities deemed disorderly or wasteful, but also encouraging education, for example, and, third, some variant of *Wirtschaft-Wissenschaft* or *Oeconomie*, focused on the direct means and techniques by which income was produced.[13] It would be wrong, however, to imagine that such boundaries were rigorously policed in practice. One of the most influential writers on this theme of the late eighteenth century, for example, Johann Friedrich von Pfeiffer, divided his *Universal-Camer-Wissenschaft* into four parts, comprising the art of securing the external borders, a *Polizeiwissenschaft* concerned with inner security, *Staatswissenschaft* that managed economic processes of production and consumption, and a *Finanzwissenschaft* by which the government raised revenue and used it wisely.[14]

In turn these could connect up to a large set of relevant cognate or sub-disciplines ranging from moral theology to agricultural studies to chemistry. The genre promoted the idea that governing also required some expert knowledge of the full range of disciplines that might usefully be applied to that government in order to understand what should be administered and whose expertise might be brought to bear. 'Nothing is more decisive than that those who wish to rule over others, come to know both themselves, and the state they will rule.'[15] The question that underlay the broader set of cameralist writing was, 'What did one need to know to rule?', or in an educational context, 'What should be on the curricula of those being educated to govern?' Many works were explicitly produced as collections of lectures, as cameralist studies became widespread in

---

[12] J. Brückner, *Staatswissenschaften, Kameralismus und Naturrecht* (Munich: C. H. Beck, 1974), 112–148. For recent discussions, see the essays in J. G. Backhaus (ed.), *Physiocracy, Anti-Physiocracy and Pfeiffer* (Heidelberg: Springer, 2011); A. Wakefield, 'Books, Bureaus and the Historiography of Cameralism', *European Journal of Law and Economics* 19 (2005), 311–320.

[13] This formal division was applied in the work and teaching of C. Dithmar, *Einleitung in die Öconomischen, Policey- und Cameral-Wissenschaften*, 5th ed. (Frankfurt an der Oder: Johann Christian Kleyb, 1755); it already owed something to the organization of Seckendorff's book. The tradition of declaring one's predecessors as impractical and lacking experience was almost universal throughout this period, but emerges as a critique of Aristotilean *Staatslehre* in Lühney. See Brückner, *Staatswissenschaftten*, 15.

[14] J. F. von Pfeiffer, *Grundsätze der Universal-Cameral-Wissenschaft* (Frankfurt am Main: Eßlingerschen Buchhandlung, 1783), 4–5.

[15] Pfeiffer, *Grundsätze*, i.

central European and Scandinavian universities from the 1750s,[16] which itself demonstrates how the audience was primarily expected to be the senior officials and counsellors of the prince, although it was equally true that an effective prince should also be a good cameralist in order to appoint effective administrators.

As a founding text in the German language we may take Ludwig Veit von Seckendorff's *Der teutsche Fürsten-Staat*, 'The German principality', of 1655. Seckendorff was a young man appointed administrator to a minor German prince who wished to escape the chaos of the Thirty Years' War, and systematically put his statelet on a path to success through sound governance. The huge text was basically a manual for everything he thought you needed to know to manage such a state, and in itself it contains virtually nothing that is not familiar to anyone who has trawled through the contemporary records of German administrations; for the most part it was simply descriptive of practices of the time. This largely descriptive approach remained, in fact, characteristic of much of cameralist writings right up until the end of the eighteenth century, for all the frequent protestations that a new work was going to be truly practical and not succumb to the generalities of its predecessors.[17] There is no need here for an extensive debate on whether this literature reflected reality, because a large amount of its content and recommendations was drawn from actual legislation (whether this was universally enforced or not is another matter of course and to be doubted).[18]

The shared viewpoint of cameralists is described neatly by Pfeiffer writing in 1782, whose economics was in part cribbed from Adam Smith but who differed on the fundamental point of the directive role of the state: 'no labour without peace, no peace without laws, no laws without

---

[16] Tribe, *Governing Economy*, 42–46, 94–95, 116; Brückner, *Staatswissenschaften*, 32, 60, 66, 73; V. L. von Seckendorff, *Teutscher Fürsten-Staat* (Jena: Johann Meyer, [1655] 1737); Dithmar, *Einleitung in die Öconomischen*.

[17] See for example the work of Dithmar in 1732, edited and issued anew as a textbook by Schreber in 1755; or at the end of the century, the textbook of Johann Heinrich Jung. J. H. Jung, *Lehrbuch der Cameral-Wissenschaft oder Cameral-Praxis* (Marburg: Neue Academische Buchhandlung, 1790), esp. iv–v. Brückner, *Staatswissenschaften*, 12.

[18] André Wakefield, on the basis of a rather limited selection, has argued that cameralist works were fantastical in their propositions, or simply mendacious, and served above all to legitimize rulers (and authors) who did not believe in the prescriptions they made; but this fundamentally misses the issue that most of its content was drawn from regulation already enacted in *some*, although rarely *all*, German states. Some works relied very heavily on printed volumes of legislation as sources. A. Wakefield, *The Disordered Police State: German Cameralism as Science and Practice* (Chicago: University of Chicago Press, 2009).

government, no government without rules'.[19] Thus the roots of prosperity lay in wise rules of government, and these were what cameralists sought to provide. This was an admittedly legalistic view of rule-making as the engine of good government, although it should be noted that since the *Polizeiordnungen* (police ordinances) of the sixteenth century it was common to mix within single Acts laws as to how the populace should conduct itself, and the procedural rules by which administrators should govern. At the same time no government could act without being able to draw on the wealth of its subjects. It would be misguided to try and find some consistent ideas of the primacy of the economy or governance in such writing; the point was that productive processes (*Oeconomie*), regulation (*Polizei*) and the organization of the state (*Camer-sachen*) were mutually reinforcing, and if anything marked out cameralism from other discourses on government or society at this time, it was a determination never to treat of any aspect of the state in isolation. In the end the goal was the 'happiness' (*Glückseligkeit*) of the populace.[20] Of course, just as a rich populace made for a rich ruler, so did a contented populace make for a contented prince. This was the case whether the happiness of ruler or ruled was seen as reciprocal and inextricably bound, or whether it was argued that a wealthy and happy populace was the best source of revenue for the ruler, which in turn could be used for the general good (positions that could quite easily appear in the same work).[21] This was the task and duty of a ruler 'who wants to ... better secure, maintain and protect his wealth, to direct all of his efforts in order that his land and people are set in an ever more flourishing condition of sustenance (*Nahrung*) and thereby in an ever greater prosperity (*Aufnehmen*)'.[22]

There were, of course, plenty of rulers who chose their own happiness over anything that very obviously benefitted the populace, while claiming it was for the general good in the long run, or at the very least that there

---

[19] J. F. von Pfeiffer, *Grundriß der Staatswirtschaft zur Belehrung und Warnung angehender Staatswirte* (Frankfurt am Main: Barrentrap, Sohn & Wenner, 1782), 6; see also A. F. Napp-Zinn, *Johann Friedrich von Pfeiffer und die Kameralwissenschaften an der Universität Mainz* (Wiesbaden: Steiner, 1955).

[20] There was, however, some difference of opinion; Sonnenfels stressed the outer security of the state as the first purpose of government, as nothing was achievable without it, but Pfeiffer argued this was merely a means to an end. Dithmar, *Einleitung in die Öconomischen*, 14; U. Engelhardt, 'Zum Begriff der Glückseligkeit in der kameralistischen Staatslehre des 18. Jahrhunderts (J.H.G. von Justi)', *Zeitschrift für historische Forschung* 8 (1981), 37–79; Pfeiffer, *Grundsätze*, i and 33.

[21] See for example A. W. Small, *The Cameralists: The Pioneers of German Social Policy* (New York: Burt Franklin, 1909), 142–143; E. F. Heckscher, *Mercantilism*, 2nd ed. (London: Allen and Unwin, 1955), vol. II, 19–20.

[22] Zincke cited in Brückner, *Staatswissenschaften*, 82; Dithmar, *Einleitung in die Öconomischen*, 19, 178, 306.

might be different ideas about what was good. Pfeiffer simply wished away this awkward separation of interests by arguing that it was the duty of the ruler to 'unify' the happiness of each individual with the 'collective best', and the obligation of the people to obey the ruler's injunctions that were given with these good intentions. His argument that people bore a sensibility orientated towards respective needs drew on writing about moral sentiment in Hutcheson, Hume, and Smith.[23] Other writers tended to take a commonality of interest for granted. What did bind this set of thinkers together was the notion that *Glückseligkeit*, while experienced individually, could be generated only by corporate endeavour. Cameralists shared a basic assumption that people were already inextricably and originally bound into a political order; they generally considered the political order as they found it as a starting point, and rarely raised questions about its origins. This was perhaps a reflection of the situation of its advocates, who nearly all sought preferment by the government or expected to spend a career working for it.[24] However, this did not lead to the conclusion that knowledge of what constituted collective or individual happiness could be determined from some panoptical sovereign viewpoint. These writings remained too resolutely attached to traditional administrative and academic demarcations for such an idea, and indeed very rarely engaged in what we might call 'joined-up' thinking today, despite efforts at universal coverage. In practice they projected a confidence that implementing long series of improvements in each individual branch of government would be to the general betterment.

Nevertheless, the goal of 'happiness', or in the sixteenth and seventeenth centuries the idea of the 'common weal' or 'common good' (*gemein nutz*), was not an entirely empty figure that could be dictated at a ruler's whim.[25] The duty to seek the collective best also related to the specific needs of the ruled, by which government could become the subject of claims to rights. Throughout early modern central Europe, it

[23] Wakefield, *The Disordered Police State*; Brückner, *Staatswissenschaften*, 235; Pfeiffer, *Grundsätze*, 8–10, 33. Also Pfeiffer, *Grundriß der Staatswirtschaft*, 1. However, even before the reception of Smith's writing, authors such as Sonnenfels were arguing for the essential autonomy of private households and the relatively unimpeded operation of the market, paving the way for a more limited conception of the state's role. J. Von Sonnenfels, *Grundsätze der Policey, Handlung und Finanzwissenschaft* (Munich, 1787).
[24] See Tribe, *Governing Economy*, 29–30, following, in many cases, Grotius and Pufendorf. See S. von Below and S. Breit, *Wald – von der Gottesgabe zum Privateigentum. Gerichtliche Konflikte zwischen Landesherren und Untertanen um den Wald in der frühen Neuzeit* (Stuttgart: Lucius & Lucius Verlag, 1998), 17; Von Justi, however, did provide an account of the origins of the state.
[25] On *gemein nutz*, see A. Landwehr, *Policey im Alltag. Die Implementation frühneuzeitlicher Policeyordnungen in Leonberg* (Frankfurt am Main, 2000), 62–68.

was thought that one's welfare was dependent on maintaining a certain level of material well-being. This was expressed in the concept of *Notdurft* in German, *necessitas domestica* in Latin and related to the idea of 'necessary use' in English common law.[26] *Notdurft* expressed the idea that the actions of others should not deprive one of the basic materials needed to sustain one's enterprise, whether this was a peasant household or a princely court. The idea, as we would say today, could be 'scaled'. A claim to *Notdurft* was a claim to the means to achieve a minimal standard of living, appropriate to one's status, not necessarily a desirable equilibrium or bare subsistence. Equally, one could not make any legally recognized claim to one's *Notdurft* (along the lines of equity claims) if no one else was causing you to fall below such a level. After equity, there was only charity for the unfortunate. Thus, as Seckendorff wrote, a task of the sovereign was to ensure that 'no subject lacks his necessary means, excepting special punishments from God, and by his own fault; but that through diligent labour and proper use of what is his he may obtain his rightful sustenance without any improper hindrance'.[27]

The concept of *Notdurft* provides the essential context for understanding early modern notions of 'sustainability'. Resources were perceived to be scarce because people feared not receiving their *Notdurft*. But the reason for this failure was perceived to lie either in the failure of will on the part of the sufferer, which was their own problem, or in them being inhibited in obtaining it because of the actions of others, in which case it became an issue for government. Indeed, the reason for misfortune that concerned cameralists above all was poor rule-making by governors. In this age, fortune was largely thought of as providential, and misfortune came from sloth, sin, and the failure of governors to tackle such *human* frailties. It was only from the middle of the eighteenth century that some natural historians began to posit that there might be some finite limit to the vital, life-giving sustenance available on earth – articulated mostly widely in the works of the Comte du Buffon[28] – but this was not thought

---

[26] R. Blickle, 'From Subsistence to Property: Traces of a Fundamental Change in Early Modern Bavaria', *Central European History* 25 (1992), 377–386; C. P. Rodgers, E. A. Straughton, A. J. L. Winchester and M. Pieracinni, *Contested Common Land: Environmental Governance Past and Present* (London: Earthscan, 2011), 7, 36. On a related argument in natural law, Below and Breit, *Wald*, 19–20. In the eighteenth century it became more frequently distinguished from 'comfort' or 'luxury' and thus was more closely associated with being 'poor', and indeed was assimilated more closely to a 'natural law' view where one enjoyed a basic right to subsistence. Engelhardt, 'Zum Begriff der Glückseligkeit', 58–59; Brückner, *Staatswissenschaften*, 231.

[27] Seckendorff, *Teutscher Fürsten-Staat*, 217–218.

[28] See for example Comte de Buffon, trans. W. Kendrick and J. Murdoch, *The Natural History of Animals, Vegetables and Minerals with the Theory of the Earth in General* (London, 1775),

to have much bearing on human affairs. Curiously, even Malthus did not imagine limits on raw material supplies as he did on food.[29] Local shortages became most obvious in the case of famine, and the governors of villages, towns, and states had long been acutely aware and fearful of harvest shortfalls or the pressure that immigrants might put on food and welfare resources; the result was centuries of regulation restricting the movement of food and the indigent. But this pressing local and regional politics of entitlement did not translate into a more general theory of a population outstripping its resource base. Such a possibility remained abstract. Pfeiffer recognized the theoretical possibility of overpopulation, for example, but reckoned in 1782 that Europe fed only a quarter of its population.[30] Similarly, in late seventeenth-century England, William Petty thought that population growth might outstrip food supply in around 1800, but in the whole world, not for two millennia yet. Such a prospect seemed irrelevantly distant, although by the second half of the nineteenth century the prospect of resource exhaustion within centuries had become a cause for alarm.[31] Johann Heinrich Gottlob von Justi, perhaps the most energetic economic writer in Enlightenment Germany, famously declared, 'A country in which subsistence and commerce flourish can never have too many inhabitants,'[32] and in the 1660s, Seckendorff had reversed the Malthusian argument by arguing that while a larger population was the basis of a land's riches (*schatz*), poor and middling families were averse to the burden more children represented, and so should receive some support.[33] Famines, wrote

---

vol. 1, 466. This will be dealt with in a forthcoming book, P. Warde, *The Invention of Sustainability: Nature and Destiny, 1500–1870* (Cambridge: Cambridge University Press).

[29] 'It should be remembered always that there is an essential difference between food, and those wrought commodities, the raw materials of which are in great plenty. A demand for these last will not fail to create them in as great a quantity as they are wanted.' R. T. Malthus, *Essay on the Principle of Population* (London: J. Johnson, 1798), 90.

[30] Pfeiffer, *Grundsätze*, 15–17; certainly, writers on wood shortage recognized that it was partly caused by the expansion of tillage and settlement, but felt that this could easily be resolved by more effective management. For example, Carlowitz, *Sylvicultura*, 2nd ed. (Leipzig: Johann Friedrich Braun sel Erben, 1732), 42–43, 49–50; J. G. Beckmann, *Gegründete Versuche und Erfahrungen der zu unsern Zeiten höchst nöthigen Holzsaat, zum allgemeinen Besten*, 4th ed. (Chemnitz: Johann Christoph Stößel, 1755), 8–9.

[31] W. Petty, *Another Essay in Political Arithmetick, Concerning the Growth of the City of London* (London, 1682), 18–19. In contrast, nineteenth-century alarm over coal supplies operated on much shorter timescales, especially Jevons's famous argument that coal supplies might be exhausted in a century. J. N. Madureira, 'The Anxiety of Abundance: William Stanley Jevons and Coal Scarcity in the Nineteenth Century', *Environment and History* 18 (2012), 395–421.

[32] Tribe, *Governing Economy*, 65.

[33] This was, of course, in the wake of the depopulating Thirty Years' War. J. V. Seckendorff, *Additiones oder: Zugaben und Erinnerungen zum teutschen Fürsten-Staat* (Leipzig: Meyer, [1664] 1737), 229.

Pfeiffer, were the result of institutional failure, generated by 'erroneous art (*Kunst*), rather than physical causes'. God had not designed a world in which the right actions of the virtuous could ever bring calamity upon themselves. In central Europe in the wake of the calamitous seventeenth century especially, rulers considered under-population to be a genuine concern.[34]

Rather than over-use, it was *under-use* of resources that appeared more problematic to eighteenth-century economic thinkers, and that threatened well-being. This was viewed as an issue of neglect, of indolence and moral failing, but increasingly, over time, a failure of expertise and dissemination of the knowledge that would raise productivity. It was not enough to admonish or punish. Discipline and industriousness were necessary, but both had to be steered by expert knowledge, which in turn implied administrative activism. From this viewpoint, a state that simply arbitrated claims of infringements to entitlements and ensured court-determined allocative justice appeared increasingly insufficient.

II.   Forests: From Proscription to Prescription

There might have been little fear that poor management of the soil could create a long-term political problem, but wood supplies presented a different case. Wood was a visually identifiable resource essential to nearly all economic activity that grew, for certain kinds of uses, on time horizons beyond the human lifespan. Wood was widely understood as 'one of the most necessary requirements of life, a thing that we can as little dispense with for necessity (*Notdurft*) or comfort, that shows its uses in all branches of industry, and where every station would be exposed to the most damaging consequences were it lacking'.[35] Literature about impending wood shortage was prolific throughout the period and across nearly all regions of Europe, irrespective of their actual endowment of trees. Equally, from the fifteenth century there was a proliferation of legislation and forestry administrations to tackle the alleged problem. This could be found from the level of village by-laws to parliamentary legislation, but was often, unsurprisingly given the context of *Notdurft*, about attempts to allocate supplies to particular users (whether peasant

---

[34] Pfeiffer, *Grundriß*, 4; Dithmar, *Einleitung in die Öconomischen*, 156.

[35] '... eine der allernöthigsten Bedürfnisse unsers Lebens, ein Stück, das wir so wenig zur Notdurft als Bequemlichkeit entbehren können, das bey allen Arten von Gewerben seinen Nutzen zeigt, und durch dessen Ermangelung dem gesamten Nahrungs Stand die allerschädlichsten Folgen zuwachsen würden'. Moser, *Grundsätze*, 5.

homes, the smelting industry or shipbuilding) as opposed to the relationship of supplies to demand *in toto*.[36]

The right of government to legislate for the conservation of woodland
and regulation of wood use, even over private property, was justified by
the responsibility of government to ensure *Notdurft* – however defined –
to its subjects. This was the explanation for the *Forstregal* (the right to
designate and regulate on 'forest matters') provided in legislation from
the late fifteenth century, and as a justification for the control of wood
supplies it was still repeated in the eighteenth: 'because this thing that is
so indispensible to human life requires the special provision of the
government'.[37] So, wrote Seckendorff, entirely conventionally, officials
were to ensure 'through their instructions that the yield of the woods is
not exceeded, rather that there might remain an ever-lasting and constant
use of wood for the lords, and a persistent supply of fuel and other
wooden necessities for the territory, from year to year in this time and
in the future for our descendants'.[38] Some 150 years later the forester
Georg Hartig wrote a famous definition of *Nachhaltigkeit*, advocating a
geometrically planned scientific forestry: 'Every wise forestry administration must ... seek to exploit [the woodlands] such that the subsequent
generations (*Nachkommenschaft*) can draw at least so much advantage
from them, as currently living generations appropriate.'[39] Thus the need
to generate an acceptable and just allocation of the resource, to domestic,
industrial and military users increasingly led government to stipulate how
woodlands themselves should be managed, and engage in surveying,

---

[36] There is a very extensive literature on the 'wood shortage' or 'timber famine' debates in
many countries in Europe, although very few examine its international breadth. See
Warde, 'Fear of Wood Shortage'; R. P. Sieferle, *The Subterranean Forest: Energy Systems
and the Industrial Revolution* (Knapwell: White Horse Press, 2001); P. Warde, 'Early
Modern Resource Crisis: The Wood Shortage Debates in Europe', in A. T. Brown,
A. Burn and R. Doherty (eds.), *Crises in Economic and Social History: A Comparative
Perspective* (Woodbridge: The Boydell Press, 2015).
[37] 'weil dieses zum menschlichen Leben unentbehrliche Stück einer besondern Vorsorge
der Regierung allerdings bedurfte.' J. G. von Justi, *Staatswirtschaft oder systematische
Abhandlung aller Oekonomischen und Cameralwissenschaften, die zur Regierung eines
Landes efodert [sic] werden* (Leipzig: Scientia, 1758), 206–207; this argument was taken
up and at times cited word-for-word by Moser, *Grundsätze*, 23–27. For some
examples of the numerous early interventions and justifications for regulating wood
resources, see P. Kissling, 'Policey der Nachhaltigkeit. Die Politik entdeckt die
knappen Ressourcen', in P. Blickle, P. Kissling and H. Schmidt (eds.), *Gute Policey als
Politik in 16. Jahrhundert. Die Entstehung des öffentlichen Raumes in Oberdeutschland*
(Frankfurt am Main, 2003), 515–547; P. Warde, *Ecology, Economy and State Formation
in Early Modern Germany* (Cambridge: Cambridge University Press, 2006); and carried
forth by Schilling into the nineteenth century, see B.-S. Grewe, *Der versperrte Wald.
Resourcenmangel in der bayerischen Pfalz (1814–1870)* (Köln: Böhlau 2004), 65.
[38] Seckendorff, *Teutscher Fürsten-Staat*, 471.
[39] Hasel and Schwartz, *Forstgeschichte*, 335, 341.

inventorization, the creation of professional managers and the diffusion of best practice. Over time, this shifted into an aspiration to engineer the forests, and eventually would become linked to the desire of governments to enhance 'well-being' or 'happiness' rather than simply secure *Notdurft*.

The process was slow and uneven, and proceeded with a variety of motives. Early and famous attempts at inventorization were undertaken from the fifteenth century by Venice, anxious to secure supplies of timber on which the city stood and from which its fleet was constructed. Naval timber was a perennial concern for maritime states, an issue more to do with sourcing the right quality of wood than shortfalls in quantity. At times, such as with Jacobean attempts to reform the crown forests, or the famous legislation of Colbert in France, a major motivation was the improvement of revenue, and commands such as imposing universal cutting cycles on forests were probably as much to do with valuing their output to draw up leases as maintaining a steady supply of wood.[40]

Thus from the sixteenth to the eighteenth centuries the ambition of forest management as a *political task* undertaken by the state shifted from a general (although not exclusive) emphasis on conservation by negative rules (do not cut too much wood, use only specific types of wood for specific tasks, do not clear the forest and so on) to engineering that supplemented this with prescriptive requirements for transformation (foresters require qualifications, property rights should be transformed, systematic planning introduced.) Earlier, Renaissance forest legislation tended to rely on moral admonishment of both the population and the foresters, to behave honestly, thriftily and equitably in the spirit of *Polizeiordnungen* (police ordinances): a population habituated to virtue would be its own guarantee of *Notdurft*. Over time, legislators

---

[40] Unsurprisingly, given their great variety of locations, states, and uses to which wood could be put, motives for regulating it could be equally varied, although historians have a tendency to generalize from their own cases. There is a large literature on the subject, of which a selection is Appuhn, *Forest on the Sea*; Warde, 'Fear of Wood Shortage'; A. Corvol, *L'Homme et l'arbre sous l'Ancien Regime* (Paris: Economica, 1984); A. Corvol, 'La decadence des forêts. Leitmotiv', in A. Corvol (ed.), *La Fôret malade. Débats anciens et phénomènes nouveaux XVIIe–XXe siècles* (Paris: L'Harmattan, 1994), 3–17; see also B. Fritzbøger, *A Windfall for the Magnates: The Development of Woodland Ownership in Denmark c. 1150–1850* (Odense: University Press of Southern Denmark, 2004); C. Ernst, *Den Wald entwickeln. Ein Politik- und Konfliktfeld in Hunsrück und Eifel im 18. Jahrhundert* (Munich: R. Oldenbourg, 2000); J. Allmann, *Der Wald in der frühen Neuzeit* (Berlin: Duncker & Humblot, 1989); R. Hölzl, *Umkämpfte Wälder. Die Geschichte einer ökologischen Reform in Deutschland 1760–1860* (Frankfurt am Main: Campus, 2010); I. Schäfer, *'Ein Gespenst geht um'. Politik mit der Holznot in Lippe 1750–1850* (Detmold: Naturwissenschaftlichen und Historischen Vereins für das Land Lippe, 1992); U. E. Schmidt, *Der Wald in Deutschland im 18. und 19. Jahrhundert* (Saarbrücken: Conte Verlag, 2002); Sieferle, *The Subterranean Forest*; P.-M. Steinsiek, *Nachhaltigkeit auf Zeit. Waldschutz im Westharz vor 1800* (Münster: Waxmann, 1999).

increasingly doubted in the efficacy of such appeals and controls, whether in terms of the management of individuals, households or a wider economy.[41] They certainly did not abandon moralizing, but increasingly viewed the rural populace as being incapable of understanding what was good for them; they had to submit to or learn from experts, and change the way the woods were managed. In doing so, governors also imposed a much more open-ended set of aspirations towards improvement (*Verbesserung*) upon themselves.[42]

This was particularly true of the German states, where the numerous and fragmented polities led to the creation of many forestry administrations, and movement of personnel between them, creating both a competitive and cooperative arena for innovation. For some states, income from wood sales, mining, smelting, and salt-making were significant sources of princely revenue and focused attention on increasing wood yields at an early date. Germany thus emerged as a centre of forestry expertise, already having been a pioneer in the creation of conifer plantations as early as the 1360s.[43] It is in this context that we come to Carlowitz writing in the state of Saxony in 1712 at the end of a long career as a forestry and mining official. Not least, in his explanation for the poor yield of woods: 'It is mostly people who are themselves guilty, when infertility is found in the earth ...', he wrote; 'ground and soil remain eternally able to harbour enough vegetation, if they are not neglected by people's lack of diligence ... but appropriately worked, planted and cultivated, coming to the aid of a seemingly powerless Nature, and thus will the soil's perpetual and continually effective power be allowed to erupt in unending fertility.'[44] This was a conventional view, and would remain so. It involved a set of 'ecological' assumptions about the resilience of nature, and the capacity of people, by correct usage, to draw out its powers of generation. Even *declines* in fertility and

---

[41] This also had much in common with the disciplining instincts so prominent in social legislation during the course of the 'long Reformation'. Warde, *Ecology*, 161–169. See also A. Landwehr, 'Die Rhetorik der "Guten Policey"', *Zeitschrift für historische Forschung* 30 (2003), 251–287; M. Raeff, *The Well-Ordered Police State: Social and Institutional Change through Law in the Germanies and Russia 1600–1800* (London: Yale University Press, 1983); P. H. Wilson, *Absolutism in Central Europe* (London: Routledge, 2000), 100–101.

[42] There is certainly some kinship between this account and the focus on sovereignty, discipline and biopolitics evoked by Michel Foucault found in *Security, Territory, Population: Lectures at the Collège de France 1977–1978* (Basingstoke: Palgrave, 2007), esp. 11 January 1977. We might note that these notions are at least as applicable to the ordering of the trees – and perhaps more so, as the concept of the *Normalbaum* appeared as a goal for forest management by the end of the eighteenth century – as the consumers of wood.

[43] See note 5.   [44] Carlowitz, *Sylvicultura Oeconomica*, 106.

productivity were attributed to human moral failings rather than either natural causes or over-exploitation. If people damaged their resource base, it was through wrong use, not over-use.

The trends in regulating forests and wood use also reflected a move in German political thought away from an idealized conception of the 'republic' as an association of the virtuous that enhanced the happiness of all (and if all were virtuous, all needs would be met), to one where happiness was the goal of the state that had to take a form and conduct itself instrumentally towards this end.[45] In turn, new controls and interventions raised the question of how to reconcile innovation with a system strongly underpinned by customary rights and practices. By the time Christoph Dithmar wrote as a professor of cameralism in 1731, he explicitly distinguished himself from the Aristotelian tradition where *Oekonomie* was a matter of morals.[46] He was more concerned with developing technical expertise. It was the combination of virtuous behaviour with this expertise that made an effective *Oeconomie*. Moral virtue was, on its own, inadequate. Morals were still to be regulated by the various manifestations of *Polizei* (including religion), but had to be augmented with the spread of *Wissenschaft* (knowledge) to enhance wealth. This interest in technical expertise had long had a place in German legislation, especially on forests, but was a literary tradition built up in so-called *Hausväterliteratur*, written at first in imitation of classical authors such as Cato and Columella on a patriarch's management of his landed estates.[47] Thinkers in this tradition had begun to assimilate work on forestry, chemistry, natural history and mathematics into their agrarian economics.[48] By the 1730s, and especially the 1750s,

---

[45] In practical terms this shifted away from the view still taken by Christian Wolff as to the essential role of virtue in political life towards a more ends-orientated and technical view of what the state provided, and what was crucial in education; following Thomasius, relations and *decorum* becoming more significant than inner virtue. See Engelhardt, 'Zum Begriff der Glückseligkeit', 42–49; Brückner, *Staatswissenschaften*, 230; see also T. C. W. Blanning, *The Culture of Power and the Power of Culture: Old Regime Europe 1660–1789* (Oxford: Oxford University Press, 2002), ch. 6.

[46] Dithmar, *Einleitung in die Öconomischen*, 14. On Dithmar, see C. Kohfeldt, 'Justus Christoph Dithmar: *Die Oeconomische Fama*. Der erste Versuch eine ökonomische Zeitschrift zu etablieren', in M. Popplow (ed.), *Landschaften agrarisch-ökonomischen Wissens. Strategien innovativer Ressourcennutzung in Zeitschriften und Sozietäten des 18. Jahrhunderts* (Münster: Waxmann, 2010), 49–60, 52.

[47] M. P. Cato, *On Agriculture*, and M. T. Varro, *On Agriculture* (Cambridge, MA: Harvard University Press, 1934); L. J. M Columella, *Of Husbandry* (London: A. Miller, 1745).

[48] Dithmar, *Einleitung in die Öconomischen*, 16–17, 26, cites a mix including ancient authors such as Columella, more recent writers such as Seckendorff and Ludwig, the Hausväter-like Rohr, foreign works on natural history and agriculture such as Bradley and Vallemont, Carlowitz on forestry, and rulers such as Erik von Gotha and Friedrich Wilhelm I of Prussia.

a diversification in the relevant literature had occurred, which ranged from encyclopaedic surveys of knowledge as taught by professors of *Cameralwissenschaft* and the vast work of Zedler and the French encyclopaedists, to highly specialized books and journal articles on soil chemistry, seed planting or geometry for foresters.[49] Learned societies and journals (usually short-lived) sought to disseminate best practice across borders and to estate managers, foresters and farmers. Somehow, the enlightened governor was supposed to maintain his grip on this proliferation of learning and apply it for the collective good.[50] A starting point was having the right men trained for the job. As Bücht-ing wrote in his 1756 *Entwurf der Jägerei* (Treatise on Hunting), 'If every district had the fortune to be managed by people well-versed in forestry, it is sure no wood shortage would arise, as experience shows.'[51] This was, as we would say, a knowledge economy, and like a modern knowledge economy it required education, property rights, means of communication and incentives to change. Marcus Popplow has described it as a 'specific culture of innovation' of the eighteenth century that sought to improve production by placing the right kind of learned personnel in positions of authority, and fostering networks of communi-cation to disseminate knowledge across borders and to the wider populace.[52] Traditional rights and communal property came to be seen as a barrier to reform, as part of the European-wide movement towards enclosure.[53] These ambitions, however, begged the question of whether there would be eventual limits to improvement born of knowledge given the actual distribution of resources.

---

[49] E.g. G. H. Zincke, *Anfangsgründe der Cameralwissenschaft* (Leipzig: Carl Ludwig Jacobi, 1755); Beckmann, *Gegründete Versuche*; J. F. Zedler, *Grosses Universal Lexicon aller Wissenschafften und Künste, welche bishero durch menschlichen Verstand und Wiß efunden worden* (Halle and Leipzig; Johann Heinrich Zedler, 1731–1754).

[50] The problem of how to integrate theoretical and abstracted specialist knowledge into *praxis* remained an ongoing debate. See S. Windelen, 'Die Vollkommene Landwirtschaft, der vernünftige Landwirt und die Erdflöhe, *Die Berliner Beyträge zur Landwirthschaftswissenschaft* (1770/74–1791)', in Popplow, *Landschaften*, 79–96.

[51] 'Wenn alle Reviere das Glück hätten, von forstverstandigen Leuten verwaltet zu werden, so rise gewiß kein Holzmangel ein; doch stehet auf die Erfahrung'. Cited in Beckmann, *Gegründete Versuche*, preface, 13.

[52] M. Popplow, 'Die Ökonomische Aufklärung als Innovationskultur des 18. Jahrhunderts zur optimierten Nutzung natürlicher Ressourcen', in Popplow, *Landschaften*, 3–48.

[53] There is a vast literature on this topic but in the German case, see H. Zückert, *Allmend und Allmendaufhebung. Vergleichende Studien zum Spätmittelalter bis zu den Agrarreformen des 18/19. Jahrhunderts* (Berlin: De Gruyter Oldenbourg, 2003), esp. pp. 295–319; for an excellent discussion of the application of arguments about 'backwardness' in Bavarian forestry, see Hölzl, *Umkämpfte Wälder*.

III.   Power through Knowledge

It is clear that Carlowitz and his cameralist contemporaries did not believe that the economy of their time was a zero-sum game with fixed resources. They have sometimes been described as a certain kind of 'mercantilist', preoccupied with the retention of bullion, discriminatory regulation of trade and beggar-thy-neighbour policies. Typically these views are contrasted with the focus on exchange and specialization found in authors such as William Petty in the seventeenth century, and most forcefully, making extensive use of a caricature of mercantilism, by Adam Smith. The conceit of the mercantilists, according to their critics, was that they considered wealth to be anchored in some material good (whether specie, resources or numbers of people), while the political economists focused on the more elastic properties of labour and its augmentation with skill and capital.[54] In truth, one can range through many of the political economists of the late eighteenth and early nineteenth centuries cherry-picking statements implying that the root of all value lay in labour, or alternatively in land – sometimes in the same book.

It might be more accurate to say that the British political economists did not write about material constraints as much as modern writers concerned with such things think they should have, rather than that they ignored the issue entirely. As E. A. Wrigley has repeatedly highlighted, Adam Smith spoke of a low-wage stationary state emerging 'in a country which had acquired that full complement of riches which the nature of its *soil* and climate, and its situation with respect to other countries allowed it to acquire'.[55] Nevertheless, it is true that the overall corpus of his writing bears greater testimony to an interest in the second part: exchange and the division of labour as a source of continuing growth. It is also true that the argument that 'the laws of nature ... have limited

---

[54] Smith did note extreme cases: 'The *soil* must be improveable, otherwise there can be nothing from whence they might draw that which they should work up and improve. That must be the foundation of their labour and industry. It is no less necessary that they should have an easy method of transporting their sumptuous produce into foreign countries and neighbouring states ... if there be no such opportunity of commerce, and consequently no opportunity of increasing their wealth by industry in any considerable degree, there is little likelyhood that they should ever ... produce more sumptuous produce than will be consumed within the country itself ... Tartary and Araby labour under both these difficulties.' A. Smith, *Works and Correspondence,* vol. 5: *Lectures on Jurisprudence,* 24 February 1763, ed. R. L. Meek, D. D. Raphael and P. G. Stein, (Oxford: Oxford University Press, 1978).

[55] A. Smith, *An Inquiry into the Nature and Causes of the Wealth of Nations,* I, [1776] ed. E. Cannan (London: Methuen, 1961), 106; and see E. A. Wrigley, *Energy and the English Industrial Revolution* (Cambridge: Cambridge University Press, 2010), 10–11.

the productive power of the land'[56] underpin Ricardo's exploration of the long-run decline in the return on capital, but he did not have much else to say on the matter. It simply does not seem to have been of very immediate concern, although some of their near contemporaries were much more preoccupied with these issues. In fact, in the middle of the nineteenth century, John Stuart Mill discussed the condition of the soil at much greater length, but he did not see it as a profound constraint on development either.[57]

German authors were much more interested in resources, but in part for reasons that may have appeared familiar enough to their British counterparts. It reflected a common observation, as William Petty wrote of the Dutch in the 1660s: 'I take the Foundation of their achievements to lie originally in the Situation of the Country, whereby they do things inimitable by others, and have advantages whereof others are incapable.'[58] In the Dutch case, situation facilitated maritime trade. Without such advantages, it made much more sense to worry about domestic resources. One of several reasons Pfeiffer gave for the promotion of agriculture was that farmers cannot substitute the source of their income, the land, and thus are likely to be much more industrious in its care, producing a more valuable asset.[59] Johann Gottlieb von Justi argued that 'a northern land which has much mineral coal will always, in relation to its other natural endowments, be able to be far more peopled, than another, that is not provided with these subterranean goods of nature, which take up no space on the surface.'[60] In other words, unlike Britain, which could effectively expand its resource base through mining downwards as well as by foreign trade, countries dependent on resources won from the surface of the land had to be much more preoccupied with the

---

[56] D. Ricardo, *On the Principles of Political Economy and Taxation* [1821], in P. Sraffa (ed.) (Cambridge: Cambridge University Press, 1951), 125–126, also cited in Wrigley, *Energy*, 21.

[57] Mill repeatedly discusses the soil in his *Principles of Political Economy* (London: John W. Parker, 1848), primarily in relation to rent but also the Corn Laws and trade. On Smith's 'ecology', see also F. Albritton Jonsson, *Enlightenment's Frontier: The Scottish Highlands and the Origins of Environmentalism* (New Haven, CT: Yale University Press, 2013).

[58] Petty, *Another Essay in Political Arithmetick*, 2; see also J. Houghton, *A Collection for the Improvement of Husbandry and Trade*, vol. 1 (London: Woodman and Lyon, 1727–1728), 441–442 [from 1 November 1695]. Such arguments should not be confused with some kind of determinism based on resource endowment, but reflected the capacity of a country both to *obtain* and *add value* to raw materials. See for example Schröder (1686) cited in Small, *The Cameralists*, 161–164.

[59] Pfeiffer, *Grundriß*, 19.

[60] J. G. von Justi, *Politische und Finanzschriften über wichtige Gegenstände der Staatskunst, der Kriegswissenschaften und des Cameral- und Finanzwesens* (Kopenhagen und Leipzig: Rothenschen Buchhandlung, 1761), 442.

allocation of that land. A century earlier Seckendorff had argued that high transport costs in largely landlocked Germany put an imperative on fostering and utilizing domestic resources. In none of these cases did anyone argue that resources were fixed, but all were highly sensitized to what might confer advantage, both now and in the future.[61] Without access to seas and rivers, and under pressure to run a positive balance of trade and maintain essential bullion for payments, the degree to which domestic resources could be exploited became of essence for Enlightenment regimes.

Cameralist thinkers thus saw fostering the provision of resources as an essential part of good government. They remained concerned with securing each household's *Notdurft*, as had been governments in the sixteenth century. But by the 1750s, Justi was arguing that the woodlands 'required the especial care of the government being an indispensible part of human life', as a 'collective necessity', (*gemeinschaftlichen Nothdurft*), or a 'national necessity' (*Landesnotdurft*). It was no longer merely a question of allowing subjects to live their lives well, but securing the future and flourishing of the polity as a unit. By extension this thus applied not just to the needs of households, but also to industry and the means to commerce, whether because there was a profitable trade to be had in the resource itself (such as metals or salt), or some other product for which they were an input. Most processed goods in turn required other natural resources in their production, above all fuel. Historically, as plenty of authors noted, greater population and labour had often summoned forth adequate resources from the land, and so long-term shortages were not a problem – an argument made explicitly, for example, by J. J. Becher in 1668.[62] Generally, the 'improving' minds of the eighteenth century concurred with Friedrich Casimir Medicus in 1774, that any question of overpopulation in his locality was being posed at least fifty years too early, and that 'the riches of the fields are immeasurable, and the more industry (*Fleiß*) and zeal one applies to it, the more productive they are.'[63] Nevertheless, if the produce of the land was not, at least in any foreseeable future, seriously limited, this did not necessarily mean that the correct *balance* of resources was available at any one place and time, for example ores and the fuel to smelt them, both heavy products (most especially the latter) and expensive to transport relative to their unit value.

[61] Seckendorff, *Additiones*, 215–218.
[62] J. J. Becher, *Politische Discurs von den eigentlichen Ursachen des Auf- und Abnehmens der Stadt, Länder und Republiken*, 3rd ed. (Frankfurt am Main, [1668] 1688), 3.
[63] M. Popplow, 'Von Bienen, Ochsenklauen und Beamten. Die Ökonomische Aufklärung in der Kurpfalz', in Popplow, *Landschaften*, 196.

Carlowitz, along with many contemporaries, suggested that God had chosen to distribute resources unevenly over the world – 'to one land or empire this, to the other that heavenly blessing' – as a deliberate way of inducing ingenuity and exchange, but nevertheless some were better placed to take providential advantage than others.[64] This argument opened up the question of the *appropriateness* of land use as well as capacity for improvement. Crops and trees should be matched with the land in which they grew best, while viewing that land as also being open, through human artifice, to improvement. It was not enough to leave the rejuvenation of trees to natural process, according to forester Johann Beckmann in 1755, because too often the seeds of trees germinated on sites that did not bring forth the best timber, or led to distributions of species by historical accident that did not optimize yields. This would lead to an insistence on intervention, 'artificial' planting and plantation forestry, although the ideas long remained controversial. Such new approaches required micro-level knowledge of the environment to get the best out of it, to better exploit it.[65]

It is anachronistic to leap directly from the *Forstwissenschaft* (forest science) that we see emerging in the Enlightenment, with its new employment of geometry and abstract mathematics to calculate the yields of trees and stands of trees, to some modern versions of monotonous, one-size-fits-all solutions in forestry imposed by technocrats with little regard to local environmental conditions. In fact, the new thinking in this period demanded more detailed local knowledge, and attributed past neglect to foresters being insufficiently acquainted with the woodlands they managed.[66] True, this was ideally to be combined with a more academic education and mastery of new theoretical (and especially mathematical) techniques for assessing and predicting productivity; indeed, it

---

[64] Carlowitz, *Sylvicultura*, 52–53, (1732 edition), 64.

[65] Beckmann, *Gegründete Versuche*, 22, 113–115; also Carlowitz, *Sylvicultura* ([1713] 1732 edition) 90, 98–102.

[66] Often, the appearance of monocultures such as spruce was the result of degradation of older mixed stands of trees over long periods of time, to be replaced by rapid-growing colonizers that were then fostered by foresters. Plantation-style forestry often thus appeared through contingency and experience rather than by the precepts of foresters. Hasel and Schwartz, *Forstgeschichte*, 294–300. Equally, when German forestry was exported to great influence abroad in the nineteenth century, they were frequently much more sensitive to local variation than modern hindsight often allows, albeit frequently not as sensitive as we might wish for. Some forestry writers very explicitly stated they could not make general rules because of divergent local conditions. E.g. Moser, *Grundsätze*, 10–11, 18, 156; on the export of German forestry overseas, see for example J. Beattie, *Empire and Environmental Anxiety: Health, Science, Art and Conservation in South Asia and Australasia, 1800–1920* (Basingstoke: Palgrave, 2011), 123–149.

was argued that this was necessarily so, because only with the calculation of site-specific growth rates could one determine the cutting cycles that would maximize yields. Writers on forestry differed, however, as to whether one should attempt this by sampling sites and direct measurement of yields, or make do with swifter ocular assessments of timber volume and growth, necessitating long experience to do so reliably.

The push for localization on the one hand and increased abstraction on the other provoked tensions. Much of the geometry introduced into forestry textbooks at this time was probably redundant and never applied in the field.[67] For G. U. Däzel, a leading forester and writer in Bavaria who sought to introduce the latest Prussian techniques to the south, the chief failing of the 'mere practical man, the empiricist' is that he 'achieved his knowledge only through the passage of time and mechanically', and hence without understanding its underlying principles he is incapable of adapting to change or innovating.[68] In one fell swoop Däzel distinguished himself from the traditional forester who in terms of knowledge, at least, was not far divorced from any other users of the woodland.

This did not mean that 'local knowledge' of woodsmen was dismissed out of hand by Enlightened foresters. As Wilhelm Moser commented, 'An old woodcutter has often noted much better what has helped this or that place to flourishing growth, or what has stopped or hindered it, than any treasury official or forester.'[69] Rather, it created a new hierarchy of expertise, by which local knowledge and experience had to be translated into a more standardized technical language. Resources became abstractly compared to capital yielding interest (although this did not mean that they were considered infinitely substitutable).[70] Eventually

---

[67] The measurement of tree volume and growth rates is a major preoccupation of most of the forestry literature published after 1750, which it would be tedious to cite here. See Lowood, 'The Calculating Forester', 332; the level of mathematical training required remained controversial. Hölzl, *Umkämpfte Wälder*, 130–132, 161–164; Lowood, 'The Calculating Forester', 322.

[68] 'der bloße Praktiker, Empyriker, der nur durch die Länge der Zeit und maschinenmäßig zu seinem kenntnissen gelangt ist.' G. U. Däzel, *Ueber Forsttaxierung und Ausmittelung des jährlichen nachhaltigen Ertrages* (München: Joseph Eindauer, 1793), vi–vii; 17–46, 50. See also Popplow, *Landschaften*, 44, 207.

[69] 'Ein alter Holzhauer hat oft viel besser angemerkt, was diesem oder jenem Platz zu so schönen Wachsthum verholffen, oder was denselben aufgehalten und verhundert hat, als alle Cammer-Räthe und Ober-Forstmeisters.' Moser, *Grundsätze*, 12.

[70] In this regard the rise of ideas of 'natural capital' and 'ecosystem services' are new glosses on old metaphors. Moser, *Grundsätze*, 76. See also Lowood, 'The Calculating Forester', esp. 330. This could lead to the idea expressed by the liberal Prussian forester Wilhelm Pfeil that the goal of forestry was not to produce a sustainable yield, but 'the highest sustainable income'. W. Pfeil, *Forstwirtschaft nach rein praktischer Ansicht*, 3rd ed. (Leipzig: Baumgärtner's Buchhandlung, 1843), 195.

such approaches opened the door to attempts to reconfigure woodlands as a *tabula rasa* of clear-cut spaces, which could be minutely managed according to local conditions and set plans.[71] But field experience and painstaking knowledge of local environments remained an essential measure of the esteem and competence of the trained forester. 'Ask the trees, how they want to be raised', declared Wilhelm Pfeil, director of Prussia's leading forestry school in the 1820 and 1830s; 'they will teach you better than books will!'[72] Certainly, emerging professional expectations coupled with the desire to raise output reconfigured the frame by which resources and the environment were viewed. It is rather less clear, indeed rather doubtful, that this represented a break with a more harmonious and respectful view of nature and the 'human condition' as some authors, notably James C. Scott, have claimed.

IV.   Sustaining Purposes

The issue of *balanced growth* lay at the heart of Carlowitz's work and his formulation of what some twentieth-century successors, especially those connected with forestry, see as the original definition of 'sustainability' (*Nachhaltigkeit* in German). 'If the annual output is fixed against the regrowth with sowing and planting, namely so that [trees] can be amply replaced and the woods are treated with care, then no wood shortage will ensue . . .' This would allow 'continual, consistent and sustainable (*nach haltende*) use' of the resource. Yet Carlowitz wrote not to maintain some kind of balanced steady-state, but to permit the *expansion* of the local metallurgical industries – this being the main source of government revenue in Saxony. His was a search to keep production in step with increasing commercial demand, and he devoted his work largely to encouraging the artificial sowing of conifers to increase yields, preferably using fast-growing species, rather than relying on the natural rejuvenation of forests.[73] He noted that people thought, erroneously, that they could rely on nature, 'as if this would always from itself proffer and furnish a superfluity of wood, without the application of people's industry

---

[71] See the prescriptions in G. L. Hartig, *Anweisung zur Taxation der Forste oder zur Bestimmung des Holzertrags* (Giessen: Buchhändler Heyer, 1795), i–vi, 78–79; on the reality in the Palatinate, Grewe, *Versperrte Wald*, 229–249.

[72] See Pfeil cited in Hasel and Schwartz, *Forstgeschichte*, 343–344: 'We set the greatest value on the observation of nature, on the study of trees and their natural behaviour, and on the careful consideration of every circumstance under which one works (*wirtschaftet*).'

[73] Carlowitz, *Sylvicultura* ([1713] 1732), 5, 48–50, 66–82. And it is in the extensive attention to technique, and the fact that the entire volume is devoted to forestry, that Carlowitz was original, rather than in any formulation about 'sustainability' or the need to match cutting to regrowth, of which there are plenty of earlier examples.

and labour'. However, if industry and labour *were* applied one would not be able to describe the plenty of wood that could ensue. Metal ores 'would not be used up ... so long as the world exists' and wood was 'the inexhaustible treasure of our land'.[74] Supply and demand were interlinked, in that it was also industry that created the incentive to maintain the forests: 'the good condition of the woodlands depends on the economic and sustainable use of the same', as Justi argued in 1758.[75]

Establishing balanced growth required information on the supply of resources, the demand for them and the spread of best practice in production and efficient use. It was essential that the authorities, remarked Justi, gathered details on how much wood was consumed in town and country. Equally, one needed to know 'how much wood could annually be felled sustainably, economically and without ruin to the woodlands', which was a job for foresters. By combining these two pieces of information, one could ensure that 'no more wood is annually felled and consumed than will annually grow back,' thus advancing Carlowitz's formula to the level of the polity. In fact, noted Justi, it was better to keep more wood than one needed to allow for the expansion of demand, while also seeing that no lands were left bare or unused.[76] Although it was beyond the capacity of authorities to make much use of the data their officials began to accumulate, we can observe expanding efforts, already under way in the late sixteenth century, to estimate consumption, production and their relations, much in the spirit of the early gathering of demographic and medical data.[77] 'How should he make it happy, if he does not know it?' queried Rößig of a ruler in a particularly elaborated version of the 'tables' required to aggregate and distribute data in 1779.[78] Thus for Enlightenment cameralist thinkers the wood economy moved into the information economy, with the state acting as a coordinating agent over time and space. This was particularly important given the long time horizons required to plan wood yields.

This reinforced, but, as we have seen, did not create the notion that only the central government was in a position to effectively manage forests: 'only the state can manage for eternity', as the early nineteenth-century

---

[74] Carlowitz, *Sylvicultura* (1732), 65.
[75] 'Kommt der gute Zustand der Wälder auf den wirtschaftlichen und nachhaltigen Gebrauch derselben an.' Justi, *Staatswirtschaft*, 227.
[76] Justi, *Politische und Finanzschriften*, 443–446.
[77] See for example L. Behrisch, 'Agrarian Statistics in Late *Ancien Régime* France and Germany', in N. Vivier (ed.), *The State and Rural Societies: Policy and Education in Europe 1750–2000* (Turnhout: Brepols, 2008), 35–55; A. N. Rusnock, *Vital Accounts: Quantifying Health and Population in Eighteenth-Century France and England* (Cambridge: Cambridge University Press, 2002).
[78] Cited in Tribe, *Governing Economy*, 33.

forester Heinrich Cotta put it.[79] The full scope of the information and cognate disciplines a cameralist virtuoso might be expected to master extended far beyond the more immediate challenges of administration. It incorporated ever-widening realms of knowledge, with (as a liberal critique might counter) obvious contradictions between an insistence on central coordination, and the view that the system to be mastered actually would operate most effectively if left to itself (as political economy and natural history might suggest).[80] However, this tension was more theoretical than real: the literature of cameralism and *Forstwissenschaft* in practice provided an encyclopaedic collection of knowledge and prescriptions, mirroring the practical day-to-day devolved coordination of government by various branches of the administration, rather than the means to command and control from the centre. With only the final metric of *Glückseligkeit* (happiness) to hand, cameralist success was measured, if at all, by having the right kind of administrator, with the right kind of knowledge, in post. Cameralist theory did not thus provide any objective means by which the usefulness of administration itself could be assessed, aside from whether it was self-financing. Nevertheless, foresters were not all of one mind on the question of what level of state intervention was for the best. Once the writings of the Physiocrats and Smith became known, some suspected that the market might do the job of coordinating and providing incentives for good management, especially when the quality of transportation improved. The possibility of long-term rational planning by centralized authorities on a grand scale was notably contested in the early nineteenth century by the liberal foresters Hazzi in Bavaria and Pfeil in Prussia, who both spent time at the head of their respective polity's forestry organizations.[81]

The importance of government intervention also rested on what one thought about the relationship between economic development and *particular* natural resources. Was a particular set of resources the essential precondition for welfare, and did this impose an obligation on existing states to future generations? With wood this seemed to be the case. It was all too easy, it seemed, to neglect to plant trees after felling, and erode woodland for tillage or pasture. This was not a new observation: an insistence on obligations to 'posterity' or one's 'descendants' (*Nachkommenschaft*) is found widely in sixteenth-century by-laws and legislation,

[79] Cotta cited in J. Radkau, *Wood: A History* (Cambridge: Polity, 2012), 150.
[80] Points made by Brückner, *Staatswissenschaften*, 71–72.
[81] A fact which should give pause to one-sided caricatures of German forestry as a monolithic enterprise. Hölzl, *Umkämpfte Wälder*, 62–65; Hasel and Schwartz, *Forstgeschichte*, 335.

and court cases as well as literature. Both the polity and property would eventually be bequeathed to descendants, and subsequent governments would also require the basic resources necessary to function and fulfil the obligations of rule. Rulers in the present were thus bound to ensure that this happened, just as landowners should not squander their inheritance held in trust for their progeny. Nevertheless, this injunction was not viewed as raising any particular ethical dilemmas about what future wants might be. It was assumed that posterity would want exactly what the present did; future generations were not conceived of as agents that should be limited in their choices. This idea was neatly expressed in a broadside against excessive wood cutting by the English pamphleteer Arthur Standish in the 1610s, decrying men 'desiring to become heyres of their owne time, without respect had to such heyres as shall succeed them'.[82] But obligations to one's own posterity, the familial inheritance, were broadened to include other duties – of patriotic sentiment and that of being true to what one knew was best. In cameralism, this justified interventions across a broad front by experts and new kinds of controls, and led to rising levels of state direction. According to Johann Beckmann, for example, the forester should 'make his provisions just as much for posterity as for the present age', and in so doing fulfil 'many duties ... which he owes to the fatherland, to the descendants, and to his own conscience'.[83]

The aims of cameralist thinkers had moved beyond those of distributional justice that had predominated during the Renaissance, and which had in the earlier period issued in measures that stressed virtuous behaviour, preservation of what existed, and a negative, juridical approach to regulation.[84] With the goal increasingly presented as enhanced *Glückseligkeit*, Enlightened policy was directed towards improvement (*Verbesserung*), which as well as a problem of jurisdiction was an issue of knowledge and communication. This did not only reflect a shift in the expressed aims of governance, but also the accumulation of knowledge about resources, and lessons drawn from agriculture, horticulture and forestry. In either case it was considered necessary for the sovereign, governing authority to have oversight of essential resources as part of its fulfilment of the basic goals of rule.

---

[82] A. Standish, *New directions of experience authorized by the king's most excellent Majesty, as may approve for the increasing of Timber and Fire-Wood, with the least waste and losse of ground* (London, 1614), 2.

[83] Beckmann, *Gegründete Versuche*, preface of 1777, 7.

[84] On Seckendorff writing in this tradition, see Brückner, *Staatswissenschaften*, 23–28.

One could also argue that what German political thinkers (in the broadest sense) were concerned about in this period was sustaining the narrative they deployed about what the state could and should do (arbitrating disputes, giving free rein to the cultivation of virtue, allowing happiness to flourish). Resources were a means to these ends, and so their maintenance came to justify new kinds of government intervention. This new politics aimed at the provision of real material returns to the gain of some and loss of others, and on a regional or national scale (for changes, it is worth noting, that came only very slowly). But despite the rising interest in developments in natural history, botany or chemistry, this was not because the resource base (never mind that later idea, 'the environment') was seen to be something fundamentally at risk. Though the cries about imminent and pressing 'wood shortage' added leverage and legitimacy to arguments for change, they were catalysts or accelerants to a resource politics that was already in place, and not a primary cause. In the end, this was not a politics that was about crisis management or tackling the environmental 'bads' left in the wake of human activities. It was geared towards fulfilling the fundamental purposes by which the existence of the state was justified, and steering the management of resources towards those ends.

4 Abundance and Scarcity in Geological Time, 1784–1844

Fredrik Albritton Jonsson

In the winter and spring of 1841, a mineralogical model became the talk of scientific London. It was displayed at the Geological Society of London and later the Institution of Civil Engineers before it was deposited at the Museum of Economic Geology. Leading aristocrats Lord Lansdowne and Lord Northumberland were among the many admirers. The educational reformer and geologist Leonard Horner brought his whole family to a viewing. Prince Consort Albert had the model sent to the royal court where he examined it with much interest.[1]

The curious object was a three-dimensional rendering of the surface and coal seams of the Forest of Dean in Gloucestershire on the Welsh border. It had been designed by the mining viewer Thomas Sopwith and built in his Newcastle cabinet-making studio. With a frame fashioned from plane tree filled with beech wood, the model was sixty inches square at a scale of 1:6,336 representing a rectangle of four miles by six miles of hills and valleys. The direction and depth of different coal seams could be examined by taking the model apart into six different sections (see Figure 4.1).[2]

Why did Sopwith's model cause such a stir? The immediate occasion for building it was a three-year Royal Commission, led by Sopwith, into the confused property claims in the mining district of the Forest of Dean. This investigation produced a detailed geological map of the district, which Sopwith then employed to make his miniature. William Buckland, the eminent Anglican geologist, hailed Sopwith's model as the beginning of a 'new era in geological science'. Much like the famous geological map of William Smith from 1815, the Forest of Dean model helped make visible the material foundation of the British economy. Sopwith pressed this point in the 1844 book *The National Importance of Keeping Mining*

---

[1] Diary of Thomas Sopwith 1828–1879 (Newcastle University Library, Special Collections, Microfilm), Journal 26, 256; Journal 27, 293–294; Journal 30, 1842, 43–45.

[2] S. Turner and W. R. Dearman, 'Thomas Sopwith's Large Geological Models', *Proceedings of the Yorkshire Geological Society* 44 (1982), 1–28.

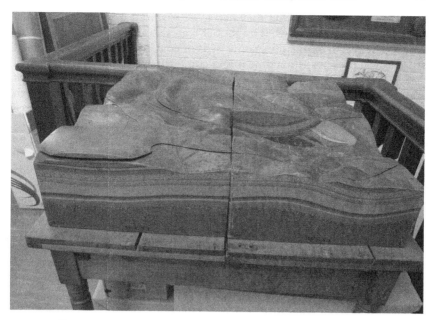

Figure 4.1 Thomas Sopwith, "The small Forest of Dean model."
Probably 1837. Oxford Natural History Museum. The model
represents 36 square miles of the Forest of Dean at a scale of 1:12,672.
This is a smaller version of the model described in this chapter.
Photograph by the author.

Records. Britain had achieved unrivalled power and unprecedented
population thanks to its coal resources. But mineral wealth differed from
other kinds of property 'chiefly in the extreme uncertainty of its existence, and the difficulty of its discovery'. Maps, models and statistical
records promised a revolution in knowledge. Buckland stressed the great
accuracy of Sopwith's work: 'the exact extent and thickness of each bed
of coal became instantaneously apparent on the removal of the upper
laminae of the model.'[3]

Sopwith's miniature landscape was at the same time a model of abundance and scarcity. Without good records, colliers might miss pockets of
coal hidden near exhausted strata. Many of the seams in the Forest of

---

[3] Diary of Sopwith, Journal 26, 242; T. Sopwith, *The National Importance of Keeping Mining
Records* (London, 1844), 17–18, 22; T. Sopwith, *Description of Sopwith's Geological Models*
(London, 1875), 55.

Dean were so fractured that they had to be assessed in three dimensions to divulge their full extent. The model was also meant as a signpost to future schemes of extraction. Some beds of coal lay too deep to be mined profitably at present. But a time might come when demand would force a rise in prices and a turn to remote seams. Indeed, the aggregation of mining statistics was meant to goad entrepreneurs towards these hidden riches. Apparently exhausted collieries would then come to life once again, an 'invaluable legacy to future generations'. But Sopwith and his allies still also could not escape a more pessimistic conclusion. The power and glory of Britain depended on the duration of a finite coal supply with no known substitute. New models and statistics could only forestall the inevitable spectre of exhaustion. The aim was merely 'to prolong, as far as possible', this wealth into the future. Sopwith's mineral cornucopia was evanescent. Increasing consumption, the badge of affluence, hastened the end of cheap coal.[4]

The dream of endless abundance has assumed many different versions over time, shaped by a variety of objects, institutions and spaces. Timothy Mitchell has argued that the ideology of endless economic growth surfaced only in the twentieth-century oil economy. Yet it is possible to find much earlier instances of this sort of confidence, from early modern natural philosophy to Victorian manufacturing. Alchemists and natural philosophers dreamt of creating artificial worlds by imitating God. Colonial boosters looked to the peripheries of empire and the bounties of new cash crops. Enlightenment naturalists imagined vertical frontiers underground. From an early stage, such projects also provoked anxieties about the physical limits to growth. Agricultural improvement at home and untrammelled expansion abroad produced evidence of environmental strain and resource exhaustion. Such predictions of exhaustion and collapse in turn provoked new forms of cornucopianism, devoted to disproving the notion of permanent limits. This dialectic was at the same time ideological and practical. As improvers became increasingly ambitious to transcend natural boundaries and remake the world, they also scaled up their demands on the life-supporting systems of the planet. Cornucopians overcame physical constraints only by increasing the ecological footprint of the economy, harvesting growing amounts of resources and overloading sinks.[5]

---

[4] Sopwith, *The National Importance*, 1844, 17, 30.

[5] T. Mitchell, *Carbon Democracy: Political Power in the Age of Oil* (London: Verso, 2011); F. Albritton Jonsson, 'The Origins of Cornucopianism: A Preliminary Genealogy', *Critical Historical Studies* 1 (2014), 151–168; D. Worster, *Shrinking the Earth: The Rise and Decline of American Abundance* (Oxford: Oxford University Press, 2016).

In the late eighteenth century, advocates of manufacturing began to associate coal and steam technology with a new era in history. The physician and inventor Erasmus Darwin celebrated the 'Giant Power' contained in coal and predicted that steam would radically transform the landscape of Britain within a generation or two. This was also the moment when geological time first entered into natural history and debates about improvement. The naturalists Comte de Buffon and James Hutton recast the conjectural history of the Enlightenment by framing it as an interlude in geological time. Hutton argued that the formation of soil, which made possible human civilization, was the product of primeval and perennial processes of erosion and uplift. Buffon suggested that the age of progress constituted the last of seven periods of geological development, when the gradual cooling of the physical globe was ameliorated by the warming effect of civilization. Paris and Quebec were situated along the same line of latitude, yet in France the climate was far milder thanks to changes wrought by human settlement, including deforestation and the draining of swamps. Savants had long reflected on the fit between human institutions and providential design in nature, but never before with a sense of prehistory so deep. These perspectives – the geological origin of human economies and the revolutionary power of coal – eventually converged in the debates over the size of the British coal reserves. The Victorian geologist William Buckland observed that fossil fuel was a gift from deep time that had to be marshalled wisely in order to sustain the new industrial economy into the remote future. Mineral endowment determined the rise and fall of nations.[6]

The argument in this chapter proceeds in two parts. We begin with the natural history of soil in the Enlightenment. James Hutton's theory of eternal cycles of uplift and erosion provides a crucial case study. Hutton was very much a product of Scottish Enlightenment, along with Adam Smith and David Hume. Hutton's writings, like Buffon's natural history, offered a new sense of how universal geological processes had shaped the soil and climate of different countries. In his natural history of the soil, natural and human cycles were connected but not always in harmony. Farmers employed the mineral elements produced by geological forces over deep time, sometimes conserving fertility and sometimes degrading it. The second part of the chapter explores the growing political

---

[6] On Erasmus Darwin, see Jonsson, 'The Origins of Cornucopianism', 161; J. Roger, *Buffon: Les Époques de la nature: Édition critique* (Mémoires du muséum national d'historie naturelle, 1988), 213; F. Locher and J.-B. Fressoz, 'Modernity's Frail Climate: A Climate History of Environmental Reflexivity', *Critical Inquiry* 38 (2012), 579–598. For Hutton and Buckland, see below.

significance of coal among British observers in the late Enlightenment. The location, abundance and scarcity of coal offered fodder for liberal, radical and protectionist arguments in debates over trade policy and popular subsistence. By the Regency and early Victorian period, geologists and mining engineers recognized that modern economies owed a significant debt to geological processes, but their focus was on the problem of mineral stock rather than soil husbandry. A fear of coal exhaustion haunted Victorian politicians and intellectuals from Sir Robert Peel to William Gladstone and John Stuart Mill. In contrast, mineral cornucopians believed that the coal stock was so abundant as to be infinite by any political or economic measure. The two camps clashed in both theory and practice over how to calculate the extent of reserves and what course to follow in commercial policy.[7]

I

At harvest time in 1785, the Edinburgh naturalist James Hutton and his companion John Clerk of Eldin found themselves scrambling over stone and heather in the steep valley of Glen Tilt, just northeast of Blair Atholl in upland Perthshire. An account of the trip to Glen Tilt was published in Hutton's magnum opus *The Theory of the Earth* in 1795. Hutton and Clerk stayed as the guests of the fourth Duke of Atholl in his hunting lodge. After exploring the valley in the immediate vicinity of the lodge, Hutton and Clerk followed the Duke on a deer hunting party into the wilderness at Fealar. Hutton was struck by the great solitude of the location: 'the most removed ... of any in Britain from the habitations of men'.[8]

Hutton had just presented his grand theory of geological change to the Royal Society of Edinburgh in March and April that year. To explain the appearance of marine fossils on mountaintops, Hutton proposed a perpetual cycle of uplift and erosion, which had shaped the rise and fall of land. His model of geological processes thus openly challenged the conventional Biblical chronology of a young earth. While moderate views of religion were commonplace in Enlightenment Edinburgh, Hutton's vision of deep time was difficult to swallow for many members of the Scottish establishment. The expedition to Glen Tilt was meant to bolster

---

[7] My argument owes a debt to two classic texts: S. Rashid, 'Political Economy and Geology in the Early Nineteenth Century: Similarities and Contrasts', *History of Political Economy* 13 (1981), 726–744; A. Briggs, *Victorian Things* (Chicago: University of Chicago Press, 1988), 289–326.

[8] J. Hutton, *Theory of the Earth*, ed. A. Geike, 3 vols. (London, 1899), I: 16; L. Leneman, *Living in Atholl; A Social History of the Estates 1685–1785* (Edinburgh: Edinburgh University Press, 1986), 34.

his theory by confirming it with fieldwork. Hutton wanted to disprove the idea that granite comprised a 'primary' stratum preceding all others in formation. By mapping the distribution of granite at Glen Tilt, he sought evidence of jumbled strata that would support his idea of never-ending cycles.[9]

Near the hunting lodge, Hutton found veins of red granite injected into the 'black micaceous' rock of 'alpine schistus'. This layering of strata was exactly what Hutton had hoped to encounter. The mixture of granite and schistus at Glen Tilt suggested that the history of geology must be understood on a temporal scale entirely different from that preached by the Church. Hutton's theory of eternal cycles was also a political wager. To what degree could humans master and manage the cycles of the geological world? What sort of political regime was best suited to control the economy of nature? A drawing of Glen Tilt by Hutton's travel companion Clerk made at the time of the visit hints at the anthropocentric vision of geology at the heart of this vision. Clerk was a gentlemen farmer, draughtsman and author of a controversial work on naval tactics. His brother George Clerk-Maxwell had served on the Board for the Annexed Estates, a government body set up to administer the thirteen Scottish estates confiscated by the state after the 1745 Jacobite rebellion. Clerk himself was a founding member of the Highland Society of Edinburgh, a private association dedicated to Highland improvement. Clerk's image of Glen Tilt strongly reflected this family legacy. He placed the hunting lodge into a vast landscape of broken rocks. A screen of leafy trees surrounded the tiny white building in the centre. The trees were in turn enveloped on the right by a low wall. On each side of the lodge, steep hillsides rose in eroded terraces towards a sky barely glimpsed. A road meandered up to the lodge between dark boulders which dominated the foreground. The sinuous line drew the observer into the funnel of the valley. The vertical fall of the sides and the gargantuan boulders at their foot prodded the observer to imagine the sublime horror of recurring landslides. Clerk in fact appears to have exaggerated the angle of the gradient. He also bathed them in a strong and hazy light. The walls of granite and schistus seemed on the verge of melting into the atmosphere, transient like clouds, a passing mirage. The presence of the many mature trees in the enclosure assured the reader that the lodge has stood safe for decades if not centuries. The violent force of erosion so visible on the hillsides acted at a rate too slow to menace the human world below.[10]

---

[9] D. Dean, *James Hutton and the History of Geology* (Ithaca: Cornell University Press, 1992), 8.

[10] Hutton, *Theory of the Earth*, I: 12–16; for Clerk's drawing, see Dean, *James Hutton*, 33.

Such a nesting of scales was characteristic of Hutton's geology. Towards the end of the survey of Glen Tilt, Hutton lifted his gaze from the veins of granite and porphyry he had followed so closely across the valley. He now invited the reader to take in the region as a whole: 'This alpine country of Scotland may be considered as a mass of strata elevated in their place and situation, being now, instead of horizontal, almost vertical; and inclined sometimes towards the north-west, sometimes again towards the south-east ...' The movement upwards was at the same time a movement inwards into the hidden strata of the mountains and backwards into geological time. In this way, Hutton made the earth lurch impossibly, from a 'horizontal' to an 'almost vertical' position, forcing plains to become alpine peaks. Next, he followed the river Tay past Atholl's estate to Dunkeld and the remnant of an 'ancient plain ... 200 feet above the present level of the water'. In this dried-out riverbed, he discovered a tell-tale 'mixture of ... broken schistus with ... white granite', which he had uncovered a few days earlier in the high valley of Glen Tarf far upstream. This was proof of the 'great operation of water, in wasting and wearing the materials of this high land, in forming the valleys between the mountains, and carrying an immense mass of matter from the summit of those mountains into the sea'. Even the most 'consolidated bodies' and 'most indestructible' substances must crumble until 'in the course of time' 'stupendous gaps' were hollowed out of the mountains. A more traditional religious observer might have taken the destructive power of water as an illustration of the evanescence of all material things. Hutton instead concluded with a theodicy of attrition. The inexorable erosion of the Highland mountains provided the soil necessary for agriculture in the Lowlands. 'The continual tendency of these operations, natural to the surface of the earth, is to diminish the heights of the mountains, to form plains below and to provide soil for the growth of plants.'[11]

The agrarian aspect of Hutton's thought has never been fully appreciated, in great part because his final treatise *Elements of Agriculture* remained unfinished and unpublished at his death in 1797. Yet the vision of geological time in Hutton was inextricably linked to a theory of soil formation and an abiding interest in agricultural improvement, as Jean Jones and Charles Withers remind us. In fact, Hutton's theory of geology bore a certain resemblance to Adam Smith's political economy. Both Smith and Hutton shared a fascination with the self-regulating properties of large-scale systems, naturalizing the economy in startlingly similar

---

[11] Hutton, *Theory of the Earth*, 26–30.

ways. Moreover, Hutton's theory of perpetual geological motion contained a political economy of the soil and climate. Conversely, Smith's faith in self-regulating markets was predicated on a deep interest in the resilience and orderliness of natural systems. At this fundamental level, Hutton and Smith shared a liberal interpretation of the natural world. In both, knowledge of nature helped justify and prop up the social structure of agrarian capitalism. The ecological differences between regions and nations were understood as spurs of specialization and exchange, not incentives for autarky. Smith and Hutton both oriented their systems towards the universal rather than the particular.[12]

Like many other naturalists of the era, James Hutton was troubled by a sense of waste within the natural economy of the world. During a visit to East Anglia in 1753, he witnessed the destructive power of water on the flooded banks of the river Yare where it emptied into the North Sea. The steady wash of disintegrating land seemed inexorable. A strong consternation is evident in a letter written to a friend two years later. 'I can't tell you what I'm about,' Hutton exclaimed. '[O]ne turn so crowds upon another, that it wou'd puzzle howdoycallum the almanac maker himself to calculate my Eclipses.' '[H]ere one Satellite stands still, there another jumps out of his Orbite and sometimes a general retrogradation will take place.' Hutton confessed in another letter that his faith had been shaken: 'you may laugh at Ovid and his fables as you please, but I find myself already more than half transform'd into a brute beast, there is nothing of the Christian left about me except some practice of piety . . .'[13]

Hutton was deeply involved in intellectual life of the Scottish Enlightenment. After a few years spent farming in East Anglia and then Berwickshire, Hutton moved to Edinburgh in 1767 where he acted as an enthusiastic advocate for the mixed husbandry model of the southeast. He also began meteorological observations of the Scottish climate in 1773–1774 to discover what crops were best suited to local weather patterns. In 1778, he founded a convivial society with Adam Smith and Joseph Black called the Oyster Club where the three savants met frequently. Both Hutton and Smith were also among the founders and

---

[12] J. Jones, 'James Hutton's Agricultural Research and Life as a Farmer', *Annals of Science* 42 (1985), 573–601; C. Withers, 'On Georgics and Geology: James Hutton's "Elements of Agriculture" and Agricultural Science in Eighteenth-Century Scotland', *Agricultural History Review* 42 (1994), 38–48; for Smith, see F. Albritton Jonsson, *Enlightenment's Frontier: The Scottish Highlands and the Origins of Environmentalism* (New Haven: Yale University Press, 2013), ch. 5.

[13] Dean, *James Hutton*, 5; National Archives of Scotland (hereafter NAS), GD 18/5749, 1–2.

officers of the Royal Society of Edinburgh in 1783. It was there that Hutton first presented his theories of precipitation and geological uplift in 1784 and 1785. When Hutton turned to Reverend William Robertson, the historian, clergyman and principal of the University of Edinburgh, for advice on how to defend his notion of perpetual geological change to the public, Robertson encouraged him to 'consult our friend Mr. Smith'. Evidently, Robertson thought that liberal political economist was well suited to render Hutton's natural history palatable to a wide audience. Robertson's own suggestions for revisions to Hutton's preamble to the *Theory of the Earth* concluded with a eulogy about the divine fit between nature and mankind. The purpose of geological change was to prepare 'such a habitation for man and other animals as Infinite Wisdom and Goodness destined it to be'.[14]

Hutton's abstract vision of natural cycles extended to the problem of climate. His 'Theory of Rain', presented to the Royal Society of Edinburgh in 1784, offered a simplified model of how atmospheric processes determined the basic weather patterns on earth. This order was explicitly providential. In Hutton's words: 'the law of nature, on which this theory of nature is founded, may be now considered in relation to its final cause; or how far it may appear to be conceived in wisdom for the purpose of this world, as affording a proper climate for plants and animals.' Hutton, like Linnaeus and other eighteenth-century savants, divided the climate into zones. But he rejected Linnaeus's five temperature bands in favour of a simpler tripartite schema with frigid, temperate and torrid regions. As in *The Theory of the Earth*, Hutton saw the problem of the natural economy as a question of how extremes interacted to produce a moderate medium, in this case the climate of the temperate zone. Frigid and torrid climates thus served as rough equivalents to the counterweights of mountains and ocean in *The Theory of the Earth*. Hutton's argument proceeded through a number of thought experiments about imperfect worlds. He imagined a planet without land, a stationary world without axial rotation, a planet where rain fell six months out of the year followed by six months of drought, and a world where currents mixed cold and warm air to generate moderate temperature but failed to produce precipitation. Through these steps, Hutton arrived at the 'wise system of things ... this useful purpose in the oeconomy of the world'. Atmospheric currents, geographic features and

---

[14] Dean, *James Hutton*, 3–4, 23; National Library of Scotland (hereafter NLS), MS 23165, James Hutton, *Elements of Agriculture*, vol. I (1797), 177/188. Hutton wrote a brief pamphlet on coal duties in this period, *Considerations on the Nature, Quality and Distinctions, of Coal and Culm* ... (Edinburgh, 1777).

the regular order of climate zones together formed a perfect machine. The centrepiece of the theory was the mechanism by which clashing masses of air produced rain. Hot and cold air circulated through the atmosphere in regular patterns. But how did these currents generate rain? Hutton argued that the temperature of the air governed the amount of moisture it could retain: the higher the temperature, the greater the level of moisture. When warm air cooled, some of the moisture in the warm air condensed into precipitation. Hence, the mixture of cold and warm air currents resulted in patterns of rainfall. This 'law of acqueous vapour' 'tempered' the atmosphere, 'by transporting the heat and cold of distant regions'. Frozen wastelands and mountain chains were crucial in 'preserving . . . a store of the winter cold for the summer season'. Providence had ruled out excessive extremes and thereby made the planet hospitable to life. 'In the actual system, now under contemplation, while both the extremes of drought and of wetness are so wisely avoided, temperate drought and moisture, rain and sunshine, so beneficial to the oeconomy of this world, are every where bestowed with the most provident attention, but not without a variety of different degrees.'[15]

Hutton's preoccupation with cosmic cycles and eternal time also shaped his understanding of improvement. The Scottish naturalist was careful to stress the link between agriculture and geology. The second chapter of the *Elements of Agriculture* was dedicated to the deep origin of soil. But the focus of the treatise on agricultural improvement involved a shift away from the homeostatic properties of the planetary machine towards problems of expert management. Like many other natural historians of the Enlightenment, Hutton saw good government as a matter of imposing human knowledge on the natural world: 'We have, at least, great reason to believe what nature has ordained every thing aright, but man a being of intelligence – a spark of the Divinity, has obtained the right of having a certain ruling power in nature.' When people first settled to farm the land, they 'redeem[ed]' the soil by cutting down the primordial forest. This action undid 'the work of nature' and replaced it with the new man-made order. Indeed, Hutton (like Buffon) believed that agriculture had ameliorated the climate across Europe: 'The face of nature upon this Earth has thus been changed; the climate of a continent improved, and bread the staff of life to man, is thus, as it were created.' From the perspective of geological time and prehistory, such fundamental changes took place with enormous speed:

[15] Hutton, 'The Theory of Rain', 49, 51, 53–55, 57–58, 66, 70.

[t]ho the constitution of this world has been designed by a wisdom infinitely superior to that of man, yet man in his proper wisdom, acquires a certain controlling power in the events of this world. He almost instantly consumes the forest which had for ages shaded the surface of the earth; and he exposes to the influences of the sun the fertilized soil which he then cultivates.

Crucially, the actions of human agents produced unintended consequences. Deforestation was not always a benign force. In late eighteenth-century Scotland, many improvers worried about real and imaginary resource shortages. Hutton singled out timber scarcity as a threat to national prosperity. Scotland was 'almost destitute of wood for houses, fuel, utensils'. His deep time perspective produced a sharpened sense of environmental fragility. In a brief time span – 'almost instantly' – Scots had destroyed mighty woodlands that had flourished 'for ages'. Good husbandry called for expert knowledge and a long-term approach to resources, what Hutton called the 'philosophy of agriculture'.[16]

This question of expertise led Hutton to attack Adam Smith's understanding of agricultural improvement in *The Wealth of Nations* (1776). Smith had failed to recognize the conflict of interest between the tenant farmer and the landlord. The right of the tenant farmer to raise good crops for the market was no doubt a 'beautiful and just principle', but Smith had 'carried' his zeal for liberty 'beyond its proper bounds'. Without checks, the tenant might resort to a short-sighted soil mining strategy:

[T]here are certain occasions when the farmer thinks it his interest to make the land bear successive crops of corn at the expence [sic] of its future fertility; he thus leaves the land which he is to quit, in the greatest poverty . . .

Smith had wrongly assumed that tenant farmers must have as much autonomy from proprietors as possible and, second, that destructive behaviour on the part of tenant farmers was not detrimental to profits because soil fertility could be easily restored. Hutton attacked this complacency as misguided: '[T]hose who have the science of the art' understood that high soil fertility once arduously achieved was a

---

[16] Hutton, *Elements*, vol. I, 50/59 (controlling power), 54 (ch. 2 on geology and soil), vol. II: 230/678 (undo nature), 644 (special spark), 645/431 (climate change). On anthropogenic climate change in the Enlightenment, see J. Golinski, *British Weather and the Climate of the Enlightenment* (Chicago: University of Chicago Press, 2007), ch. 6, passim; A. Zilberstein, *A Temperate Empire: Making Climate Change in Early America* (Oxford: Oxford University Press, 2016): Jonsson, *Enlightenment's Frontier*, ch. 3, passim. For anxieties about deforestation in Scotland, see F. Albritton Jonsson, 'Adam Smith in the Forest', in S. B. Hecht, K. D Morrison and C. Padoch (eds.), *The Social Lives of Forests: Past, Present and Future of Woodland Resurgence* (Chicago: University of Chicago Press, 2013), 45–54.

'public good' which must not be squandered by myopic profit seeking. Hence the 'legislature' should take an interest in supporting 'covenants' that restricted the freedom of tenant farmers – forbidding short leases and high rents.[17]

Soil husbandry and tree planting demanded a broader view beyond immediate self-interest. Soil was easily exhausted by tenant farmers bent on maximizing profits rather than maintaining the precious store of fertility indefinitely. Likewise, woodlands were quickly decimated, but much more difficult to regenerate since landowners must plant for distant heirs rather than present gain. Planting and soil husbandry were the environmental counterparts of canals and roads in national infrastructure. They were aspects of the public good of the nation and therefore special responsibilities of the elite:

In the rural oeconomy of a country there are three things which should be carefully looked after; these are first the high roads of the country, secondly the woods, fences, and farm houses, and lastly the proper condition of the land in order to be productive.[18]

Hutton hoped that patriotic landowners would check the destructive tendency of tenant farmers towards short-term gain. But if civil society failed to protect woodlands and soils, then the government should step in to safeguard this public good:

it concerns the state to such a degree, that nothing could be more worthy of the wisdom of the legislature, than to provide in some shape against the neglect of a duty which men of landed property owe to themselves in the first place, and to their country in the second.[19]

Hutton's natural history of soil fertility thus incorporated two levels of time. The eternal cycle of uplift and erosion produced the soil required for agriculture and forestry. This economy of nature was benign, imbuing the universe with a sense of justice and purpose. But within the larger cycle of uplift and erosion in geology lay nestled the lesser cycle of soil fertility and exhaustion in agriculture. On this human scale, every bit as vital for the maintenance of life, the interests of profit-making and public welfare clashed. Crucially, Hutton saw this conflict as a struggle over human conceptions of temporality. The small cycle of soil fertility had to

[17] J. Hutton, *Elements*, vol. II, 138/587–139/588, 257/705–263/711; cf. J. Jones, 'James Hutton's Agricultural Research and Life as a Farmer', 600. Hutton probably had the following sections from *The Wealth of Nations* in mind: I: 392–393, II: 831. Since Smith supported long leases for tenant farmers, the disagreement was not quite as grave as Hutton imagined.
[18] Hutton, *Elements*, vol. II, 250/698.   [19] Ibid., vol. II, 254/702.

be monitored by knowledgeable landowners or legislators. Without a proper understanding of the philosophy of agriculture, improvers might fall prey to the myopic perspective of the soil miner, forgetting that soil was also a public good, which had to be safeguarded and transferred from one generation to another.

II

At the same time as James Hutton was wrestling with the nested temporalities of soil husbandry, other savants began to debate the state of the national coal supply. The first great pessimist in the history of peak coal was closely connected with the same currents in the Scottish Enlightenment that shaped Hutton's work. John Williams was of humble birth from a small Welsh village. After receiving a parish school education, he turned to mining for a career. By mid-century he moved to Scotland and made a name as a surveyor. During the 1760s and 1770s he was employed as a naturalist by the Board for the Annexed Estates. Williams was brought in to discover useful minerals in the Highlands but his mission was a bitter disappointment. Almost the entirety of northern Scotland appeared to be bereft of coal. Despite Williams's failure to improve the Annexed Estates, he secured a position as overseer in a Lowland colliery afterwards. During this time, he composed *The Natural History of the Mineral Kingdom* (1789). The eclectic character of his book reflected the different strands of his career, including mineral prospecting, the natural history of Scripture, and problems of internal improvement. It seems to have circulated widely, reaching an audience in America, Russia, Italy and the German lands. Williams did not shy away from controversy. He locked horns with James Hutton over the latter's theory of deep time, presenting himself as a man of practical experience, deeply sceptical of theory, while he dismissed Hutton as a lofty intellect who had become deranged by irrational attachment to the spirit of system.[20]

Williams occupies a curious position in the history of mineral energy. Unlike most savants in the Scottish Enlightenment, he recognized the role of coal in the expanding manufacturing economy of Great Britain.

[20] H. S. Torrens, 'Williams, John (c. 1732–1795)', in the *Oxford National Dictionary of Biography* (Oxford University Press, 2004), www.oxforddnb.com/view/article/56916, accessed 8 September 2017; A. Smith, *The Jacobite Estates of '45* (Edinburgh: John Donald, 1982), 32, 98; for Williams's reports on coal, see National Archives of Scotland, E 727/46/1–27; H. Torrens, 'The British "Mineral Engineer" John Williams (1732–1795), in id., *The Practice of British Geology, 1750–1850* (Aldershot: Ashgate, 2002), II, 170; J. Williams, *The Natural History of the Mineral Kingdom*, 2 vols. (Edinburgh, 1789), I, xxxviii.

Yet paradoxically, Williams expressed his appreciation of fossil fuel in a precocious prediction about coal exhaustion. His forecast combined three basic arguments which would afterwards become commonplace among pessimists. Williams assumed that the rate of consumption was rising. He also insisted that better technology could not overcome the problem of limits to supply. Because coal fuel was so important to British manufacturing and urban life, the growing scarcity of the mineral would have catastrophic consequences. Williams predicted that the end of coal must reduce '[o]ur cities and great towns' to 'ruinous heaps for want of fuel' and destroy 'the commerce, wealth, importance, glory, and happiness of Great Britain'. Anticipating a common theme of post-apocalyptic literature, he warned that the 'future inhabitants of this island must live, like its first inhabitants, by fishing and hunting . . .' This emphasis on the vital place of coal in British society contrasted sharply with the political economy of his Scottish contemporaries. The famous section of the pin manufacture at the beginning of Adam Smith's *Wealth of Nations* celebrated dexterity in the division of labour, not the power of coal-fuelled steam technology. In Hutton's *Theory of the Earth*, the production of soil rather than coal was the final end of the earth machine. Hutton's *Elements of Agriculture* in turn gave agriculture rather than manufacturing pride of place as the economic activity that sustained human life and virtue.[21]

Williams began *The Natural History of the Mineral Kingdom* by rejecting all the fundamental assumptions behind Hutton's theory of the earth: the formation of sediment in the oceans, the force of internal heat and the uplift of new strata. Above all, he denounced Hutton's notion of eternal cycles. The idea of endless time was heretical and subversive of the social order. It encouraged scepticism, and in the final instance, the 'abyss' of unbelief. 'Sceptical notions have a pernicious influence in damping the sacred fire in our hearts.' An eternal, self-reproducing world had no use for the 'interposition of a governing power'. In Williams's tautology, the belief in a loving God was both the proper premise and conclusion of natural history. The wisdom of the Creator had been imprinted on everything in the world, a fact evident to all careful observers. A significant portion of Williams's book was dedicated to reconciling the natural history of the earth with the events described in the Old Testament. Williams's denial of geological time probably served to

[21] Williams, *The Natural History of the Mineral Kingdom*, I, 159–160, 167–168, 172–173; P. Sieferle, *The Subterranean Forest: Energy Systems and the Industrial Revolution* (Cambridge: White Horse Press, 2001), 186; for more on the pre-industrial tenor of classical political economy, see E. A. Wrigley, *Continuity, Change and Chance: The Character of the English Industrial Revolution* (Cambridge: Cambridge University Press, 1990).

heighten his concern with coal exhaustion. In the relatively short time span of Christian history since Creation, coal had formed through the decay of timber into fossils. It was a legacy of the forests that once covered the 'greatest part of the antediluvian earth'. The many fossilized plants and pieces of timber found in collieries proved this point. Coal was a providential gift, produced by a forested world now irrevocably lost to mankind. From this scriptural version of geology, Williams arrived at a prescription for long-term conservation of a fuel. (Evidently he saw no contradiction between the idea of a wise and bountiful providence and the problem of the finite coal supply.) The right response to resource scarcity was active government. 'If our coals really are not inexhaustible, the lavish consumpt of them calls aloud for the attention of the Legislature.'[22]

Williams blamed the neglect of the coal question on the cornucopian tendency of public opinion. 'I have not the smallest doubt that the generality of the inhabitants of Great Britain believe that our coal mines are inexhaustible.' This suspicion was not without some foundation. William Jowett declared that British mines were 'inexhaustible' in a House of Commons speech in support of the Anglo-French trade treaty of 1786. The coal endowment of the nation would last 'millions of years'. Jowett's figure was no doubt a rhetorical flourish in favour of free coal export rather than an expression of geological theory, yet even so, it borrowed the scale of geological time to imagine the future. Cornucopian views were in fact quite widespread in the period. The anonymous author of *Considerations on the present scarcity and dearness of coals in Scotland* in 1793 suggested that the problem of the Edinburgh coal supply lay with the cartel organization regulating the coal trade since the mines themselves were 'in a manner inexhaustible'. Writing about the same question, Henry Grey Macnab instead blamed the coal duties, but agreed that the mines themselves were not at fault. Even if one counted only the collieries that had already been discovered, those alone would not 'be exhausted for many ages to come'. Such notions of infinite coal were not a monopoly of economic liberals. Radical pamphleteers also employed the idea to defend the right of the poor to a comfortable livelihood. In the pamphlet *Cursory Remarks on Bread and Coal,* the anonymous author insisted that the government regulate the market in coal and institute a just price on the commodity in times of dearth.[23]

[22] Williams, *The Natural History of the Mineral Kingdom,* I: lxii (abyss), 91 (divine creation and improvement), 160 (government intervention), 239 (timber into coal).
[23] Ibid., I: 159 (public opinion); *Cobbett's Parliamentary History,* XXVI: 900–901; Citizen of Edinburgh, *Considerations on the present scarcity and dearness of coals in Scotland; and on the*

In response to Williams's forecast, both critics and supporters tried to estimate the precise extent of British coal fields. Henry Grey Macnab seems to have been the first savant to attempt a quantitative estimate of the supply. Born in Northumberland, Macnab was educated at the University of Edinburgh and another product of the Scottish culture of improvement. In a series of letters to Prime Minister William Pitt published in 1793, he urged the abolition of the coal duties to further improvement in Highland Scotland. He also defended the economic rationality of the Limitation of the Vend – the Newcastle cartel of coal-mine owners. Macnab argued that the market suffered from glut rather than scarcity. In a simple calculation of potential output from the Northumberland collieries, he estimated that each square mile of the Newcastle region could produce 3,845,000 tons. After adding to this number the supply on the west coast at Whitehaven, he suggested that the nation had more than 1200 years of coal left to consume.[24]

John Bailey and George Culley sided with Williams against Macnab in *The General View of the Agriculture of the County of Northumberland* (1797). Like Williams, they took aim at the notion of boundless plenty: 'It has been asserted that "the coals in this country are inexhaustible."' From 'our investigation it appears, that Mr. Williams' apprehensions are not so chimerical as have been represented.' Bailey was trained as a land surveyor with some background in mathematics. He served as the land agent on the estate of Chillingham north of the Tyne and Wear coalfields of Newcastle. Bailey's formula began with the assumption that seams were six yards thick and that one acre of ground equalled about 29,000 cubic yards. He deducted one-third as waste and arrived at 19,000 cubic yards to 'be wrought' per acre. Bailey then converted his measure into Newcastle chaldrons: one chaldron per three cubic yards. He computed that annual consumption amounted to 1,000,000 chaldrons from the Newcastle region. This meant that an average of 155 acres of coal seam was exhausted each year. Finally, he assumed that the Newcastle fields covered 200 square miles, or 128,000 acres. At a constant rate of consumption, the seams would last 825 years. But Bailey immediately began

---

means of procuring greater quantities at a cheaper rate ... (Edinburgh, 1793), 4; H. G. Macnab, *Letters addressed to the Right Honourable William Pitt ... pointing out the inequality, oppression and impolicy of the taxes on coal* ... (Edinburgh, 1793), 130; Anon., *Cursory remarks on Bread and Coal* (London, 1800), 10–12. For more examples, see Jonsson, *Enlightenment's Frontier*, 313, note 23. On the eighteenth-century politics of coal generally, see W. Cavert, *The Smoke of London: Energy and Environment in the Early Modern City* (Cambridge: Cambridge University Press, 2016).

[24] H. G. Macnab, *Letters addressed to the Right Honourable William Pitt, Chancellor of the Exchequer of Great Britain; pointing out the inequality, oppression* (London, 1793), 132–136; cf. Jonsson, *Enlightenment's Frontier*, 184–185.

to question his own measures. What if seams were only four or three feet thick on average? At three feet, the fields would last little more than 400 years. He also worried about the effects of peak coal on the price of the commodity: 'before the half of that time be elapsed, the price to the consumer will be considerably increased, from the increased expense of obtaining them, and the increased length of carriage from the pits to the river.' Bailey and Culley repeated their claim and the same calculations in the third edition of the Report (1805, reprinted 1813). However, they avoided policy advice: 'how far it may be right for the legislature to interfere, we leave to the consideration of those more conversant in political speculations.'[25]

The quarrel between Williams, Macnab and Bailey established a pattern that was repeated with regular intervals in the next few decades.[26] Robert Edington, a utilitarian reformer and coal merchant who specialized in providing fuel to British garrisons, deployed the concept of exhaustion as a kind of wrecking bar to pry open Newcastle's Limitation of the Vend. He predicted that the seams of the Newcastle field would all be gone 'within fifty years'. Indeed, he went further to predict the imminent collapse of individual collieries, including the famous Wallsend mine. In the enlarged version of the work from 1813, he offered a detailed list of dozens of mines, which he predicted would collapse within a seven-, fourteen-, or twenty-one-year interval. 'The time must come ... when the long wrought mines of Newcastle must fail, and that long before they fail, there must be an intolerable advancement of price.' To prevent such painful spikes, Edington wanted to open up sources of inland supply, in Staffordshire and elsewhere. In other words, exhaustion was for Edington a local problem rather than a national threat.[27]

[25] J. Bailey and G. Culley, *General view of the agriculture of the county of Northumberland, with observations on the means of its improvement; drawn up for the consideration of the Board of Agriculture and Internal Improvement* (Newcastle, 1797), 11, 18–19; cf. J. Bailey, *General view of the agriculture of the County of Durham: with observations on the means of its improvement; drawn up for the consideration of the Board of agriculture and internal improvement* (London, 1810), 27–29. For Bailey's background, see the *Oxford Dictionary of National Biography*. Bailey co-authored this work with the agriculturist George Culley but as a mathematician and surveyor he was likely the force behind the attempt to quantity remaining coal stock. Indeed, Robert Bakewell attributed the calculation to Bailey alone in *An Introduction to Geology* (London, 1828), 178–179.

[26] T. Thomson, 'A Geognostical Sketch of the Counties of Northumberland, Durham, and Part of Cumberland', in *Annals of Philosophy*, ed. T. Thomson, vol. IV (July to December 1814), 81–83, 410–412; R. Bakewell, *An Introduction to Geology...*, 3rd ed. (London, 1829), 178–181.

[27] R. Edington, *An essay on the coal trade ...* (London, 1803), 23, 30; id., *A treatise on the coal trade; with strictures on its abuses, and hints for amelioration* (London, 1813), 115, 122, 126, 141–143.

The question of the coal supply became fodder for a debate in the House of Commons between liberals and conservatives in the summer of 1834. The budget was showing a great surplus that year, and the question at stake was whether this might be an opportune moment to cut the duties on coal exported abroad. One of the leading liberals, the Whig representative for Manchester, Charles Poulett Thomson, proposed a wholesale abolition of the export. His laissez-faire principles left him unconcerned about the state of the domestic coal supply. There was no reason to protect national coal as a vital strategic asset. Instead, Poulett Thomson simply noted that England could not hope for a 'perfect monopoly' in coal now that new fields were opening on the continent. His sanguine outlook probably owed something to the views of his brother, the geologist and political economist George Poulett Scrope. The year before, Scrope had launched a broadside against every kind of Malthusian pessimism in his work *Principles of political economy deduced from the natural laws of social welfare and applied to the present state of Britain*. Against Malthus and his disciples, he insisted that scientific agriculture could keep pace with a growing population. Fuel too was available in astonishing abundance: there were coalfields in the middle portion of North America that would cover half of Europe.[28]

For Thompson's opponent Sir Robert Peel, this sort of liberal reasoning was perverse since fuel must be understood as a *national* strength or liability. The problem of coal was fundamentally one of cheap access within the limits of the nation. 'That somewhere in the bosom of the earth there was supply that might last for centuries he did not deny,' but if the cost of extraction rendered the 'price of coal in this country equal to what it was in foreign countries, there must be an end at once to the great advantage for manufacturing which we now enjoyed.' To husband coal and limit exports was to defend the public good over the long term: 'The Legislature was surely not to contemplate merely the present interest of the country – it was bound to look forward – to look forward even for a period of 400 or 500 years.' When the House of Commons returned to Peel's question the following week, both sides explicitly spoke of the threat of exhaustion, whether to endorse the idea or dismiss it. The clause about reduction was agreed to and passed with the rest of the budget, thanks to the Whig majority. Though Peel was defeated, the debate marked the introduction of the coal question into national politics. The issue continued to haunt the next generation of

---

[28] Hansard, vol. XXV (1834), 527–529; J. P. Scrope, *Principles of political economy deduced from the natural laws of social welfare and applied to the present state of Britain* (London, 1833), 272, 274.

political economists and politicians, including major Victorian figures such as John Stuart Mill, William Armstrong, William Gladstone and William Stanley Jevons.[29]

The most important influence on Peel when it came to questions of coal was his friend and associate William Buckland, the first reader in geology at Oxford and Canon of Christ Church in later life. Buckland played a pivotal role in presenting the notion of deep time to a broad Christian audience in the early nineteenth century. His research set out to reconcile the conventional chronology of Scripture with a new understanding of Creation as a geological event. Buckland made room for deep time by arguing that the first days of Genesis had extended across many ages before the appearance of Man in the Garden of Eden. In contrast with Hutton's eternal cycle, Buckland stressed the historical particularities of geological periods. It was this synthesis of religion and natural science that earned him such favour with the establishment of the day. The crowning glory of his career was the Bridgewater treatise on the natural history of the earth – *Geology and Mineralogy considered with reference to Natural Theology* – published in 1836. A central theme in the book concerned the origin and formation of coal. Coal mines contained fossils of early vegetable life that marked the Carboniferous order. Buckland's interest in coal led him to form friendships with men experienced in the mining trade, including John Buddle and Thomas Sopwith, both mining engineers from the northeast of England. Such connections also gave Buckland insights into the practical and economic side of the industry. He first seems to have become interested in the problem of coal husbandry when he learned about the common practice of burning 'small coal' on the side of the pitheads in the North. From Buckland's perspective, this was both economically irrational and morally insupportable. In the House of Commons hearings on the state of the coal trade in 1830, he testified to the folly of wasting the nation's resources. Mine owners burned in a few instants a finite resource that had been created for the glory of British manufacture and trade and should be husbanded for posterity.[30]

---

[29] Hansard XXV, 533–534, 908; P. Thorsheim, *Inventing Pollution: Coal, Smoke in Britain since 1800* (Columbus: Ohio State University Press, 2006), 45–47.

[30] W. Buckland, *Geology and Mineralogy considered with reference to Natural Theology*, 2 vols. (London, 1836), I: 536–538 (small coal); M. Rudwick, *Bursting the Limits of Time: The Reconstruction of Geohistory in the Age of Revolution* (Chicago: University of Chicago Press, 2005), 540–541, 610; for fossil hunting in the coal district, Durham County Record Office, NCB I/JB 83; House of Commons Report of the Select Committee on the State of the Coal Trade (1830), 244–247. To be fair, Buckland did not mention providence in his testimony but spoke instead of the position of coals beds as the 'accidental and successive accumulations of drifted vegetables'; cf. ibid., 247.

Buckland opened the Bridgewater Treatise with a brilliant meditation on economic geology and the destiny of the nation. Basic trends of economic and historical development could be explained by geological conditions. Three different forms of mineral endowment had given rise to three distinct regions of industry and agriculture in the island of Great Britain. Significant patterns of population, industry and prosperity had its origin in the ages before mankind appeared on the scene. British consumers were connected 'in almost every moment of our lives' with the 'geological events of those very distant eras'. This was not just a curious fact for the learned to analyze, but a matter of 'personal concern, of which but few are conscious'. The Bridgewater Treatise was meant to raise the material basis of daily consumption to full religious and economic awareness. 'My fire now burns with fuel,' Buckland observed, 'derived from coal which has been buried for countless ages in the deep and dark recesses of the earth.' The simple act of cooking and eating a meal called forth to Buckland an image of decaying forests and 'ferruginous mud ... lodged at the bottom of ... primeval waters'. Indeed every form of 'art and industry' in the age of industry rested on these carbon riches. 'We are all brought into immediate connection with the vegetation that clothed the ancient earth before one half of its actual surface had yet been formed.' This double vision recognized in the commodity of coal the work of divine intelligence, operating through the medium of geological change. Later in the book, Buckland warned about the consequences of coal exhaustion to British power and prosperity. Coal had to be husbanded carefully, like every 'precious gift' of providence to the nation. Moderation in consumer desire went hand in hand with new practices of production and government oversight. Buckland suggested that mine owners be forbidden from screening coal and destroying any part of it deemed inferior. An appreciation of the deep time origin of coal would move the public to understand the need for long-term conservation to the benefit of 'future Generations'. Throughout the 1830s, Buckland promoted coal husbandry in a variety of ways. Besides supporting Peel's tariffs on exports, he took a keen interest in new kinds of coal fuel, including the technique of making coal briquettes from small coal patented by William Wylam. Buckland also joined Thomas Sopwith in campaigning to create a national register of mining records. Local and national statistics were essential in measuring the rate of production and the extent of remaining reserves.[31]

[31] Buckland, *Geology and Mineralogy considered with reference to Natural Theology*, I: 1–4, 66–67, 536, 538; British Library (hereafter BL), MS 40540 f. 8.; Eight Report of British Association for the Advancement of Science, 85.

III

By recovering this forgotten battle over the geological fate of the nation, we stand to gain a new perspective on one of the fundamental problems of our own historical moment. Dipesh Chakrabarty has suggested that the beginning of the era of anthropogenic climate change marks the collapse of the old distinction between civil and natural history. The human species has become a geological force that can alter the physical cycles of the biosphere over deep time scales. In climatological terms, we have left behind the relatively stable climate of the Holocene and entered into a new geological epoch: the Anthropocene. For Chakrabarty, this moment also forces us to reckon with a new kind of history. No longer can we separate histories of human agency from the biophysical context that conditions life on earth. An adequate account of anthropogenic climate change must include both this conception of species as a collective physical force and the more familiar notion of agency in the realm of politics. Yet there are good reasons to worry about the coherence of this kind of enterprise: what sort of historical understanding can contain both registers?[32]

As it happens, the concept of the Anthropocene has generated a fair amount of debate already. The atmospheric chemist Paul Crutzen and biologist Eugene Stoermer pioneered the idea to describe the escalating impact of industrial society on the biosphere in the last two hundred years. In their 2000 essay, they located the beginning of the Anthropocene in Britain's Industrial Revolution, settling on James Watt's 1784 invention of the double condensing steam engine as the event to mark the origin of the epoch. The concept of the Anthropocene is now under formal investigation by a special working group convened by Jan Zalasiewicz as a step towards formal validation by the geological community. The working group is considering a variety of starting points for the epoch, from the Neolithic Revolution to postwar consumer society. The aim is to identify the stratigraphic signature of the new epoch: what sort of fossils will we leave behind? At present, there is increasing support for the end of the Second World War as the 'golden spike' of the new epoch. The Great Acceleration in economic growth after 1945 has given rise to a number of durable stratigraphic signals, including the proliferation of nuclear isotopes, plastics and synthetic nitrogen. But some critics worry that this short chronology for the Anthropocene overlooks the deeper causes of environmental change. They also resist the notion of

---

[32] D. Chakrabarty, 'The Climate of History: Four Theses', *Critical Inquiry* 39 (2009): 197–222.

geological agency at the level of the species, preferring conceptual frame-works centred on capitalism and empire.[33]

Arguably, the orientation towards the far past and remote future is a cardinal feature of earth system science and the discourse on the Anthropocene. This distinct sensibility stands in sharp contrast to the deficient attention span of contemporary politicians and many social scientists. Their reluctance to embrace the long term is hardly surpris-ing. An orientation towards deep time scales generates a host of difficult, some would say intractable, problems. The first is the epistemological question of long forecasts. By what means can the social order of the far future become known and relevant to the present? How can a long-term view of the future accommodate historical contingencies like unforeseen consequences of technological innovation or social change? The second is one of ethical obligation: what does the present owe unborn gener-ations? Why should anyone care about the fate of distant descendants? The third is one of political will and planning: how will political action be brought to bear on a scale of multiple generations? The historical case at hand – the constellation of theories and projects between Hutton and Buckland – offers some important clues as to how conceptions of geological time first entered into political economy and ideologies of improvement.[34]

James Hutton's geology reflected many of the peculiarities of Scottish economic and intellectual development. He was an active agent in the rapid agrarian change experienced in the region after 1760. Hutton's practical experience with farming and his unpublished treatise on the science of agriculture obviously informed his teleological interpretation of geology as pedogenesis (soil formation). Arguably, the most unusual feature of Hutton's natural history, his commitment to eternalism,

[33] P. Crutzen and E. Stoermer, 'The Anthropocene', *IGBP Newsletter* 41 (May 2000), 17–18; J. Rockström et al., 'Planetary Boundaries: Exploring the Safe Operating Space for Humanity', *Ecology and Society* 14, 2 (2009), 32; C. N Waters, J. A. Zalasiewicz, M. Williams, M. A. Ellis and A. M. Snelling (eds.), 'A Stratigraphical Basis for the Anthropocene', *Geological Society, London, Special Publications* 395 (March 2014), 1–21; J. Moore, *Capitalism in the Web of Life* (London: Verso, 2015); A. Malm and A. Hornborg, 'The Geology of Mankind: A Critique of the Anthropocene Narrative', *The Anthropocene Review* 1 (2014), 62; C. Bonneuil and J.-B. Fressoz, *L'Événement Anthropocène* (Paris: Editions du Seuil, 2013); J. Brooke and C. Otter, 'The Organic Anthropocene', *Eighteenth Century Studies* 49 (2016), 281–302.

[34] D. Archer, *The Long Thaw; How Humans Are Changing the Next 100,000 Years of Earth's Climate* (Princeton, NJ: Princeton University Press, 2009); S. Gardiner, *A Perfect Moral Storm: The Ethical Dilemma of Climate Change* (New York: Oxford University Press, 2013); M. Stafford Smith, L. Horrocks, A. Harvey and C. Hamilton, 'Rethinking Adaptation for a 4C World', *Philosophical Transactions of the Royal Society A* 369 (2011), 196–216.

reflected an idealized version of soil husbandry as a process of endlessly renewed fertility. Another signature feature of Hutton's system, the fascination with homeostatic order, echoed the liberal intellectual project of David Hume and Adam Smith. For Smith in particular, the natural order of agriculture provided the benign and resilient foundation that made liberal commerce and opulence possible (at least in corn countries in temperate climate zones). Self-regulating markets reflected the tendency towards equilibrium in natural economies. Hutton departed from Smith's liberal ecology on the question of long-term management of soil and forest resources, as we have seen. Profit was an insufficient motive to guide tenant farmers towards sustainable practice.[35]

For William Buckland, geological time was historical through and through. Martin Rudwick charts the transition from the 'eternalism' and 'deterministic purity' of Hutton's 'geotheory' to Buckland's 'geohistory' informed by contingency and the particularities of historical periods. One might add to this schema another perspective, the movement from Hutton's world of agricultural improvement to Buckland's mineral energy economy. If the geological past in Hutton mirrored the ideal cycle of soil husbandry, then Buckland's prehistory was informed by the linear logic of mineral stock. Coal was the product of a distinct period of prehistoric flora and climate, transformed by providence into fossils and fuel for the 'future use' of man. Coal mining followed its own linear logic from unregulated extraction towards increasing husbandry, but always with the spectre of exhaustion looming. The calendar of depletion introduced by Macnab and his critics produced new mineral chronologies of the future. The moment of peak production was either frighteningly close or reassuringly distant. Buckland agreed with Hutton and Williams on the need for political regulation to shape resource use.[36]

We are dealing here not with an embryonic Enlightenment version of Anthropocene in the sense of a precise foreshadowing of our current crisis, but rather with an unfamiliar variation on a common theme. Clearly, the naturalists and mining engineers of the late Enlightenment were not preoccupied with climate change or environmental degradation in our own sense. Buffon and Hutton imagined anthropogenic change as a benign effect of colonization and settlement on a continental scale. Buckland and Sopwith thought of the coal consumption as a force of material and spiritual depletion, leaving behind empty collieries and an

---

[35] For Smith's liberal ecology, see Jonsson, *Enlightenment's Frontier*, ch. 5.

[36] Rudwick, *Bursting the Limits of Time*, 235; compare the calendar of exhaustion with our own calendar of emissions.

exhausted nation. Yet for all these obvious differences, the case at hand also reminds us that the entanglement of geology and political economy goes back quite far. The boundaries between natural history and civil history, the present and deep time, have been breached before.[37]

---

[37] For a trenchant critique of embryonic modernity, see L. Daston, 'The Nature of Nature in Early Modern Europe', *Configurations* 6 (1998), 149–172.

5   Slack

Malcolm Bull

Environmentalists are always saying that human beings should consume less of the planet's natural resources. In some cases this involves the temporary or permanent non-use of a specific resource; in others, a reduction in the level of its consumption. The latter may involve resource substitution, the absolute or relative decoupling of economic growth from resource use, or else the adoption of policies designed to limit or reduce growth itself. In all cases, however, the result is the same. Irrespective of whether the goal is an overall reduction in the human consumption of natural resources or merely their more intelligent allocation, the effect of environmentalist policies is to ensure that some resources that could be used are left unexploited, and that a gap opens up between potential and actual levels of resource use.

What sort of political ideal does this represent? Save in those instances where capping use at any one time is necessary to maximize use across time, the non-use of usable resources is, by most standards, sub-optimal if not downright irrational. Those environmentalists who consciously advocate global strategies of this kind (as opposed to the short-term, targeted conservation of specific resources) often do so on the basis of a non-anthropocentric ethics where what is best for the planet takes precedence over what is best for human beings. In consequence, there has been little focus on the idea of sub-optimality itself, or on its historical parallels and antecedents.

By looking at the arguments that led to the acceptance of non-use value within environmental economics in the United States in the mid-twentieth century, and at the contemporaneous development of the concept of 'organizational slack', it is possible to get a clearer sense of the intellectual traditions to which these arguments relate. Slack was defined by Albert Hirschman as a gap between actual and potential performance, and in his account becomes closely aligned with the chronic under-use of political resources that Machiavelli termed corruption. Might the non-use of natural resources then be seen as a form of idleness akin to Machiavelli's corruption, and if so, from what perspective could such idleness appear a constructive political strategy?

I.   Idle Resources

Within the field of environmental economics, the first person to advocate the non-use of natural resources appears to have been the Dartmouth College economist L. Gregory Hines. At the Eighteenth North American Wildlife Conference in 1953, he presented a paper entitled 'The Myth of Idle Resources: A Reconsideration of the Concept of Nonuse in Conservation'. It had, he complained, 'become commonplace ... to point out that conservation does not imply the nonuse or idleness of resources'. To an alarming degree, 'emphasis upon full use or "full employment" of all resources' had diverted attention from the appropriate use for given resources, and afforded 'a basis for attack upon conservation programs by those who wish to bring all resources under commercial exploitation'.[1] It was, instead, Hines's contention that

The needs of mankind cannot be revealed and met within the perimeters of the market economy alone, but require conscious appraisal of social goals and the means of obtaining them. High in the scheme of social goals to fulfil basic human needs must be a definite provision for idle resources – idle to permit replenishment of productivity and to provide an emergency buffer for a future that seems more uncertain than ever before.[2]

As Hines explained, the problem with the market is that the pricing system simultaneously 'fails to restrict commercial utilization of some resources that should remain idle, [and] provides no effective means by which an individual can express his desire for commercial nonuse'. The lack of 'a socially adequate criterion for resource allocation' applies both to wilderness as 'a unique antidote to the pace of a highly industrialized civilization' and to 'renewable resources ... [which] may require periodic disuse or idleness to preserve a given level of productivity through time'.[3]

The myth to which Hines refers had several strands. One was embodied in government thinking about conservation after the First World War. In the late nineteenth century, John Muir, the pioneer of American environmentalism, had argued for the preservation of natural environments in absolute terms. Believing that 'every natural artefact is a

[1] L. G. Hines, 'The Myth of Idle Resources: A Reconsideration of the Concept of Nonuse in Conservation', in *Transactions of the Eighteenth North American Wildlife Conference* (Washington, DC: Wildlife Management Institute, 1953), 28.
[2] Ibid., 34.   [3] Ibid., 32.

reflection of the beauty, magnificence and abundance of the Creator', Muir thought of nature as 'God's first temple'. It was therefore axiomatic that it should receive similar respect. Muir likened the sheep grazing around Shadow Lake to the money-changers in the temple, and when, in 1908, it was proposed that Hetch Hetchy Valley in California should be flooded to create a reservoir for San Francisco he responded: 'As well dam for water-tanks the people's cathedrals and churches, for no holier temple has ever been consecrated by the heart of man'.[4]

But Muir lost the battle over Hetch Hetchy to his fellow environmentalist and former friend Gifford Pinchot, the Chief of the United States Forest Service.[5] To Muir's ideal of 'preservation' Pinchot had counterposed the idea of 'conservation', by which he understood 'the greatest good of the greatest number for the longest time'. On this view, 'the first principle of conservation is development, the use of natural resources on this continent for the benefit of the people who live here now' and the second is the 'prevention of waste'. However, the two were not entirely distinct for Pinchot considered that 'there may be just as much waste in neglecting the development and use of certain natural resources as there is in their destruction'.[6]

It was on the basis of this philosophy that the 'myth of idle resources' developed. Speaking in his later role as Governor of Pennsylvania on Conservation Day in 1926 Pinchot said:

We have vast stretches of idle forest land. It brings no good to anyone. It pays little or no taxes, keeps willing hands out of work, builds no roads, supports no industries, kills railroads, depopulates towns, creates a migratory population, all of which work against a good and stable citizenship. Idle forest serves no one well. It is a menace to our normal national life.[7]

The address was frequently reprinted and quoted in the following decades in order to sustain the argument that 'We need to ... put idle forest land to work.'[8] But during the Depression, the concern with idle forests came to intersect with wider anxiety about the idleness of resources. Now idle land was just one element in the litany of idleness:

[4] J. Muir, *Nature Writings* (New York: Penguin, 1997), 387 (journal entry, 24 July 1869); 'The Hetch-Hetchy Valley', *Sierra Club Bulletin* (January 1908), 220.
[5] See R. W. Righter, *The Battle over Hetch Hetchy: America's Most Controversial Dam and the Birth of Modern Environmentalism* (Oxford: Oxford University Press, 2006).
[6] G. Pinchot, *The Fight for Conservation* (New York: Doubleday, Page, 1910), 17, 15–16.
[7] 'Address of Governor Pinchot on Conservation Day', *Forest Leaves*, 20 (December 1926), 177–178.
[8] US Dept of Agriculture Forest Service, *Forests and National Prosperity: A Reappraisal of the Forest Situation in the United States*, Miscellaneous Publication 668 (Washington, DC, 1948), 4.

'a composite of idle men, idle land, idle machines and idle money'.[9] In line with Keynes's view that the remedy for the trade cycle was to be found not in abolishing booms but in abolishing slumps, popular writers such as Stuart Chase imagined how all of America's idle resources might be employed in future public works:

We have idle money and we have idle men. This world we have sketched can use them to the last dollar and the last man. Great sections of the American landscape must be torn down, redesigned, rebuilt; and this will demand intensive investment on a colossal scale.[10]

The US government largely agreed. There was, as the US Department of Agriculture Forest Service stated in 1941, 'a great need and opportunity to put idle men and idle land to work again'.[11]

By mid-century, therefore, it appeared that the Muir–Pinchot debate had been settled decisively in Pinchot's favour. Even before the Depression, his policy of achieving a sustainable yield from the national forests had taken priority over the ideal of preserving the American wilderness. But with the spread of Keynesian ideas in response to the economic crisis, this approach gained a wider economic rationale. The idleness of land was taken to be another example of what Keynes considered capitalism's 'chronic tendency to the under-employment of resources'.[12] It was therefore the government's duty to ensure the full employment of a nation's natural resources just as much as its human ones. As Ezra Taft Benson, Eisenhower's Secretary of Agriculture, said at the American Forestry Association (AFA)'s Fourth American Forest Congress in October 1953, 'I hope we no longer have any citizens who look upon conservation and preservation as synonymous terms.' We must not 'fail to make the land yield up to its full potential of the resource for which it is best fitted'.[13]

II.   The Defence of Idleness

Hines's defence of idleness may not be couched in religious terms like that of Muir, but it derives in part from Muir's follower Aldo Leopold,

---

[9] Temporary National Economic Committee, *Investigation of Concentration of Economic Power* (Washington, DC: US Government Printing Office, 1940), 178. Cf. H. C. Moser, *Idle Lands ... Idle Men* (St. Paul: Minnesota State Planning Board Forestry Division, 1938).

[10] S. Chase, *Idle Men, Idle Money* (New York: Harcourt Brace, 1941), 194.

[11] US Department of Agriculture Forest Service, *New Forest Frontiers: For Jobs, Permanent Community, a Stronger Nation*, Miscellaneous Publication 414 (Washington, DC, 1941), 44.

[12] J. M. Keynes, 'Some Economic Consequences of a Declining Population', *Eugenics Review* 29 (1937), 17.

[13] Quoted in P. W. Hirt, *A Conspiracy of Optimism: Management of the National Forests since World War Two* (Lincoln: University of Nebraska Press, 1994), 107.

who had developed a less mystical version of the argument for the non-exploitation of natural resources in his 1949 essay 'The Land Ethic'. Although referring to 'conservation' rather than 'preservation', Leopold distinguished between the different attitudes to conservation represented by group (A), which regards 'the land as soil, and its function as commodity-production' and 'is quite content to grow trees like cabbages', and group (B), which 'regards the land as a biota, and its function as something broader', and so 'worries about whole series of secondary forest functions: wildlife, recreation, watersheds, wilderness areas'. In Leopold's opinion, any system of conservation which assumed that the 'economic parts of the biotic clock will function without the uneconomic parts' was mistaken.[14]

Hines echoes Leopold's view, but he writes as an economist, and seeks to develop an account of how those 'uneconomic parts' function within the economy of the whole. In this respect, his critique of full employment resonates with the arguments not just of ecologists, but of anti-Keynesian economists. Even in the Depression there were some who argued against the Keynesian view that full employment should be maintained and that idle resources were necessarily undesirable. In *The Theory of Idle Resources* (1939) William Hutt argued that 'full employment', in the sense of a 'wasteless economy', was neither a definable nor a desirable goal.[15] According to Hutt, value and use must be distinguished because there are many ways in which what looks like non-productive idleness may actually be very productive, indeed essential to the smooth working of the system.

Primarily concerned with employment, Hutt argued that in this regard there was no distinction between the idleness of labour and the idleness of other resources. In his opinion, it was obvious that 'in any given state of knowledge and institutions, there are resources which perform their most wanted services through their mere passive existence, – the service of availability'. Such 'pseudo-idleness ... exists when resources are being retained in their specialized form ... because the productive service of carrying them through time is being performed', because no other value (e.g. their scrap or hire value) will exceed their capital value at some future time.[16]

Although Hines makes no direct reference to Hutt's work in 'The Myth of Idle Resources', he offers a similar argument against the 'full

---

[14] A. Leopold, *A Sand County Almanac* (New York: Oxford University Press, 2001), 186 and 179 (first pub. 1949).
[15] W. Hutt, *The Theory of Idle Resources* (London and Toronto: Jonathan Cape, 1939), n. 9.
[16] Ibid., 25, 24.

employment' of natural resources on the basis that 'wilderness ... yields social returns that become greater with each increase in population, extension of cultivation, and mechanization of production ... [and] will increase in social value, undoubtedly at a progressive rate, as our economy continues to expand'.[17] As he explained in an earlier article, 'Wilderness Areas: An Extra Market Problem in Resource Allocation', 'for wilderness to be most useful to society, it must remain unused in the traditional commercial sense because such an area has greater economic value in its primitive state' not least because the gain from grazing rights (Hutt's 'hire value') will never be greater than the loss from destruction of topsoil and the elimination of plants and animals.[18] Though less sonorous than Muir's denunciation of sheep as the money-changers to be driven from the temple, Hines's argument that hire value will never exceed future capital value in wilderness areas has the same effect.

In Hines's account, the economic value of 'non-use' is affirmed without any explicit argument as to why it will increase at a progressive rate or of how that value should be quantified. But in 'Conservation Reconsidered' (1967), another environmental economist, John Krutilla, specifies both. The value of an unused natural resource may be calculated in terms of the minimum that would be required to compensate those who enjoy or appreciate its existence in an unspoiled natural state ('the spiritual descendants of John Muir') for its loss in perpetuity. Over time, this value is likely to exceed the value to be derived from commercial exploitation because the inelasticity of natural resources means that 'the marginal trade-off between manufactured and natural amenities will progressively favor the latter', while 'the learn-by-doing phenomenon' will simultaneously allow more people to acquire the knowledge and skills needed to access and appreciate natural amenities and so change tastes in their favour. The conjunction of the two means that 'Natural environments will represent irreplaceable assets of appreciating value with the passage of time.'[19]

Krutilla's claim that conservation 'requires a present action (which may violate conventional benefit–cost criteria) to be compatible with the attainment of future states of affairs' aligns it with Hutt's definition of 'pseudo-idleness' which exists 'whenever resources are withheld from immediately more profitable specialization or despecialization because of

[17] Ibid., 31.
[18] L. G. Hines, 'Wilderness Areas: An Extra Market Problem in Resource Allocation', *Land Economics* 27 (1951), 310–311.
[19] J. Krutilla, 'Conservation Reconsidered', *American Economic Review* 57 (1967), 783.

expectations of a different situation in the future'.[20] And Krutilla main-
tains that such option value may exist 'even though there is no current
intention to use the area or facility in question and the option may never
be exercised', rather in the way that Hutt says unutilized domestic goods
such as a fire-extinguisher may bring '*continuous* satisfactions simply
through my knowledge that they are there'.[21]

For Muir, non-use had been a spiritual imperative; for Leopold it had
been an ecological one, but for Krutilla and subsequent environmental
economists non-use has a value that can be specified in economic terms.
It is clear that in the transition from the transcendental value Muir
ascribed to nature to the development of economists' accounts of non-
use value, Hines and other defenders of idleness played a pivotal role.
But in order to appreciate the wider intellectual context in which this
transition took place, it is helpful to track contemporary developments in
both macro- and microeconomics.

III.   Slack

Whether articulated in terms of idle resources or non-use values, the
policies of non-exploitation advocated by environmentalists have an
obvious, though unremarked, affinity with another concept that emerges
over the same time period – first in macroeconomics, and then in
organization theory. During the 1940s (and perhaps before) one word
that was frequently used to sum up the litany of 'idle men, idle machines,
idle money' was 'slack'.[22] With the onset of war, the value of this unused
capacity became more apparent. As the economist T. W. Schultz testified to the Select Committee Investigating National Defense Migration
in 1941:

Our defense program has had at least one happy result. It has taught us how
exceedingly large our unused capacity was. We had not only idle acres but idle
resources of almost every kind – labor, plants, finance, technical knowledge,
organization and management capacity – a large supply of each waiting to be
put to use. Because of this slack, it has been possible thus far to actually produce
both more butter and guns.[23]

---

[20] Ibid., 784–785; Hutt, *Idle Resources*, 27–28.
[21] Krutilla, 'Conservation Reconsidered', 780; Hutt, *Idle Resources*, 27.
[22] E.g. *The Magazine of Wall Street and Business Analyst* 69 (1941), 474; See also B. M.
Anderson, *Economics and the Public Welfare* (Princeton, NJ: D. Van Nostrand Company,
1949), 490–491.
[23] US Congress, House of Representatives, *National Defense Migration: Hearings before the
Select Committee Investigating National Defense Migration* (Washington, DC: Government
Printing Office, 1942), 8505.

However, it was not until the first two Economic Reports of the President in the Kennedy administration that the question of slack received more focused attention. In the 1961 report, there was an entire subsection on 'The Problem of Chronic Slack and Full Recovery' in which it was stated that 'Economic recovery ... is far more than a cyclical problem. It is also a problem of chronic slack in the economy – the growing gap between what we can and what we do produce.'[24] And in 1962, the received wisdom that 'periods of slack and recession in economic activity lead to idle machines as well as idle men' was once again repeated.[25]

The appearance of the phrase 'chronic slack' in the *Economic Reports* ensured that the term had wide currency during the Kennedy presidency. But although the second report acknowledged that the slack economy of the previous year meant that 'additional demand from both private and public sources was readily converted into increased production',[26] this was not translated into an appreciation of the benefits of slack itself. Most commentators echoed the 1961 report in supposing that all will 'look ahead to the day when the slack will be taken up and high levels of output and employment will again be the norm'.[27]

At a microeconomic level, however, 'idle capacity' was already being reinterpreted as 'organizational slack', and interpreted more positively. The concept of 'organizational slack' was first developed in a journal article by Richard M. Cyert and James G. March in 1956, but it was only when represented in their book *A Behavioral Theory of the Firm* (1963) that it gained wider attention. Cyert and March defined slack as 'the allocation of organizational resources to the satisfaction of subunits in excess of the minimum required for maintenance of the system'. In practice this meant that 'significant amounts of individual energies potentially utilizable by the organization are, in fact, being directed to the satisfaction of other roles'.[28]

Cyert and March enumerated some of the forms that slack might take within the firm: the payment of excessive dividends to stockholders; prices set too low or wages too high; subunits allowed to expand without generating additional revenue; excessive executive compensation, and the provision of unnecessary public services.[29] None of these things might in itself be aligned with organizational goals, but as Cyert and

[24] J. Tobin and M. Weidenbaum (eds.), *Two Revolutions in Economic Policy: The First Economic Reports of Presidents Kennedy and Reagan* (Cambridge, MA: MIT Press, 1988), 25.
[25] Ibid.,139.   [26] Ibid., 157.   [27] Ibid., 52.
[28] R. M. Cyert and J. G. March, 'Organizational Factors in the Theory of Oligopoly', *Quarterly Journal of Economics* 70 (1956), 46, 53.
[29] Ibid., 42.

March point out, the slack so created nevertheless represented 'a cushion ... [which] absorbs a substantial share of the potential variability in the firm's environment'. Slack therefore operates 'to stabilize the system in two ways: (1) by absorbing excess resources, it retains upward adjustment of aspirations in good times and (2) by providing a pool of emergency resources, it permits aspirations to be maintained (and achieved) during relatively bad times'.[30]

The essential ambivalence of slack has remained one of its defining characteristics in the specialist literature.[31] Given that slack means that organizations and individuals are refraining 'from using all the resources available to them', it necessarily 'describes a tendency not to operate at peak efficiency'.[32] It can therefore be viewed as 'synonymous with waste and as a reflection of managerial self-interest, incompetence and sloth'.[33] On the other hand, without slack 'a company cannot survive in an unstable environment, because the slack acts as a buffer against shock ... [and] enables a company to take risks and promote innovative behaviour'.[34]

Although now very extensive, the literature on slack produced within the context of organizational theory and management studies has had limited impact beyond those fields, and none at all within environmental thought. Nevertheless the analogies are clear enough. Not only did the concept of slack originally include 'idle land' along with 'idle men and idle machines', but the defining characteristic of slack – the non-use of usable resources – is precisely that enjoined by environmental economists from Hines onwards. For Hines too, idle resources were required 'to permit replenishment of productivity and to provide an emergency buffer for a future that seems more uncertain than ever before'.[35]

IV.   Slack, Corruption and Idleness

In *Exit, Voice and Loyalty* (1970), Albert O. Hirschman picks up the concept of slack from Cyert and March, links it to Herbert Simon's idea

---

[30] R. M. Cyert and J. G. March, *A Behavioral Theory of the Firm* (Englewood Cliffs, NJ: Prentice Hall, 1963), 43–44.

[31] For a summary, see W. Y. Oi, 'Slack Capacity: Productive or Wasteful', *American Economic Review* 71 (1981), 64–69.

[32] A. Riahi-Belkaoui, *Organizational and Budgetary Slack* (Westport, CT: Greenwood Publishing, 1994), 1.

[33] Y. Wu, C. Zhang and Y. Cui, 'A Study on the Influence of Organizational Slack on Firm Growth', in J. Luo (ed.), *Affective Computing and Intelligent Interaction* (Berlin: Springer, 2012), 420.

[34] T. Kato, M. Karube and T. Numagami, 'Organizational Deadweight and the Internal Functioning of Japanese Firms', in H. Itami et al. (eds.), *Dynamics of Knowledge, Corporate Systems and Innovation* (Berlin: Springer, 2010), 134–135.

[35] Hines, 'The Myth of Idle Resources', 34.

of 'satisficing' (not seeking the best possible outcome, but one that meets some acceptable threshold), and then applies it more widely. Describing slack as 'a gap of a given magnitude between actual and potential performance of individuals, firms, and organisations', Hirschman contrasts it with the 'image of a relentlessly *taut economy* [which] has held a privileged place in economic analysis'. He argues 'not only that slack has somehow come into the world and exists in given amounts, but that it is *continuously being generated* as a result of some sort of entropy characteristic of human, surplus-producing societies'. On this view, 'firms and other organizations are conceived to be permanently and randomly subject to decline and decay, that is, to a gradual loss of rationality, efficiency, and surplus-producing energy'.[36]

Hirschman acknowledged that there was an affinity between his understanding of slack and Machiavelli's account of corruption (*corruzione*). Asked 'How much community spirit does liberal society require?', he rephrased the question as 'How can society avoid the ever present dangers coming from what Machiavelli called *corruzione*?' and noted that 'contemporary analysts have rediscovered these dangers and attempted to discuss them under more neutral or technical labels such as "slack"'.[37] He does not elaborate on this, though he later characterizes Machiavelli's *corruzione* as 'the loss of public spirit, the exclusive concentration of individual effort on personal or sectional interests'.[38] This not only echoes Machiavelli's emphasis on the need 'to live without factions, [and] to esteem the private less than the public good', but aligns it with Cyert and March's account of slack being produced when energies are 'directed to the satisfaction of other roles (e.g. clique member, husband) within which individual members of the business organization operate'.[39]

Hirschman read Machiavelli throughout his life, and would therefore have been aware of Machiavelli's emphasis on the role of idleness in the corruption of the state.[40] According to Machiavelli, the usual cause of disunity in a republic is 'idleness (*ozio*) and peace' for if a nation 'has no

[36] A. O. Hirschman, *Exit, Voice and Loyalty: Responses to Decline in Firms, Organizations and States* (Cambridge, MA: Harvard University Press, 1970), 14, 9 and 15. Although he tries to differentiate his account of slack from that used in depression economics, he too first considered slack at the macroeconomic level in his work on development (10).
[37] A. O. Hirschman, *A Propensity to Self-Subversion* (Cambridge, MA: Harvard University Press, 1995), 5.
[38] Ibid., 151.
[39] N. Machiavelli, 'The Art of War', in *The Chief Works*, trans. A. H. Gilbert (Durham, NC: Duke University Press, 1958), 726 (translation modified); Cyert and March, 'Organizational Factors', 53.
[40] J. Adelman, *Worldly Philosopher: The Odyssey of Albert O. Hirschman* (Princeton, NJ: Princeton University Press, 2013), 489–491.

need to go to war, it will then come about that idleness will either render it effeminate or give rise to factions; and these two things, either in conjunction or separately, will bring about its downfall'.[41] Machiavelli's most sustained exposition of this theme appears in the first book of the *Discourses on Livy*:

> Since men work either of necessity or by choice, and since there is found to be greater virtue where choice has less to say to it, the question arises whether it would be better to choose a barren place in which to build cities so that men would have to be industrious and less given to idleness, and so would be more united because, owing to the poor situation, there would be less occasion for discord ...[42]

Machiavelli's answer to the question is that if men did not try to gain dominion over each other, the former would be more advisable. However, since no community is able to develop independently without also having to defend itself against its neighbours, the latter is preferable. There can be no security without power, and power comes from establishing a city in a fertile place where it has scope to grow. The city then has the resources both to defend itself from enemy attack and to conquer those who stand in the way of its expansion:

> As to the idleness which such a situation may encourage, it must be provided for by laws imposing that need to work which the situation does not impose. It is advisable here to follow the example of those wise folk who have dwelt in most beautiful and fertile lands, i.e. in such lands as tend to produce idleness and ineptitude for training in virtue of any kind, and who, in order to obviate the disasters which the idleness induced by the amenities of the land might cause, have imposed the need for training on those who were to become soldiers, and have made this training such that men there have become better soldiers than those in countries which were rough and sterile by nature.

Machiavelli therefore concludes that 'it is more prudent to place a city in a fertile situation, provided its fertility is kept in due bounds by laws'.[43]

Hirschman's account of slack is developed in the same terms. Most human societies (unlike primate societies) are characterized by 'the existence of surplus over subsistence', and

> the wide latitude [they] have for deterioration is the inevitable counterpart of man's increasing productivity and control over his environment. Occasional decline as well as prolonged mediocrity – in relation to achievable performance levels – must be accounted among the many penalties of progress.[44]

---

[41] N. Machiavelli, *The Discourses*, trans. L. J. Walker (Harmondsworth: Penguin Press, 1970), 360 (2.25) and 123 (1.6).
[42] Ibid., 102 (1.1).   [43] Ibid., 102–103 (1.1).   [44] Hirschman, *Exit*, 6.

On this view, economic progress and latitude for deterioration are positively rather than negatively correlated. According to Hirschman, this
accounts for

man's fundamentally ambivalent attitude toward his ability to produce a
surplus ... while unwilling to give up progress he hankers after the simple rigid
constraints on behaviour that governed him when he ... was totally absorbed by
the need to satisfy his most basic drives.[45]

Machiavelli's suggestion that those who live in fertile lands must have
'laws imposing that need to work which the situation does not impose'
would count as an example of this pattern. But so too is the reaction of
those who in the modern economy 'search for ways and means to take up
the slack, to retrieve the ideal of the taut economy'. Hirschman describes
various 'pressure mechanisms' through which 'additional investment,
hours of work, productivity, and decision making can be squeezed out'.
If the pressures of competition prove insufficient, then the 'pressures of
adversity will be invoked', exogenous forces such as strikes, war and
revolution. For advocates of social revolution, for example, 'only revolutionary changes can tap and liberate the abundant but dormant, repressed
or alienated energies of the people'.[46]

However, Hirschman argues, the search for pressure mechanisms
could be mistaken, for slack may be a blessing in disguise. Slack permits
firms to ride out adverse market conditions, and contributes to the
stability and flexibility of a political system. As he indicates later in the
book, 'for voice to function properly it is necessary that individuals
possess reserves of political influence which they can bring into play',
which requires that there be 'considerable slack in political systems'.[47]
The artificial attempt to reproduce the conditions of necessity through
pressure mechanisms may succeed only in squeezing out the slack that is
necessary for reform and the long-term health of the state.

To this, Machiavelli's retort would probably be the same as the one he
offers to Christian reformers, namely that by allowing slack, reform
becomes increasingly difficult. This, he suggests, is what had happened
in the Italy of his own time where the failure to instil martial virtues had
inhibited active citizenship. This was the fault of 'those who have interpreted our religion in terms of idleness not in terms of virtue'. Whereas
pagan religion had glorified army commanders and princes, 'Our religion
has glorified humble and contemplative men, rather than men of action.
It has assigned as man's highest good humility, abnegation, and contempt for mundane things.'[48] In consequence, its prophets come

---

[45] Ibid., 9.   [46] Ibid., 2–3.   [47] Ibid., 70–71.   [48] Machiavelli, *Discourses*, 278 (2.2).

unarmed.[49] Not just Savonarola, but also the original Dominicans and Franciscans who, Machiavelli complains, 'prevented the depravity of prelates and of religious heads from bringing ruin on religion' yet also taught that it was 'a good thing to live under obedience to such prelates' and so permitted the perpetuation of the very abuses they sought to reform.[50]

Machiavelli does not see idleness as ambivalent, only as a creator of discord, and as part of the cycle of corruption he describes in the *Florentine Histories*:

Change is the lot of all things human and when they reach their utmost perfection and can ascend no higher they must of necessity decline. So, too, when they have sunk to the lowest point, and can sink no lower they begin to rise ... Virtue is the mother of peace, peace produces idleness, idleness begets disorder, and disorder brings ruin. So order springs out of ruin, virtue out of order, and then follows a glorious fortune.[51]

Hirschman would not necessarily have disagreed with this sequence, for in *Shifting Involvements* (1982) he developed his own cyclical account of the oscillation of private interest and public action in modern societies, within which disappointment with and disengagement from the public sphere allows attention to be diverted to the pursuit of private interest and vice versa.[52] Unlike Machiavelli, who valued only public life, Hirschman presents private interest as the foundation of commercial society and gives equal weight to both spheres of action. Disengagement from one sphere permits the re-investment of resources in the other, so that, for example, exit from the private sphere may facilitate voice in the public one.

Although Hirschman does not use the world 'slack' in *Shifting Involvements* or refer to Machiavelli's cycle of corruption and renovation, it is clear that the transfer from the public to the private corresponds both to his definition of Machiavelli's *corruzione* as 'loss of public spirit, [and] the exclusive concentration of individual effort on personal or sectional interests', and to Cyert and March's account of slack being produced when energies are 'directed to the satisfaction of other roles'. What the 'Hirschman cycle' demonstrates is that slack provides the latitude needed not only to meet unexpected problems, but to redirect resources to other objectives altogether.

[49] N. Machiavelli, *The Prince*, trans. G. Bull (London: Penguin Press, 1999), 20.
[50] Machiavelli, *Discourses*, 389 (3.1).
[51] N. Machiavelli, *The Florentine Histories*, trans. C. E. Lester (New York: Paine and Burgess, 1845), vol. 2, 6.
[52] A. O. Hirschman, *Shifting Involvements* (Princeton, NJ: Princeton University Press, 1982).

By expanding the concept of slack to encompass the various ways in which social bodies may be 'permanently and randomly subject to decline and decay', Hirschman enables it to fulfil both the specific role of idleness in Machiavelli's account and the larger one Machiavelli assigns to corruption in a world where 'human affairs are ever in a state of flux and cannot stand still'. But Hirschman always retains Cyert and March's insistence that the effects of slack are not exclusively deleterious. Whereas Machiavelli sees idleness as both a form and a source of corruption, slack is a form of corruption that permits renovation because it can furnish the idle resources needed to achieve renewal or change. Machiavelli seems to miss this possibility. In his account, order arises from ruin only because when things cannot get any worse they must get better; idleness is a step on the road to ruin, but has no equivalent role in the ascending part of the cycle. Although seemingly a welcome benefit of peace and surplus production, idleness leads only to disorder. Machiavelli has no sense that it might also be the means through which the cycle of corruption is arrested and renovation begun. But what sort of idea is that? And where does it come from?

V.   Decadence and Renewal

It is easy to find such thinking around the *fin de siècle* when, according to Frank Kermode, 'decadence and renewal [were] indistinguishable, or rather contemporaneous'.[53] For W. B. Yeats, 'the end of an age, which always receives the revelation of the character of the next age, is represented by the coming of one gyre to its place of greatest expansion and of the other to its place of greatest contraction'.[54] The spatial configuration Yeats envisages is formed by double vortices with the apex of one at the base of the other, so that the forms assumed by the 'inrushing gyre' take their shape from the contrary movement of the other.

As Yeats acknowledges, the idea that 'our civilisation was about to reverse itself or some new civilisation was about to be born from all that our age had rejected' could be traced back to the work of the twelfth-century interpreter of the apocalypse, Joachim of Fiore.[55] Joachim conceived of history in terms of the Christian doctrine of the Trinity (the three *status* of the Father, Son and Holy Spirit) and argued that the

---

[53] F. Kermode, 'Waiting for the End', in M. Bull (ed.), *Apocalypse Theory and the Ends of the World* (Oxford: Oxford University Press, 1995), 258.

[54] W. B. Yeats quoted in A. N. Jeffares, *A Commentary on the Collected Poems of W. B. Yeats* (Stanford, CA: Stanford University Press, 1968), 210.

[55] Ibid., 285.

interpenetration of the members of the Godhead indicated periods of overlap between one *status* and the next. Each *status* itself contains a sequence of germination, fructification and consummation, and so the consummation or decay of the first *status* is simultaneously the fructification of the second, and so on. One consequence of this is that the tribulation that marks the end of every age coincides with the coming of a new age, so that the transition between the two has a double aspect.[56]

Machiavelli's cyclical account of corruption and renovation, derived from the Roman historian Polybius, is a rejection of the apocalyptic mode of thought that had nearly triumphed in Savonarola's Florence. As J. G. A. Pocock observes:

The air of Florence was heavy with apocalyptic, and Machiavelli could not have been as impervious to it as he may have liked to pretend. Innovation at the highest level, the creation of a just and stable society, had been attempted under the protection of the greatest concepts of Christian thought – nature, grace, prophecy and renovation; and the attempt had failed, so that it must have been falsely conceived.[57]

Not all this apocalyptic speculation was directly inspired by Joachim, but 'the Joachimist marriage of woe and exaltation exactly fitted the mood', and Savonarola's expectation that God would renew his church with the sword of tribulation was characteristic of it.[58] Rather than missing the possibility that decline and renewal might happen together, Machiavelli rejected it by emphasizing that unarmed prophets do not succeed and that renovation requires political action rather than divine grace. He merely mocked the idea that 'Without you for you God fights / While you are on your knees and nothing do.'[59] For Machiavelli, imagining that the endurance of persecution led to renewal was just another aspect of the religion of idleness.

This historical digression reveals something that might otherwise be missed about Hirschman's reinterpretation of Machiavelli's *corruzione*. In his insistence that the latitude provided by slack might be beneficial, he is undermining Machiavelli's insistence that idleness and passivity were

---

[56] On Joachim's theory of history, see M. Reeves, 'The Originality and Influence of Joachim of Fiore', *Traditio* 36 (1980), 269–316, and B. McGinn, *The Calabrian Abbot: Joachim of Fiore in the History of Western Thought* (New York: Macmillan, 1985).

[57] J. G. A. Pocock, *The Machiavellian Moment: Florentine Political Thought and the Atlantic Republican Tradition*, 2nd ed. (Princeton, NJ: Princeton University Press, 2003), 113.

[58] M. Reeves, *The Influence of Prophecy in the Later Middle Ages* (Oxford: Clarendon Press, 1969), 43. On Savonarola and Joachim, see D. Weinstein, *Savonarola and Florence: Prophecy and Patriotism in the Renaissance* (Princeton, NJ: Princeton University Press, 1970).

[59] Quoted in M. Viroli, *Machiavelli's God* (Princeton, NJ: Princeton University Press, 2010), 180.

never the means through which renewal might be engendered, but rather the means through which both republics and religions come to ruin. And in allowing an ambivalence to slack, he is unconsciously reintroducing a duality that Christian apocalyptic encouraged, but which Machiavelli sought to exclude.[60] So, although Hirschman's slack is configured in the same terms as Machiavelli's corruption, it is not interpreted in the same way. Slack may be a form of corruption, but Hirschman reads it from a perspective that is closer to that of apocalyptic thought, for in his account slack is that form of decline which permits renewal.

VI.   Double Time

All of this may seem rather remote from the concerns of the eighteenth North American Wildlife Conference of 1953, and it is. Nevertheless, the sequence of parallels traced above may suggest something unexpected about the sort of political thinking represented by environmentalist policies of non-use or low growth.

If allowing environmental resources to remain idle is what Hirschman would have called slack, then any demand that nature should be preserved forever, or that its resources should be conserved for use by future generations, or that consumption should be reduced to limit environmental damage, is in effect a demand to introduce greater slack into both the economy and the environment. And if Hirschman's slack is a modern version of what Machiavelli would have called corruption, then advocating greater slack is tantamount to allowing the spread of corruption without any of the laws or pressure mechanisms needed to contain or reduce it.

In this context, it becomes easier to see why idle land is so often thought of in terms of human decadence.[61] When Edward P. Cliff, Chief of the US Forest Service, stated in 1961 that 'nonproductive, misused and idle woodlands will add nothing to the economic and cultural foundation upon which our future as a nation and a civilization depend',[62] he was not just repeating the arguments of Gifford Pinchot, but rehearsing the republican argument against the corrupting effects of idleness that stretches back to Machiavelli – the idleness of trees just as

---

[60] However, Hirschman cannot have remained oblivious to the apocalyptic background after reading Pocock's *The Machiavellian Moment*, in which the interweaving of the discourses of apocalypse and corruption is a significant theme. On Hirschman and Pocock, see Adelman, *Worldly Philosopher*, 505–506 and 514.

[61] E.g. *The World's Work*, 59 (July 1930), 30.

[62] Quoted in W. D. Klemperer, 'Is Idle Forest Land Always Economic Folly?', *Journal of Forestry* 67 (1969), 222.

much a menace to society as the idleness of men or other resources. Like those Christians who, according to Machiavelli, interpreted religion according to idleness, environmentalists are advocates of policies that are in themselves both forms of, and a stimulus to, economic decline and political decadence. Rather than warning of decline and disaster, environmentalists are in a sense advocating it.

However, unlike Machiavelli's corruption, the non-use or conservation of natural sources is, like slack, always double-edged. By wasting one set of opportunities it simultaneously creates others, and every loss can be counted as credit for the future. In this respect, environmental idleness resembles the more ambiguous transitions of apocalyptic thought, where periods of decay, tribulation and decadence are the means of change and renewal. If so, it may be necessary to reconsider the relationship of environmentalism to religion. It has long been suggested that ecological thought transposes ideas of sacredness from religion to nature.[63] And critics of the ecology movement have often located predictions of environmental degradation within the context of religious prophecies of doom.[64] On this reading, however, conservation, rather than being the preservation of the pristine or the primitive, is revealed as a form of decadence. And rather than being an eschatological mode of thought, focused on the proximity of the end, environmentalism emerges as apocalyptic in the sense that the decadence or dissolution of one order is recognized to be simultaneously constitutive of the new.

Joachim called periods of overlap between historical periods, in which more than one person of the Trinity was at work, 'double time'.[65] It is a concept that lends itself to wider application in the context of the 'tyranny of the contemporary' that so often stands in the way of thinking about the future.[66] Slack, of its very nature, seems to call for some form of double accounting across time, for its existence is not just the precondition of change, but actually constitutes both the opportunity and the means of renewal. As such, it posits the present as a form of double time in which the unused resources of today are simultaneously (not at some future time, but already) the resources of the future, the buffer that gives future generations the latitude needed to address their problems.

---

[63] D. Worster, 'John Muir and the Roots of American Environmentalism', in *The Wealth of Nature: Environmental History and the Ecological Imagination* (New York: Oxford University Press, 1993), 182–202.

[64] E.g., J. E. Foss, *Beyond Environmentalism: A Philosophy of Nature* (Hoboken, NJ: John Wiley & Sons, 2009), 21–40.

[65] See Reeves, 'Originality and Influence', 290–291.

[66] See S. Gardiner, *A Perfect Moral Storm: The Ethical Tragedy of Climate Change* (New York: Oxford University Press, 2011), 143–184.

But thinking of conservation as a form of slack also carries more counter-intuitive implications. It suggests that rather than treating environmental problems like climate change as pressure mechanisms galvanizing us into political mobilization and the creation of a taut green economy, it might be better to leave both natural and political resources unused, the better to deal with the uncertainties of the future. It is well known that the largest reductions in greenhouse emissions since 1990 are not the results of environmentally friendly policy, but the unintended consequence of economic decline in Eastern Europe after the fall of Communism. Perhaps economic decline and political inertia will turn out to be among the more useful instruments in the tool-kit we are assembling for the future. As Joseph Schumpeter famously remarked, 'A system – any system that at *every* given point of time fully utilizes its possibilities to its best advantage may yet in the long run be inferior to a system that does so at *no* given point of time, because the latter's failure to do so may be a condition for the level or speed of long-run performance.'[67]

[67] J. Schumpeter, *Capitalism, Socialism, and Democracy* (London: Routledge, 1943), 83.

Science, Agency and the Future

6   The Nature of Fear and the Fear of Nature from Hobbes to the Hydrogen Bomb

Deborah R. Coen

There are good reasons to be suspicious of claims for a 'scientific' approach to natural disasters. Disasters are, by definition, events that elude the predictive knowledge of the sciences,[1] and to pretend otherwise places a society at risk. Technical responses to catastrophe have often provided false security, as in the tragic failure of Japan's sea walls to defend against the 2011 tsunami. Just as disturbingly, technical responses can distract from the underlying societal problems exposed by disasters.[2] Reconstruction after Hurricane Katrina, for instance, failed to address the unequal distribution of risk in New Orleans, placing low-income and African American residents at comparatively even greater danger in the event of another extreme storm.[3] What's more, history offers many examples of self-confidently 'scientific' responses to natural catastrophes that turned out to be mere pretexts for the centralization of power and the curtailment of liberty. For instance, it was in the aftermath of major earthquakes in Italy and Japan in the early twentieth century that the concept of the state of emergency was first articulated.[4] In light of examples like these, disaster science may seem like little more than a tool for the manipulation of popular fears. Jean Baudrillard has argued in this

---

[1] M. Voss, *Symbolische Formen: Grundlagen und Elemente einer Soziologie der Katastrophe* (Beilefeld: Transcript, 2006), 13.

[2] T. Steinberg, *Acts of God* (Oxford: Oxford University Press, 2000); S. Hoffman and A. Oliver-Smith (eds.), *The Angry Earth: Disaster in Anthropological Perspective* (London: Routledge, 1999).

[3] J. Schwartz, 'A Billion Dollars Later, New Orleans Still at Risk', *New York Times* (12 August 2007), https://nyti.ms/2mUcmZO.

[4] M. Orihara and G. Clancey, 'The Nature of Emergency: The Great Kanto Earthquake and the Crisis of Reason in Late Imperial Japan', *Science in Context* 25 (2012), 103–126; G. Agamben, *State of Exception*, trans. K. Attell (Chicago: University of Chicago Press, 2005); W. Scheuerman, *Between Norm and Exception: The Frankfurt School and the Rule of Law* (Cambridge, MA: MIT Press, 1997). For other examples, see C. Walker, *Shaky Colonialism: The 1746 Earthquake-Tsunami in Lima, Peru, and Its Long Aftermath* (Durham, NC: Duke University Press, 2008); J. Buchenau and L. L. Johnson, *Aftershocks: Earthquakes and Popular Politics in Latin America* (Albuquerque: University of New Mexico Press, 2009).

vein that any state capable of predicting and controlling natural catastrophes would be so coercive that its citizens would *prefer* a catastrophe.[5]

Our twenty-first century intuitions thus tell us that the very idea of disaster science poses a threat to democracy. Intuitions like these have undoubtedly helped to feed skepticism of the science of global warming. Yet those intuitions have little to say about how knowledge of natural disasters is actually produced. This chapter uses the tools of the historian of science to open up the black box of knowledge production. It sketches some key elements of a history of disaster science from the Scientific Revolution to the Cold War, with a particular focus on the political and epistemic functions of fear. I look first at Thomas Hobbes's notion of a 'civil and moral science' that would defend against future 'miseries'. Then I turn to the European sciences that took shape in response to the Lisbon earthquake of 1755 and other natural disasters of the eighteenth and nineteenth centuries. Finally I consider the rise of a sociology of disaster in the United States during the Cold War. Not until the twentieth century, I argue, did the aspiration to a science of disaster come to connote the circumvention of a democratic process of evaluating threats. Until then, there was no reason to assume that a more scientific approach to disasters would mean a less political one. It was also not until the twentieth century that states conceived the ambition of exerting total control over the emotion of fear. Though fear had long been subject to manipulation from above, it had also drawn respect from earlier philosophers and scientists as a motivation to knowledge and a clue to the analysis of natural hazards.

I.   The Fear of Nature after the State of Nature

For all men are by nature provided of notable multiplying glasses, (that is their passions and self-love) through which, every little payment appeareth a great grievance; but are destitute of those prospective glasses (namely moral and civil science) to see afar off the miseries that hang over them, and cannot without such payments be avoided.[6]

Thomas Hobbes recognized already in the middle of the seventeenth century that fear is a principal motivator of men's actions, and he was the first to appreciate the potential of fear to act as the glue binding civil society together. Hobbes also knew that individuals are often poor judges of the dangers that represent their most serious long-term threats. They

---

[5] J. Baudrillard, 'Paroxysm: The Seismic Order', European Graduate School, available at www.egs.edu/faculty/jean-baudrillard/articles/paroxysm-the-seismic-order.

[6] T. Hobbes, *Leviathan*, ed. J. C. A. Gaskin (Oxford: Oxford University Press, 1998), 122.

might be unable to see, for instance, how paying their taxes might one day ensure their safety against a still invisible danger. Hobbes therefore reasoned that the sovereign must have absolute authority to decide what constitutes a danger to his subjects. On these grounds it has been claimed that Hobbes anticipated the politics of fear in the modern liberal state. The political scientist Corey Robin argues that liberalism has followed Hobbes in using the rhetoric of fear to create the appearance of consensus.[7] Liberalism posits supposedly apolitical objects of fear and makes them the grounds for concerted action. Without disputing Robin's characterization of the modern politics of fear, I want to suggest that his historical claim for continuity rests on certain misleading assumptions about what Hobbes meant by 'science'. Robin tells us that Hobbes trusted the sovereign to identify appropriate objects of fear because 'the sovereign would be able to act on behalf of an impartial, disinterested, and neutral calculation of what truly threatened the people as a whole and of what measures would protect them'; he would be able to 'get the calculations right'.[8] This may describe what modern states expect of science, but I will argue that it bears no resemblance to Hobbes's expectations.

To be sure, Hobbes recognized that the fear of disasters, natural and civil, was a potent political tool. He explained that religious leaders used the fear of 'sickness, earthquakes' and other misfortunes in order to ensure their followers' obedience. He exposed the manipulations of prognosticators, who prey on men's 'fear' and 'ignorance' to convince them of approaching calamities. He was equally suspicious of 'natural' as of 'supernatural' forecasters, evincing little faith in the possibility of a predictive natural philosophy.[9] With good reason: the only branch of physics whose predictions could be trusted in the early seventeenth century was celestial mechanics, since earthly mechanics was still beset by a poor understanding of friction and the lack of a reliable method for measuring experimental error. Early modern meteorology, for instance, as taught at universities, took almost no interest in forecasting, while the predictions of popular almanacs did not meet Hobbes's causal definition of science.[10] This was a world where natural disasters were, understandably, 'acts of God', and where particular facts and instances still did not

---

[7] C. Robin, *Fear: The History of a Political Idea* (Oxford: Oxford University Press, 2004).

[8] C. Robin, 'The Language of Fear: Security and Modern Politics', in J. Plamper and B. Lazier (eds.), *Fear across the Disciplines*, (Pittsburgh: University of Pittsburgh Press, 2012), 118–131, at 120.

[9] Hobbes, *Leviathan*, ch. 12, 'Of Religion.'

[10] C. Martin, *Renaissance Meteorology: Pomponazzi to Descartes* (Baltimore: Johns Hopkins University Press, 2011), 11–14.

fit comfortably into the epistemological frameworks of natural philosophy. From this perspective, an uncertain natural science might be more dangerous to the polity than none at all. Thus Hobbes stressed that the fear of nature was just as vulnerable to political manipulation as the fear of other people. Indeed, Hobbes himself became a victim of it in the wake of the disastrous plague and fire that struck London in the 1660s. In 1666 'the House of Commons cited the atheism of Hobbes and of his friend the Roman Catholic priest Thomas White as a probable "cause" of the Great Fire and Plague of London, and ordered an investigation of their works.'[11] Hobbes thus gained direct experience of the manipulation of the fear of nature to political ends.

Even so, Hobbes never made the modern move of arguing that nature trumped politics, that it constituted a body of facts about which agreement could be achieved without resorting to a political process of decision-making. On the contrary, he strenuously rejected this step when it was taken by proponents of the new experimental philosophy.[12] When the Royal Society claimed to have created a space in which matters of fact could be decided on strictly apolitical grounds, Hobbes cried foul. To cordon off nature from the sovereign's authority in this way, he argued, was to open the door to cancerous disagreements, and ultimately to civil war. Thus Hobbes in no way called for a 'disinterested' science of civil security. As Steven Shapin and Simon Schaffer showed in their classic study of Hobbes's natural philosophy, Hobbes was his generation's fiercest critic of the emerging ideology of disinterested science. Hobbes saw all too clearly the power plays involved in such claims.

In addition, Hobbes did not make a distinction that political theorists are prone to make today: between human and non-human objects of fear (between civil hazards like warfare, on one hand, and natural hazards, on the other). Robin, for instance, intentionally leaves aside environmental hazards in his treatise on the politics of fear.[13] Writing circa 2004, he insists that a natural disaster like a tidal wave does not generate the kind of fear that inspires political commitments. A decade later, this statement is no longer plausible. Certainly, Hurricane Katrina brought a surge of social-justice activism in its wake. In the age of global warming, the

[11] S. Mintz, *The Hunting of Leviathan: Seventeenth-Century Reactions to the Materialism and Moral Philosophy of Thomas Hobbes* (Cambridge: Cambridge University Press, 1962), 62.

[12] S. Shapin and S. Schaffer, *Leviathan and the Air Pump: Hobbes, Boyle and the Experimental Life* (Princeton, NJ: Princeton University Press, 1985).

[13] He explains: 'If fear is to commit us to political values like the rule of law or liberal democracy, we must confront a political threat to those values. After all, a coastal city threatened by a tidal wave may be incited to public action, but natural disaster seldom provokes citizens to embrace or enact specific political principles.' Robin, *Fear*, 4.

public is better able to spy the injustices that leave some populations more vulnerable to natural disasters than others. The notion that the risks associated with the natural world are apolitical has become as untenable as the claim that terrorism is a threat that transcends politics.

Hobbes never made the mistake of overlooking the politics involved in dealing with 'natural dangers'. Indeed, as Shapin and Schaffer observed, Hobbes 'allowed no boundaries between the natural, the human, and the social'.[14] Hobbes vehemently opposed the efforts of his contemporaries to separate natural 'matters of fact' from other objects of knowledge. In his insistence on the indivisibility of natural knowledge from politics, Hobbes was distinctly pre-modern, or perhaps post-modern. By no means was he – or his notion of science – modern in Robin's sense of the term.

Nor did Hobbes think that fear could or should be controlled by the state. For fear was not simply, for Hobbes, a motivation for civic union and collective action. Following an ancient tradition, he saw fear equally as a path to knowledge.[15] 'Anxiety for the future time, disposeth men to inquire into the causes of things: because the knowledge of them, maketh men the better able to order the present to their best advantage.' As he explained, fear needs to have an object if it is not to devolve into a generalized and paralyzing anxiety. In an age of *scientia*, fear finds its object in the restless search for *causes*. In this sense, anxiety gives rise to another passion, curiosity: 'Curiosity, or love of the knowledge of causes, draws a man from the consideration of the effect, to seek the cause.'[16] Lorraine Daston and Katharine Park describe Hobbes as the most 'voluble' thinker of the seventeenth century on the topic of curiosity, which he believed was the passion that distinguishes man from animals.[17] As J. W. N. Watkins observes, Hobbes viewed reason as the servant of the passions: we read in *Leviathan* that 'the thoughts are to the desires, as scouts, and spies, to range abroad, and find the way to the things desired.'[18]

For Hobbes, then, fear is the force that opens people's eyes to the natural world. Indeed, if fear can drive people to superstitious beliefs, it

---

[14] Shapin and Schaffer, *Leviathan*, 21.

[15] See Plamper and Lazier, 'Introduction', in *Fear across the Disciplines*, 5. On fear and knowledge, see too L. Daston, 'Life, Chance, and Life Chances', *Daedalus* 137 (2008), 5–14.

[16] Hobbes, *Leviathan*, 70.

[17] L. Daston and K. Park, *Wonders and the Order of Nature: 1150–1750* (Cambridge, MA: Zone Books, 1998), 307.

[18] Quoted in J. W. N. Watkins, *Hobbes's System of Ideas: A Study in the Political Significance of Philosophical Theories* (London: Hutchinson, 1965), 94.

can also help to unmask those beliefs, exposing natural causes in the place of supernatural ones. Sometimes this exposure removes the fear, as when an oracle's effects are explained by 'the intoxicating vapour' of 'sulphurous caverns', or a heavenly portent is explained as a consequence of celestial mechanics.[19] Even if the impulse to explain nature at times serves to eliminate fear, nonetheless fear is its point of origin.

Moreover, Hobbes was too sophisticated an epistemologist to believe that security is merely a matter of 'getting the calculations right.' As Leibniz observed, Hobbes was a nominalist: truth depended on proper logical relations among signs, without regard to what they signified. 'No man can know by discourse that this, or that, is, has been, or will be; which is to know absolutely: but only, that if this be, that is; if this has been, that has been; if this shall be, that shall be: which is to know conditionally, and that not the consequence of one thing to another; but of one name of a thing, to another name of a thing.'[20] From this perspective, differences of opinion cannot be settled by appeal to an external reality. If the disputants cannot reach agreement, Hobbes argues, they 'must, by their own accord, set up, for right reason, the reason of some arbitrator, or judge, to whose sentence they will both stand, or their controversy must either come to blows, or be undecided, for want of a right reason constituted by nature; so is it also in all debates of what kind soever'.[21] In this way, Hobbes's conventionalist theory of knowledge was meant to guarantee that disputes could be resolved peacefully.

We are now in a position to ask about the nature of Hobbes's 'prospective glasses'. What exactly was this science of 'far-off miseries' that Hobbes envisioned? What was the sovereign if not a scientist intent on 'getting his calculations right'? Answering these questions will help to throw into relief the peculiarities of more modern interpretations of disaster science.

Watkins observes that Hobbes modeled his civil science on Galileo's natural philosophy: begin with absolutely true principles, deduce consequences from them and confirm those by experiment.[22] Experiential knowledge thus has a role to play in this science, but a circumscribed role. To be sure, Hobbes expected the sovereign to rely on expert advisers: 'to the person of a commonwealth, his counsellors serve him in the place of memory, and mental discourse.'[23] Yet it is probably an exaggeration to claim, as Loralea Michaelis does, that Hobbes conceived of governance as 'a science over which the expert, and not the ruler,

---

[19] Hobbes, *Leviathan*, 77.   [20] Hobbes, *Leviathan*, 42.
[21] Ibid., 28, quoted in Watkins, *Hobbes's System*, 147.   [22] Watkins, *Hobbes's System*, 44.
[23] Hobbes, *Leviathan*, 172.

ultimately presides'.[24] At issue here is what this science was supposed to achieve. As we have seen, science was only of use to the Hobbesian state insofar as it drew absolute assent by demonstrative force. Predictive claims, whether based on natural or supernatural theories, were inherently uncertain and potentially destructive of social disorder. A merely probabilistic science might inform, but could not constrain, the sovereign's deliberations. If the future looks more predictable in Hobbes's commonwealth than in the state of nature, it is not because the sovereign relies on the predictions of experts. Hobbes was not counseling blind trust in expertise.

On the contrary, it is precisely because scientific expertise does not have the last word in Hobbes's commonwealth that its 'prospective glasses' work. The quest for natural knowledge always remains subordinate to the need to maintain civil order. By guaranteeing order, the absolute power of the sovereign guarantees a more predictable future – or, at least, the appearance thereof. We catch a glimpse of this reading in Michaelis: 'Such a science does not make the future more transparent', she concedes, 'but it does make it more available as an object of planning and control: one might say that the future becomes all the more stable and predictable.'[25] This point can be fleshed out with reference to the broader context of the Enlightenment. Lorraine Daston has proposed that the rise of probabilistic reasoning in the seventeenth and eighteenth centuries reflected the experience of a more predictable world: 'A safer life could have been experienced as a more stable, predictable one, for it encouraged planning for the future in a way that periodic fortunes did not. Children that usually survived past infancy; ships that usually returned from exotic destinations; dwellings that usually withstood fires for generations: in a mathematical sense these patterns were no more regular than the worst consistently coming to pass, or even cycles of prosperity and want, but they promoted a sense of security that the other equally well-defined patterns did not.'[26] For readers in Hobbes's own day, there was thus no need to imagine a predictive science behind his 'prospective glasses'. It was enough to believe that a Hobbesian state would bring about a more certain future.

By framing the question of what to fear as a matter for 'science', Hobbes did indeed hope to build consensus around objects of fear. But

---

[24] L. Michaelis, 'Hobbes's Modern Prometheus: A Political Philosophy for an Uncertain Future', *Canadian Journal of Political Science* 40 (2007), 101–127, at 121.
[25] Michaelis, 'Hobbes's Modern Prometheus', 122.
[26] L. Daston, *Classical Probability in the Enlightenment* (Princeton, NJ: Princeton University Press, 1988), 183.

he rejected the familiar modern move that would force consensus by framing the matter at hand as *above* politics. For Hobbes, there was no knowledge without fear, no science without politics. The Leviathan could not afford to sever any domain of knowledge from the sovereign's authority, for doing so could lead to ungovernable disputes. This might well sound like a recipe for something like Lysenkoism. However, Hobbes did not expect the sovereign to preside over the formulation of predictive sciences, as Stalin would do.[27] For predictive science was not the path to order and security, in Hobbes's view. In the 1640s there was good reason to believe that forecasting would always be playing with fire, and that a more orderly world could be achieved only by fiat. The clarity of the view through the sovereign's 'prospective glasses' came about because, in that 'far off' future, many competing wills would have been reduced to one.

II.   The Lisbon Earthquake and Nineteenth-Century Disaster Science

If Hobbes is not the source of our modern view of natural disasters, it is plausible to look for it instead in the aftermath of the catastrophic Lisbon earthquake of 1755. Philosophers tell us that natural disasters were thereafter removed from the purview of theology and moral philosophy and set squarely in a framework of technical analysis, prediction and control.[28] Once again, however, the historical reality is not so clear cut. To be sure, philosophers like Kant and Rousseau roundly rejected theological interpretations of the disaster in favor of strict naturalism. Rousseau blamed the victims for the location of their homes, while Kant offered (in Walter Benjamin's estimation) the very first work of seismology. In the aftermath of the disaster, earthquakes received scientific attention throughout Europe. The French Academy of Sciences rapidly organized a system of empirical studies of seismic activity on French soil.[29] In the 1780s, a series of temblors in Calabria offered European naturalists prime conditions for the elaboration of an enlightened account of earthquakes.[30] Thus, in the late eighteenth century,

---

[27] E. Pollock, *Stalin and the Soviet Science Wars* (Princeton, NJ: Princeton University Press, 2006).

[28] D. N. Robinson, 'Wisdom through the Ages', in J. R. Sternberg (ed.), *Wisdom: Its Nature, Origins, and Development* (Cambridge: Cambridge University Press, 1990), 22–23.

[29] G. Quenet, *Les Tremblements de Terre aux XVIIe et XVIIIe Siècles: La Naissance d'un Risque* (Paris: Editions Champ Vallon, 2005).

[30] S. B. Keller, 'Section and Views: Visual Representation in Eighteenth-Century Earthquake Studies', *British Journal for the History of Science* 31 (1998), 129–159.

earthquakes came to be studied from the modern perspective of risk: not as acts of divine retribution, but as expected consequences of a seismically active landscape.[31]

However, if we agree with the many commentators, then and now, who insist that seismology became a modern science after 1755, then we need to use the term 'modern science' more cautiously than usual. To begin with, religious explanations of earthquakes hardly disappeared after 1755, even among savants. Theological interpretations not only endured but sometimes even motivated the seismological investigations of the Enlightenment.[32] Nor did seismology become a science of prediction and control. On the contrary, those who claimed to be able to predict earthquakes, even on the basis of natural causes, were quickly deemed quacks by the scientific elite. Scientists studying earthquakes in the nineteenth century were remarkably modest about what they claimed to know, and they typically urged the public to err on the side of caution when it came to earthquake-sensitive construction. Instead, most seismological investigators of this period in Europe and North America saw their task as a quest to *understand* the forces that had shaped the earth over the course of its history, not to control them.

To that end, many scholars of earthquakes turned to the public for help. They organized networks of lay observers to watch for seismic activity. As I have shown elsewhere,[33] many of these projects were undertaken in a populist spirit by naturalists with democratic leanings. As the California seismologist John Casper Branner put it in 1913, 'To our requests for information about earthquakes we are frequently told apologetically that "I don't know anything about earthquakes." There is but one reply to be made to such remarks, and that is that "we know precious little about them ourselves; we are just now trying to find out, and we want your help."'[34]

Most fundamentally, seismology remained untroubled by the mingling of natural and human phenomena that constituted its object of study. Like Hobbes, early seismologists understood themselves to be studying the workings of nature alongside those of society. They

[31] Quenet, *Les Tremblements de Terre.*
[32] M. Gisler, *Göttliche Natur? Formationen im Erdbebendiskurs der Schweiz des 18. Jahrhunderts* (Zurich: Chronos Verlag, 2007).
[33] D. R. Coen, *The Earthquake Observers: Disaster Science from Lisbon to Richter* (Chicago: University of Chicago Press, 2013), from which this section of the current chapter is adapted.
[34] J. C. Branner, 'Earthquakes and Structural Engineering', *Bulletin of the Seismological Society of America* 3 (1913), 1–5, at 5.

certainly saw their enterprise as a modern one, yet they did not make the move that, as Latour tells us, defines modernity: to delimit a strictly apolitical realm of 'nature'.[35]

Instead, nineteenth-century seismologists pursued what they termed the 'monographic' method. This meant studying an earthquake 'in and for itself', in its 'unique aspects'.[36] They drew their evidence from field observations of the affected site, from eyewitness reports of the event and from records of past events in provincial archives. Human observations of earthquakes are surprisingly rich in scientific information. They demonstrate – in a way that geophysical observatories cannot – the local variability of the impacts of earthquakes, which is a complex function of factors such as tectonic structure, soil type and building style. They also profit from the familiarity of local observers with the normal state of their surroundings: locals are in the best position to recognize anomalies before and after earthquakes, such as variations of groundwater levels, unusual weather, remarkable animal behavior or changes in the surface of the land. The methods of nineteenth-century seismology thus combined geology, sociology, psychology and history. Scientists sought both a better understanding of fundamental geophysics and a means of protecting the public against future disasters.[37]

The principal tool for turning lay observations into scientific evidence was the intensity scale, which quantified the *felt* effects of ground movement. A standard scale was introduced in 1883 and still forms the basis for those used today. These scales operated (and still operate) in part by calibrating the public's reactions. The most widely used version in the late nineteenth century distinguished, for instance, between a degree 6 event, in which 'some frightened people leave their dwellings', and a degree 7, characterized by 'general panic'.

As this suggests, nineteenth-century seismology did not treat fear as an irrational response to geophysical hazards. On the contrary, scientists were invested in documenting fear as a legitimate emotional response to changes in the physical environment. In this vein, the seismologist Alexander McAdie distinguished between the 'depression of spirits which is physical and real, brought about by some as yet unknown relation between the nervous system and conditions of air-pressure, humidity, and purity', and the 'unnecessary' fear that was 'largely the

[35] Cf. B. Latour, *We Have Never Been Modern*, trans. C. Porter (Cambridge, MA: Harvard University Press, 1993).
[36] Quoted in D. Coen, *The Earthquake Observers*, 22.
[37] On lay observers in seismology, see too the essays by F. Fan and C. Valencius in *Science in Context* 25 (2012), and C. Bolton Valencius, *The Lost History of the New Madrid Earthquakes* (Chicago: University of Chicago Press, 2013).

work of the imagination'.[38] Nineteenth-century seismology thus activated an ancient tradition in which fear is not merely a motivation to or a consequence of knowledge; rather, fear is in itself knowledge of the state of the world. In Martha Nussbaum's elegant formulation of this point of view, it is through emotion that 'the world enters into the self'.[39]

In this framework, lay seismic observers functioned partly as human seismographs, as passive registers of the physical event. Yet intensity scales also treated laypeople as naturalists in their own right. Witnesses were expected to be discerning observers of nature. A shock of degree 3, for instance, was described as 'strong enough that the duration or direction could be appreciated'. A shock of degree 6 would produce an '*apparent* shaking of trees and bushes'.[40] These phrases hinted at the mindfulness expected of laypeople. Intensity scales codified their dual status as both experimental subjects and amateur naturalists; they were expected to react to ground movement with an appropriate degree of fear while remaining accurate observers.

What is perhaps most remarkable about this particular disaster science is the way that it distributed the power to determine appropriate objects and levels of fear. Rather than dictating what the public *should* fear, nineteenth-century seismology made ongoing adjustments between its evaluation of geophysical hazards and of social psychology. Seismologists were not only interested in what could be learned about the physical nature of earthquakes from human perceptions; occasionally, they turned the tables, using their physical data to analyze human phenomena. In an influential paper of 1900, 'The Effects of Earthquakes on Human Beings', the British mathematician and seismologist Charles Davison grouped responses to earthquakes into four 'rough' categories: 'A) No persons leave their rooms. B) Some persons leave their houses. C) Most persons run into the streets, which are full of excited people. D) People rush wildly for open spaces, and remain all night out of doors.' Applying these categories to the Charleston, North Carolina, earthquake of 1884, Davison was able to identify a culturally specific reaction. In some areas where the shaking was 'not even strong enough to cause doors and windows to rattle', nonetheless 'some persons were so alarmed that they left their houses, and public meetings were dispersed. Whether these effects were due to the rarity of the phenomenon or to the highly-strung

---

[38] A. McAdie, 'Needless Alarm during Thunderstorms', *The Century Magazine* 58 (1899), 604–605, at 605.

[39] M. Nussbaum, *Upheavals of Thought: The Intelligence of Emotions* (Cambridge: Cambridge University Press, 2001), 78.

[40] Quoted in Coen, *The Earthquake Observers*, 86.

nerves of the American people, it may, I think, be inferred that in no
other civilized country would such alarm be shown at a sudden and
unexpected occurrence.'[41]

In this judgment, Davison offered an important corrective to a widespread Victorian prejudice. Nineteenth-century British and German
writers, reflecting on the difference between Europe and its colonies,
and between the north and south of Europe itself, argued that human
reason could not withstand repeated exposure to natural dangers – least
of all to earthquakes. Consider this passage from Henry Thomas Buckle,
the Victorian who famously hoped to turn history into a science:

The mind is thus constantly thrown into a timid and anxious state; and men
witnessing the most serious dangers, which they can neither avoid nor
understand, become impressed with a conviction of their own inability, and of
the poverty of their own resources. In exactly the same proportion, the
imagination is aroused, and a belief in supernatural interference actively
encouraged. Human power failing, superhuman power is called in; the
mysterious and the invisible are believed to be present; and there grow up
among the people those feelings of awe, and of helplessness, on which all
superstition is based, and without which no superstition can exist.[42]

According to this widely held view, the *physical* destruction due to
earthquakes was secondary to the *psychic* devastation they caused.
Repeated earthquakes could impair the use of reason and destroy all
chance of progress in science and industry. In the place of such stereo-
types, Davison pointed the way to a systematic evaluation of the fear that
was warranted in different places at different times.

The appropriate level of fear could not be judged from geophysical
data alone, since it also depended on variables such as construction
standards and on the social conditions that shaped a society's ability to
cope with disasters. Nineteenth-century seismology effectively distinguished between a background fear *of earthquakes*, and a situational fear
in an earthquake, such that the former partly determined the latter.[43] In
other words, an individual's emotional response in the moment of danger
depended on a lifetime of experience with that danger. Thus Alexander
von Humboldt noted with approval that natives of earthquake-prone
lands had learned to keep their wits about them when the ground began
to shake.[44]

[41] C. Davison, 'The Effects of Earthquakes on Human Beings', *Nature* 63 (1900),
165–166.
[42] H. T. Buckle, *History of Civilization in England*, 2nd ed., vol. 1 (New York: Appleton,
1884), 88.
[43] See Nussbaum, *Upheavals of Thought*, 67–76.
[44] See Coen, *Earthquake Observers*, 109–112.

For all these reasons, the fear of nature – or the absence thereof – could not be dictated from above; it required empirical study jointly from the perspectives of the natural and human sciences. In the nineteenth century, then, the scientific identification of natural hazards took a form that was both democratic (reflecting the perceptions of ordinary people) and pluralistic (allowing for variation across cultures).

Other branches of natural science developed similarly integrated approaches to disaster in the eighteenth and nineteenth centuries. Famines, droughts, and epidemics all became objects of scientific investigation in the late eighteenth century, in frameworks that encompassed both natural and social factors.[45] For instance, as Mike Davis has shown, famines in colonial India were analyzed not simply in terms of weather and soil conditions but as 'complex economic crises induced by the market impacts of drought and crop failure'.[46] Victims' experiences were a valued form of evidence for all these sciences. In the field of medical geography, for instance, experts were interested in a patient's own accounts of illness, her own observations of triggering factors in her natural environment.[47] In scientific accounts from this period, victims of disaster would have seen their own experiences reflected clearly.

Then, beginning in the 1870s, explanations of natural disasters turned increasingly reductive. Theories of climate-related catastrophes like drought came to focus on sunspot cycles and global atmospheric oscillations. Simultaneously, the hunt for microbes replaced the early nineteenth century's more multifaceted, socio-environmental explanations of disease. And seismologists gradually turned to the 'hard' evidence of seismographs and accelerometers, rejecting data filtered by human bodies. By the 1950s, Georges Canguilhem could argue that 'the essential function of science is to devalue the qualities of objects that make up the milieu proper, by offering itself as a general theory of the real, that is to say nonhuman, milieu. Sensory data are disqualified, quantified, and identified.'[48] Whether this devaluation is inevitable or historically contingent remains open to debate. What is clear, however, is that the histories of climatology, epidemiology and seismology since the 1870s

---

[45] K. Anderson, *Predicting the Weather: Victorians and the Science of Meteorology* (Chicago: University of Chicago Press, 2005); L. Nash, *Inescapable Ecologies: A History of Environment, Disease, and Knowledge* (Berkeley: University of California Press, 2006).

[46] M. Davis, *Late Victorian Holocausts: El Niño Famines and the Making of the Third World* (New York: Verso, 2001), 19.

[47] C. B. Valencius, 'Histories of Medical Geography', *Medical History Supplement* 20 (2000), 3–28, and *The Health of the Country: How American Settlers Understood Themselves and Their Land* (New York: Basic Books, 2002).

[48] G. Canguilhem, 'The Living and Its Milieu', trans. J. Savage, *Grey Room* 3 (2001), 6–31, at 26.

all involve the construction of incommensurability between scientific expertise and common experience. Scientists no longer culled their evidence from survivors of disaster, and they no longer worried about the fit between their account and the public's. They tended to abandon field studies and to narrow their focus to non-human data – observatory-based instrumental measurements replaced eyewitness reports, laboratory germ cultures replaced victims' bodies. In this way, they eliminated the disaster itself from their field of study. Victims of natural disasters today have little hope of recognizing their own experiences in the models and theories of the environmental sciences.

III.   Disaster Science in the Twentieth Century

As these natural scientists retreated to their laboratories and observatories in the early twentieth century, others began to step in to create a new social science of disaster. It was in the wake of the Second World War that this project gained momentum. In the United States, the National Research Council inaugurated a 'Committee on Disaster Studies' in 1952 (renamed the 'Disaster Research Group' in 1957), including members from the social sciences, law, engineering and medicine. In the absence of a history of this research, I will consider it here through the lens of the report published by members of the Disaster Research Group in 1962, *Man and Society in Disaster*.[49]

The goal of the new disaster science was to learn to predict and control social behavior in the event of a nuclear war by studying responses to natural disasters. 'Many of the physical effects of more common disasters are not unlike the physical effects we might expect from an atomic bombing.'[50] Despite the overlap in subject matter, however, *Man and Society in Disaster* marked a break with nineteenth-century studies of natural disasters. Indeed, it emphasized the distinctly twentieth-century origins of its research. The inspiration lay in 'the Depression of the early thirties and the Second World War, when the challenges to understand and control behavior during periods of extreme national and international stress were most urgent'.[51]

Reversing the move made by Kant in 1755, the new disaster scientists eliminated from their fields of view the physical phenomena responsible

---

[49] G. W. Baker and D. W. Chapman (eds.), *Man and Society in Disaster* (New York: Basic Books, 1962). For a participant history, see E. L. Quarantelli, 'Disaster Studies: An Analysis of the Social Historical Factors Affecting the Development of Research in the Area', *International Journal of Mass Emergencies and Disasters* 5 (1987), 285–310.
[50] Baker and Chapman, *Man and Society in Disaster*, 309.   [51] Ibid., 407.

for the disaster; they would attend only to the human response. Indeed, they noted that their research did not even require the occurrence of a 'destructive event', since cases of 'hoaxes and false alarms' could serve their needs equally well. 'It is the perception of threat and not its actual existence that is important.'[52] By contrast, for nineteenth-century scientists, as we have seen, the study of the threat and of its perception could not be separated. *Man and Society* was thus described as 'a scientific report on the behavior of individuals and groups in response to stress'.[53] By ignoring the source of the stress, the new disaster science was able to apply the common Cold War analytical lenses of cybernetics, systems theory and information theory. The disaster itself was reduced to 'an increase in entropy'.[54]

In these senses, Cold War–era Disaster Studies was not a disaster science of the kind Hobbes had envisioned. It was not about identifying appropriate objects of fear, since the objects of fear were not in question. Either the 'stressors' were irrelevant or there was only one worth mentioning. As one reviewer of *Man and Society* reflected: 'Should a surviving historian chance upon a preserved copy of this book in the conceivable future, he may think it disastrous that in 1962 seventeen behavioral scientists had nothing to say about the gravest question of their times: How might international behavior have been controlled to *prevent* a nuclear disaster?'[55] In addition, the project was defined in such a way that it foreclosed discussion of the ways in which nuclear war would *not* resemble natural disasters. The research approach precluded acknowledging the rationality of fear of a nuclear war or discussing the means to avert one. The one and only task of this science was to learn to control fear. 'Every effort must be bent in the direction of modifying behavior *now* and increasing the tolerance for disruption *now* in order to reduce in some way the almost total disruption that would face an unprepared nation if the disaster were to occur.'[56] So it was that in 1962 disaster science adopted the model that has been misleadingly attributed to Hobbes, in which 'danger is whatever the state says it is.'

The new Disaster Studies was predicated on a new understanding of fear itself, one that had emerged in the early twentieth century, inspired by the ideas of Darwin and Freud.[57] Fear in this new sense was void of the moral and epistemic significance that Hobbes and his contemporaries

---

[52] Ibid., 30.   [53] Ibid., vii.   [54] Ibid., 117.

[55] N. J. Demarath, 'Review of *Man and Society in Disaster*', *Journal of Health and Human Behavior* 4 (1963), 220–222.

[56] Baker and Chapman, *Man and Society in Disaster*, 36–37.

[57] R. Leys, 'How Did Fear Become a Scientific Object and What Kind of Object Is It?', in Plamper and Lazier (eds.), *Fear across the Disciplines*, 51–77.

had attributed to it. It was an evolutionarily conditioned, physiologically defined and politically manipulable phenomenon. Fear no longer needed an object, as Hobbes had insisted; researchers now expected it to take the generalized form of 'anxiety'. The new Disaster Studies condemned fear as a poison to rational thought – even as it acknowledged an alternative interpretation. Thus the sociologist Pitirim Sorokin, author of the 1942 *Man and Society in Calamity*, described the mental effect of disasters as 'undulatory' – 'the general trend toward impairment of mental function being interrupted by intermittent flashes of enlightenment, penetrating and inspirational thought'.[58] Where nineteenth-century seismology had recognized fear as a form of knowledge about the world, Sorokin concluded that disasters deprive the mind of its 'requisite autonomy'. When the evidence contradicted their emotionless model of cognition, disaster sociologists ignored it.

More weight was placed on the role of the emotions in the chapter of the 1962 report titled 'The Psychological Effects of Warnings'. The author described an attitude that he termed 'vigilance', involving 'increased attentiveness to environmental events and readiness to take protective action in response to any cue perceived as indicating the onset of danger'. He theorized that vigilance was possible only with a high degree of 'ego development', which made it possible to 'bear the emotional tension that goes along with vigilance. Even many adults find it difficult to adopt a set of watchfulness, alertness, and readiness to take protective action in the face of known danger.'[59] Thus far, the account of vigilance echoes pre-twentieth-century notions of the path from fear to knowledge. In 1962, however, vigilance was no longer of interest as a condition under which ordinary citizens might produce scientific knowledge. Instead, it was regarded as a form of mass therapy. The author of the chapter on 'Disaster and Mental Health' called for a 'moral equivalent of disaster, which, like William James' moral equivalent of war, would provide a stimulating and unifying outer challenge without unfortunate side-effects such as the destruction of life and property. Certainly disaster encourages Freud's dual prescription for the healthy mental life: love and work.'[60] The new disaster sociology thus adopted the Freudian conception of emotions as the non-intentional expression of inner drives.[61] In this way, it voided fear of its epistemic and moral value and promoted it merely as an exercise in psychic self-regulation.

---

[58] P. A. Sorokin, *Man and Society in Calamity* (New York: E. P. Dutton, 1942), 36.
[59] Baker and Chapman, *Man and Society in Disaster*, 62.   [60] Ibid., 132.
[61] Leys, 'How Did Fear Become a Scientific Object?'.

Where earlier scientists and philosophers had assumed that fear was the driving force behind the production of knowledge at a scene of disaster, the new disaster scientists argued instead that knowledge was motivated by a desire for 'environmental mastery':

Perhaps the greatest ally in the attempt to promote effective handling of crisis is the general human propensity to strive for environmental mastery ... The intense desire to perform capably, in the deepest sense to *know* one's environment, offers substantial theoretical help in assessing the reasons for good disaster performance.[62]

Knowledge was now equated with control – control of the self and of the environment. Oddly, there appears to be no emotional source of this 'intense desire' for control. The philosophical chain between fear and knowledge had been severed, and fear was no longer to be trusted as an indicator of hazard.

IV.   Conclusion

The history of science shows that a scientific approach to disaster is compatible with a democratic and pluralistic method of identifying the appropriate objects and levels of fear. Only in the twentieth century did disaster science come to mean a top-down imposition of phobic norms. Twentieth-century disaster science broke with its predecessors by abstracting away the object of fear. Cold War–era social science analyzed human responses in isolation from what earlier scientists had termed the disaster 'in and for itself'. It thus paved the way for the framework of risk analysis that emerged in the late twentieth century and that still dominates thinking about natural disasters today.

Social scientists today theorize risk as a discourse unconstrained by the reality or unreality of 'hazards'. Paradigmatic for this trend was Mary Douglas and Aaron Wildavsky's *Risk and Culture: An Essay on the Selection of Technological and Environmental Dangers* (1983), which argued that 'public perception of risk and its acceptable levels are collective constructs, a bit like language and a bit like aesthetic judgment.' Douglas and Wildavsky acknowledged that their analysis would need to be supplemented by attention to the 'reality of physical dangers' and the 'conditions of knowledge', but insisted that the first was 'beyond our scope' and the second 'beyond our capacity'.[63] In the absence of such

---

[62] Baker and Chapman, *Man and Society in Disaster*, 131.
[63] M. Douglas and A. Wildavsky, *Risk and Culture: An Essay on the Selection of Technological and Environmental Dangers* (Berkeley: University of California Press, 1983), 186.

extensions, social scientists persist in analyzing environmental fear as a purely discursive phenomenon, isolated from the environment and from the production of environmental knowledge. In this vein, Nikolas Luhmann's influential systems-theoretical model of environmental politics assumes that the self-referentiality of risk discourse prevents a direct coupling between the social and natural 'systems'.[64]

It is only in these last few decades that the term 'hazard' has taken on its current meaning of an objective, 'natural' condition, in opposition to the human-centered concept of 'risk'. Yet etymology belies this overly neat distinction. The term 'hazard' derives from the French for a game of chance; it is thus by definition something that eludes our full knowledge and predictive abilities. It is an inherently expansive concept, pointing beyond material facts towards perceptions and possible courses of action. The concept of hazard singles out the perspective of the victim of an unpredictable world, not of a disinterested observer. Its etymological origins remind us that a hazard is a hazard not merely because of 'natural' conditions, but also because of a given state of knowledge and affect, a certain balance between certainty and uncertainty, between confidence and fear.

Therein lies a weakness of today's discourse on climate change. Those who label global warming a catastrophe stand accused of 'alarmism', both by critics who believe there is cause for alarm and by those who do not. The former critics contend that the rhetoric of catastrophe risks overwhelming the public with anxiety, thereby inflicting general paralysis. The skeptics, meanwhile, suspect an attempt to manipulate public fear in order to undermine capitalism. Both sides converge in their assumption that science should serve to eliminate fear, not provoke it. Why? There is no reason to expect that greater knowledge should produce a stronger sense of security.[65] Moreover, science sometimes serves us best when it delineates the scope of our ignorance, the limits of our predictive capacities. Despite the optimism of the Cold War sociology of disaster, comfort is not always to be found in 'the healthy exercise of rationality involved in submitting the inconceivably terrible to scientific scrutiny'.[66] In this vein, science can generate anxiety that successfully provokes public debate and political reform.

---

[64] N. Luhmann, *Soziologie des Risikos* (Berlin: De Gruyter, 1991).
[65] Daston, 'Life, Chance, and Life Chances', 14.
[66] M. Brewster Smith, 'Preface', *Journal of Social Issues* 10 (1954), 1, at 1, cited in J. Bourke, *Fear: A Cultural History* (Emeryville, CA: Shoemaker & Hoard, 2005), 283.

7 Between Frankfurt and Vienna
Two Traditions of Political Ecology

*John O'Neill and Thomas Uebel**

In this chapter we consider the conflicts between two traditions of political ecology. The two traditions might be crudely characterized as physicalist and culturalist. The first is apparent in much of the work in ecological economics in particular, but also in the materialist left and more practically in conservation policy. It is concerned with the physical and biophysical conditions for human and non-human flourishing. It typically employs physical indicators of human well-being and biophysical indicators of environmental change. It is typically concerned with the ways in which current economic and social systems meet physical limits in the capacity of the environment for resource provision, waste assimilation and climate regulation. It is science based. In the tradition of ecological economics one can trace the influence of an older physicalist tradition found in the work of the left Vienna Circle, and in particular of Otto Neurath. The second tradition is apparent in a body of work that sees the environmental crisis as part of a wider cultural crisis in 'Western reason'. It is typically more critical of science and scientism as forms of ideology that are taken to underpin the environmental crisis. The reduction of practical reason to modes of instrumental rationality limits the possibility of a critical perspective on our environmental problems. One of the main sources of this body of work is the Frankfurt School.

This outline of the two traditions is crude. However, it does reflect a real tension within political ecology and the environmental movement more generally, in particular in its ambivalent relation to the natural sciences. On the one hand, the environmental movement is one that is science dependent. More than any other political movement it is reliant on scientific claims. Most environmental problems, such as those associated with climate change or rates of biodiversity loss, could not

* Earlier versions of this chapter were read at the conference on 'Political Thought and the Environment', Cambridge University, 25–26 May 2012 and the University of Helsinki, 7 May 2012. Our thanks for the many helpful comments made on those occasions.

be even identified without the natural sciences. However, on the other hand, it is a movement that contains within it strong elements of science scepticism ranging from the concerns about the conflicts between scientific expertise and demands of democratic participation through to views that the sciences themselves are one source of the very environmental problems the sciences have identified.[1]

In this chapter we examine one of the historical roots of the opposition between these two traditions of political ecology, in the debates between the left Vienna Circle and the Frankfurt School. In doing so we suggest the basis for at least a partial reconciliation. The chapter is in five sections. In Section I we outline the history of the conflict between the two traditions in some largely forgotten debates between Neurath and Horkheimer in the 1930s. In Sections II, III, and IV we examine the history and influence of the Vienna Circle and Frankfurt traditions by placing Horkheimer's and Neurath's papers in a larger narrative arc: the second and third outline the influence of the work of the Vienna Circle in the development of the tradition of ecological economics; Section IV considers the critique of instrumental reason that emerged from the Frankfurt School, developed in part in opposition to the positivism of the Vienna Circle. In Section V we consider the legacy of the debate and outline some of the virtues of the approach offered within the tradition of the Vienna Circle, in particular as developed by Neurath, for understanding the tensions between science dependence and science scepticism within modern political life.

I.   The Tale of Two Papers

In 1937 issue no. 1 of volume 6 of the Frankfurt School's journal, *Zeitschrift für Sozialforschung* (Journal for Social Research) contained two papers that might look unlikely cohabitants of the journal.[2] The first was Max Horkheimer's 'The Latest Attack on Metaphysics', which developed a systematic critique of positivism which became central to the tradition of critical theory.[3] The paper marked a shift in the history of

---

[1] For different perspectives on this tension, see S. Yearley, *The Green Case* (London: Harper Collins, 1991), and J. O'Neill, *Ecology, Policy and Politics: Human Well-Being and the Natural World* (London: Routledge, 1993), chs. 8 and 9.

[2] For further detail about the 1937 papers and their background, see J. O'Neill and T. Uebel, 'Horkheimer and Neurath: Restarting a Disrupted Debate', *European Journal of Philosophy* 12 (2005), 75–105. Parts of this chapter draw on this paper.

[3] M. Horkheimer, 'Der neueste Angriff auf die Metaphysik', *Zeitschrift für Sozialforschung* (hereafter *ZfS*) 6 (1937), 4–53, translated as 'The Latest Attack on Metaphysics', in M. Horkheimer, *Critical Theory: Selected Essays* (New York: Seabury Press, 1972), 132–187.

the Frankfurt School, from the interdisciplinary empirical research programme of the early work of the Institute for Social Research (*Institut für Sozialforschung*) to the central themes of critical theory that defined its second stage – in particular the criticism of instrumental reason that became central to one tradition of political ecology. In doing so it also marked a significant turn in the reception of the Vienna Circle, who were identified as the central object of the critique of instrumental reason. Here originated the familiar picture of the logical empiricists as committed to a technocratic and instrumentalist view of politics, unable to sustain any critical standpoint on existing society.

Given this, the second paper in the issue, 'Inventory of the Standard of Living', might look a strange companion piece.[4] The author, Otto Neurath, was a central target of Horkheimer's paper. Neurath's paper reformulated some of the themes in Neurath's long-standing attack on the attempt to capture changes in welfare in purely monetary terms. The paper belonged not to a politically conservative ideology unable to critically engage with existing social conditions, but rather to the politically radical tradition of the left Vienna Circle. It was continuous with Neurath's own critique of capitalism and his engagement in the socialization debates that followed his involvement in the Bavarian revolution as director of the Central Economic Office. A feature of Neurath's contribution to the socialization debates was the introduction of an environmental dimension into the debates.[5] Neurath's contributions to the debates had a subsequent influence on the development of ecological economics, in particular through the work of K. William Kapp.

The unlikely juxtaposition of these two papers had its own history and its own afterlife. The Frankfurt School and the Vienna Circle had first come into contact through an earlier meeting between Horkheimer and Neurath at The Hague in January 1936, where the two had explored the possibilities for cooperation between the two groups of émigrés from Nazi Germany. In October and November 1936, Neurath twice visited the

---

[4] O. Neurath, 'Inventory of the Standard of Living', *ZfS* 6 (1937), 140–151, reprinted in Neurath, *Economic Writings: Selections 1904–1945*, ed. T. Uebel and R. S. Cohen (Dordrecht: Kluwer, 2004), 513–526.

[5] See J. O'Neill, 'Socialist Calculation and Environmental Valuation: Money, Markets and Ecology', *Science and Society* 66 (2002), 137–151; J. O'Neill, 'Ecological Economics and the Politics of Knowledge: The Debate between Hayek and Neurath', *Cambridge Journal of Economics* 28 (2004), 431–447; J. O'Neill, 'Austrian Economics and the Limits of Markets', *Cambridge Journal of Economics* 36 (2012), 1073–1090; T. Uebel, 'Incommensurability, Ecology and Planning: Neurath in the Socialist Calculation Debate 1919–1928', *History of Political Economy* 37 (2005), 309–342; T. Uebel, 'Calculation in Kind and Marketless Socialism: On Otto Neurath's Utopian Economics', *European Journal for the History of Economic Thought* 15 (2008), 475–501.

Institute for Social Research (then relocated to New York) for seminars on philosophy of science, metaphysics and dialectics, and the Institute provided financial support for Neurath's standard of living research reported in the 1937 issue of *Zeitschrift für Sozialforschung*. Horkheimer's subsequent letter to Neurath expressed a 'desire to continue to concern ourselves with logical empiricism'.[6] But although to Neurath the scene looked set for cooperation, the Frankfurt School saw things differently. In correspondence, Horkheimer made clear that a central aim of the meetings was to learn more of logical empiricism in order to develop a more effective critique. The perhaps clearest expression of the intention can be found in a letter from Horkheimer to Karl Wittvogel of October 1936:

The scientific discussions, which are taking place in the Institute partly by invitation of external colleagues, currently concern mainly the problem of the so-called scientific philosophy ... Since this philosophy is oriented exclusively towards the natural sciences and thus does not yield anything else but the meagre world view of some physicists, who in their own field may do excellent work but are barely competent in these more general theoretical questions, the whole thing amounts to an apology for the conduct of natural science, to a misunderstanding of history and its theory and to a fight against the methods of thinking that are shared by us ... In light of the confusion which this philosophy currently inspires in academic and non-academic circles, the Institute intends in the near future to effect a critique of this tendency, perhaps even by means of several articles in the *Zeitschrift*. To this end we seek to orient ourselves by means of lectures by members of this circle and to become expert in it.[7]

Following further exchanges with Adorno about the work of logical empiricists, Horkheimer wrote in February 1937: 'I have completed the work very quickly since basically it does not merit spending too much time on it.'[8]

---

[6] Horkheimer to Neurath, 24 November 1936, in M. Horkheimer, *Gesammelte Schriften*, Band 15: *Briefwechsel 1931–1936*, ed. G. Schmid Noerr (Frankfurt am Main: Suhrkamp, 1995), 15, 743. Translations from sources for which no translation is indicated are by the present authors.

[7] Horkheimer to Karl Wittvogel, 19 October 1936, in Horkheimer, *Gesammelte Schriften*, 15, 778–779. See also Horkheimer to Adorno, 22 October 1936, in ibid., 688–689, which anticipates the essence of Horkheimer's later article, and Horkheimer to Henryk Grossman, 27 November 1936, in Horkheimer, *Gesammelte Schriften*, Band 16: *Briefwechsel 1937–1940*, ed. G. Schmid Noerr (Frankfurt am Main: Suhrkamp, 1995), 750. Both are quoted in H.-J. Dahms, *Positivismusstreit: Die Auseinandersetzungen der Frankfurter Schule mit dem logischen Positivismus, dem amerikanischen Pragmatismus und dem kritischen Rationalismus* (Frankfurt am Main: Suhrkamp, 1994), 85–86, which provided the first discussion of these interactions between the Frankfurt School and the Vienna Circle.

[8] Horkheimer to Adorno, 22 February 1937, in Horkheimer, *Gesammelte Schriften*, 16, 48.

In June 1937, Neurath was still considering Horkheimer as an author for his International Encyclopedia of Unified Science.[9] Unsurprisingly, given the different understanding of the possibilities for cooperation, the polemical nature of Horkheimer's published critique – 'The Latest Attack on Metaphysics' – came as a surprise: 'At first the shock rendered me speechless.'[10] Neurath drafted a response but Horkheimer declined to publish it, claiming that the *Zeitschrift* 'is not intended to furnish a platform for opposing views'.[11] The cooperation between the two schools thus came to an end; the scene was set for the subsequent history of mutual suspicion.

Along with the criticisms of the Vienna Circle and Neurath by Hayek, who as we show below developed a remarkably similar account of their technocratic politics and scientism, Horkheimer's paper and the critical accounts of logical empiricism that followed in subsequent issues of the *Zeitschrift* played a large role in defining the subsequent picture of the Vienna Circle and the use of 'positivism' as a term of academic abuse.[12] The picture was always a caricature. On the one hand, Horkheimer's criticism of logical empiricism echoed some of Neurath's criticisms of what was to emerge as the mainstream orthodoxy of 'logical positivism', in particular the relative neglect of history and social science. Moreover, the view ascribed to logical positivism as committed to a technocratic politics was one that Neurath himself explicitly rejected. On the other hand, Neurath's reply to Horkheimer invoked features of Horkheimer's own early materialism which were rejected in the later developments of Critical Theory, such as the re-autonomization of philosophy and the increasingly radical criticism of science. Neurath developed a response to the problems which afflicted Horkheimer's later work – problems which were highlighted by later theorists in the Frankfurt tradition like Habermas: the very radicalness of the Frankfurt School critique of reason made it difficult to sustain without undermining itself. Indeed, it is in its own critical engagement with the place of science in modern political life that Neurath's anti-technocratic politics retains a theoretical and practical significance that has been obscured by the Frankfurt School critique.

---

[9] Neurath to Horkheimer, 10 June 1937, quoted in Dahms, *Positivismusstreit*, 147–148.

[10] Neurath to Horkheimer, 21 June 1937 in Horkheimer, *Gesammelte Schriften* 16, 178.

[11] Horkheimer to Neurath, 29 December 1937, in Horkheimer, *Gesammelte Schriften* 16, 344, 348; cf. 30 January 1938, ibid., 37.

[12] See Section IV below.

II.   Neurath: Socialist Calculation and Ecological Economics

Neurath's 1937 paper 'Inventory of the Standard of Living' developed a set of claims about the measurement of 'life-conditions' that persist in more recent discussions of well-being in ecological economics. The first was that the concept of standard of living is multidimensional: 'The attempts to characterize the standard of living are like those which try to characterize the "state of health". Both are multidimensional structures.'[13] The different components of the standard of living will include health, free time, the interest of work, social relationships, aesthetic experiences etc. many of which, like health, are themselves multidimensional. Some of these will have specific cardinal measures, some only ordinal measures. However, Neurath argued, none can be caught in a single measure, particularly a single monetary measure. More generally, he rejected any summative view of well-being: 'We cannot regard [the standard of living] as a weight made up of the sum of the weights of the various parts.'[14] Decision-making and social planning on this account need to use specific in-kind measures of the components of human well-being:

'Measurement in kind' characterises the point of departure in furnishing the data for further deduction. These fundamental data we shall designate as the 'basis of life', the environment in the broadest sense: supplies of raw material, all sorts of sources of energy, inventions, human abilities, existing towns, streets, trains, canals, etc. . . .[15]

Those welfare measures themselves would form part of a larger system of in-kind measurement for decision-making which would consider the wider determinants of well-being.

Neurath's argument for an economy in kind had formed the starting point for both Weber's and Mises's contributions to the socialist calculation debates.[16] His plans for 'total socialisation' presented during the Bavarian revolution of 1919 (during which he acted as director of socialization) were radical in rejecting not only monetary units for calculation

---

[13] Neurath, 'Inventory', 146/520.   [14] Ibid., 143/516.   [15] Ibid., 149/524.

[16] See L. v. Mises, 'Die Wirtschaftsrechnung im sozialistischen Gemeinwesen', *Archiv für Sozialwissenschaft* 47 (1920), translated as 'Economic Calculation in the Socialist Commonwealth', in F. A. Hayek (ed.), *Collectivist Economic Planning* (London: Routledge and Sons, 1935), 89–130; L. v. Mises, *Die Gemeinwirtschaft* (Jena: Fischer, 1922), trans. J. Kahane (of the 1932 2nd ed.), *Socialism: An Economic and Sociological Analysis* (London: Cape, 1936); M. Weber, *Wirtschaft und Gesellschaft. Grundriss der verstehenden Soziologie* (Tübingen: Mohr, 1921; 4th rev. ed. 1956), translated as *Economy and Society: An Outline of Interpretive Sociology* (Berkeley: University of California Press, 1978), ch. 2, sections 12–14.

in a socialized economy, but any single unit of calculation, including the labour time units advocated by many socialists. Because a socialist economy would consider only the use-value of goods, it would have to be a non-market 'economy in kind' in which money-values would no longer form the basis for economic calculation:

We must at last free ourselves from outmoded prejudices and regard a large-scale economy in kind as a fully valid form of economy which is the more important today in that any completely planned economy amounts to an economy in kind. To socialize therefore means to further an economy in kind. To hold on to the split and uncontrollable monetary order and at the same time to want to socialize is an inner contradiction.[17]

While specific in-kind measures would be necessary for different determinants of living standards in such an economy, there would be no single unit of comparison or measurement for decision-making. Choice would therefore require direct comparisons of alternatives. 'There are no units that can be used as the basis of a decision, neither units of money nor hours of work. One must directly judge the desirability of the two possibilities.'[18]

In his opening contribution to the socialist calculation debates, Mises agreed with Neurath that no single unit for comparing options was available in a fully socialized economy. However, he argued that in virtue of this fact a full socialized economy could not be rational.[19] Rational choice about the employment of higher-order production goods requires commensurability; i.e. rational economic decision-making requires a single measure on the basis of which the worth of alternative states of affairs and uses of productive resources could be calculated and compared in order that we can choose between 'the bewildering mass of intermediate products and potentialities of production'. In market economies, money provides a common unit of measurement for comparing options: 'calculations based upon exchange values enable us to reduce values to a common unit'.[20] Non-market economies, in particular

---

[17] O. Neurath, *Wesen und Weg der Sozialisierung* (Munich: Callwey, 1919), translated as 'Character and Course of Socialisation', in O. Neurath, *Empiricism and Sociology*, ed. M. Neurath and R. S. Cohen (Dordrecht: Reidel, 1973), 135–150, at 145.

[18] Ibid., 146.

[19] Weber's argument was more careful than that of Mises. Weber distinguishes formally rational economic action concerned with the degree to which quantitative calculation is possible and substantively rational economic action which is concerned with how far economic provision is in accordance with some ultimate values. Weber argues that formally rational economic action is not possible in an economy in kind, but allows for a departure between formally rational economic action and substantively rational economic action. Mises makes no such distinction.

[20] Mises, *Socialism*, 99.

socialist economies, lack such a common unit of comparison. Hence, rational economic choices are possible only in market economies; socialist economies do not allow for rational choices.

‾ Much of the subsequent socialist calculation debate focused either on the possibility of the use of monetary measures within a socialist economy – a possibility raised in particular by the more neo-classical defences of socialism offered by Oskar Lange and Fred. M. Taylor – or on the possibility of alternative single units such as labour time or energy units. Neurath rejected both alternatives:

Even some socialists have agreed with Mises' thesis – without calculation with *one* unit, an economy is *not* possible; socialism does not acknowledge any calculation with *one* unit; it follows that socialism is impossible – and therefore try to establish that in the socialist society there also can be such a calculation. For us it is essential that *calculation in kind in the economic plan has to be the moneyless basis of socialist calculation of economic efficiency.*[21]

His arguments for this position in part revolved around the multidimensional nature of well-being. Decisions founded on monetary measures would not be able to incorporate the full range of constituents of human well-being into social choices. However, the arguments also had a directly intergenerational component. With respect to intergenerational decision-making in particular, neither money nor the main alternatives – labour time and energy units – could deal with the different dimensions of value involved.

The question might arise, should one protect coal mines or put greater strain on men? The answer depends for example on whether one thinks that hydraulic power may be sufficiently developed or that solar heat might come to be better used, etc. If one believes the latter, one may 'spend' coal more freely and will hardly waste human effort where coal can be used. If however one is afraid that when one generation uses too much coal thousands will freeze to death in the future, one might use more human power and save coal. Such and many other non-technical matters determine the choice of a technically calculable plan ... we can see no possibility of reducing the production plan to some kind of unit and then to compare the various plans in terms of such units ...[22]

The arguments here with Mises turn on different conceptions of practical reasoning. Neurath's arguments presuppose his rejection of a conception of practical reasoning that assumed that any choice could be subject to a

[21] Neurath, *Wirtschaftsplan und Naturalrechnung* (Berlin: Laub, 1925), translated as 'Economic Plan and Calculation in Kind', in *Neurath, Economic Writings*, 405–465, at 430.
[22] O. Neurath, *Lebensgestaltung und Klassenkampf* (Berlin: Laub, 1928), excerpts translated as 'Personal Life and Class Struggle', in Neurath, *Empiricism and Sociology*, 249–298, at 263.

purely formal procedure which would result in a particular optimal outcome. Neurath characterized this view as 'pseudorationalism' – the view that the job of reason is to discover an 'optimal' decision and that there exist formal rules of reason that unequivocally determine that decision. Such rules or optimal choices were not always possible: 'Rationalism sees its chief triumph in the clear recognition of the limits of actual insight.'[23] It is a mark of the pseudorationalist to believe that there are such rules of insight that determine answers to all decisions. Pseudorationalism exists in the domain of both action and thought, for example in the belief that there are rules for the scientific method which if followed eliminate falsehood and lead to ever nearer approximations to the truth.[24]

Neurath's contributions to the socialist calculation debates have had a lasting influence in ecological economics.[25] His influence is not to be found in any specific model of socialism; rather it lies in his defence of the two claims, articulated in the 1937 paper on the standard of living and in his early contributions to the calculation debates, about the multidimensionality of welfare and its dependence on a variety of environmental conditions. These claims later found their way into ecological economics through the work of Kapp, whose own doctoral dissertation, *Planwirtschaft und Aussenhandel*, had been concerned with Mises's arguments against socialism.[26] Kapp argued that as economists had become concerned with market models of socialism, they had forgotten what was at stake in the original debates between Neurath, Mises and Weber.[27] That

[23] O. Neurath, 'Die Verirrten des Cartesius und das Auxiliarmotiv', *Jahrbuch der philosophischen Gesellschaft an der Universität Wien 1913*, 45–59, translated as 'The Lost Wanderers of Descartes and the Auxiliary Motive', in O. Neurath, *Philosophical Papers*, ed. R. S. Cohen and M. Neurath (Dordrecht: Reidel, 1983), 1–12, at 8.

[24] See also O. Neurath, *Was bedeutet rationale Wirtschaftsbetrachtung?* (Vienna: Gerold, 1935), translated as 'What Is Meant by Rational Economic Theory?', in B. McGuinness (ed.), *Unified Science* (Dordrecht: Kluwer, 1987), 67–109. For discussions of this aspect of the socialist calculation debate, see J. O'Neill, 'Who Won the Socialist Calculation Debate?', *History of Political Thought* 27 (1996), 431–442; J. O'Neill, *The Market: Ethics, Knowledge, Politics* (London: Routledge, 1998).

[25] This is not to say that Neurath himself was always a particularly ecologically minded thinker, in particular in the way the terms are currently understood. For example, he wrote sympathetically about monoculture in agriculture; see Neurath, 'Das gegenwärtige Wachstum der Produktionskapazität der Welt', in M. L. Fledderus (ed.), *World Social Economic Planning: The Necessity for Planned Adjustment of Productive Capacity and Standards of Living*, 2 vols. (The Hague: International Industrial Relations Institute, 1932), 105–141, translated as 'The Current Growth in Global Productive Capacity', in Neurath, *Economic Writings*, 475–504, at 489.

[26] K. W. Kapp, *Planwirtschaft und Aussenhandel* (Geneva: Georg & Cie, 1936).

[27] K. W. Kapp, 'Review: *Einführung in die Theorie der Zentralverwaltungswirtschaft* by K. Paul Hensel', *American Economic Review* 45 (1955), 682–685, at 682.

was the problem of whether human well-being and its environmental conditions could be captured by monetary valuations:

> By stating that 'useful effects' or free 'disposable time' are the measure of real wealth and thus of the quality of life Engels and Marx must have been convinced to have specified at least in general terms the alternative criteria for the planning and decision-making process in a socialist planned society. Few Marxist writers have taken up these hints while many have simply followed the general trend toward a subjective theory of value and price. The great exceptions were Otto Neurath and Max Weber ... The formulation of environmental policies, the evaluation of environmental goals and the establishment of priorities require a substantive economic calculus in terms of social use values (politically evaluated) for which the formal calculus in monetary exchange values fails to provide a real measure – not only in socialist societies but also in capitalist economies. Hence the 'revolutionary' aspect of the environmental issue both as a theoretical and a practical problem. In short, we suggest that environmental values are social use values for which markets provide neither a direct measure nor an adequate indirect indicator.[28]

Neurath's work therefore laid the groundwork for two important claims central to recent ecological economics: first, that rational social choices need to recognize the ways that economic institutions and relations are embedded within the physical world and subject to resource and ecological constraints; second, in part in virtue of this fact, that economic choices cannot be founded upon purely monetary valuations. Neurathian contributions to the socialist calculation debates thus formed one of the historical predecessors of the physicalist tradition of modern political ecology.[29]

III.   Neurath and Hayek

These two claims were also at the centre of a lesser-known exchange between Neurath and Hayek that had significant parallels with that between Neurath and the Frankfurt School. Hayek's epistemic arguments against social planning were aimed not just at socialism, but at scientistic tendencies in a wider group of theorists who, with Neurath, are typically seen as earlier precursors of the physicalist tradition of political ecology.[30]

Hayek's criticisms of scientism and social engineering in his essays of the 1940s, 'The Counter-Revolution of Science' and 'Scientism and the Study of Society', included amongst its targets writers such as

---

[28] K. W. Kapp, *Environmental Policies and Development Planning in Contemporary China and Other Essays* (Paris: Mouton, 1974), 38.

[29] See J. Martinez-Alier, *Ecological Economics* (Oxford: Blackwell, 1987), 2nd ed. 1990.

[30] Ibid.

Wilhelm Ostwald, Patrick Geddes, Frederick Soddy and Ernest Solvay, whose work on energy and economics was taken to exemplify a form of 'scientistic objectivism' characteristic of an engineering mentality. All assumed that calculations in kind using physical in-kind – *in natura* – calculation units could replace monetary calculation in economic decision-making.[31] Hayek criticized 'the characteristic and ever-recurrent demand for the substitution of *in natura* calculation for the "artificial" calculation in terms of price or value, that is, of a calculation which takes explicit account of the objective properties of things'.[32] Everything that Hayek opposed – scientism, 'objectivism', 'physicalism', socialism and *in natura* calculation – was united in the person who became his primary target: the 'protagonist of modern "physicalism" and "objectivism"', Neurath.

Hayek took all these theorists to commit the same epistemic errors that underpin the socialist project: the scientistic identification of all know-ledge with scientific knowledge; the belief that all this knowledge could be communicated to a single planning agency of technical experts; the assumption that this body of experts could use this knowledge to calcu-late a socially optimal outcome. They succumbed to a rationalist illusion typified by the social engineer: 'The engineer's ideal which he feels the "irrational" economic forces prevent him from achieving, based on his study of the objective properties of the things, is usually some purely technical optimum of universal validity.'[33] The belief in the possibility of a technical optimum achievable by experts fails to acknowledge the limits on the knowledge that any particular individual can possess:

The application of the engineering technique to the whole of society requires . . . that the director possess the same complete knowledge of the whole society that the engineer possesses of his limited world. Central economic planning is nothing but such an application of engineering principles to the whole of society based on the assumption that such a complete concentration of all relevant knowledge is possible.[34]

The illusion of what is called 'rationalism', 'superrationalism' or 'Cartesian rationalism' involves a failure to understand the limits of scientific reason: 'it may . . . prove to be far the most difficult and not the least important task for human reason rationally to comprehend its own limitations.'[35]

---

[31] See F. A. Hayek, 'The Counter-Revolution in Science', *Economica* 8 (1941), reprinted in Hayek, *The Counter-Revolution of Science: Studies in the Abuse of Reason* (New York: Free Press, 1952), 183–356, and 'Scientism and the Study of Society', *Economica* 9–11 (1942–1944), reprinted in Hayek, *The Counter-Revolution of Science*, 17–182.
[32] Hayek, *The Counter-Revolution of Science*, 170.   [33] Ibid.
[34] Ibid., 173.   [35] Ibid., 162.

144   *John O'Neill and Thomas Uebel*

The scientistic identification of knowledge with scientific knowledge fails to comprehend the significance for economic life of forms of knowledge that can be stated in universal terms, in particular of knowledge that is specific to time and place, and practical knowledge – knowledge how – that cannot be stated in propositional form. Such knowledge is distributed amongst different individuals in society and cannot in principle be passed on to a single planning agency. In contrast to a centrally planned economy, Hayek argued that the market acts as a coordinating procedure which through the price mechanism distributes to different actors that information that is relevant for the coordination of their plans – without requiring the centralization of knowledge.[36] It allows different individuals to use their local and practical knowledge to best effect in coordination with others. Monetary prices on this account cannot be substituted by in-kind measurement. They are required in a complex and changing economy marked by a division of knowledge. There is no *in natura* alternative to the monetary measures. On this view, the tradition of ecological economics that is concerned with the physical preconditions of economic activity and in particular its ecological pre-conditions, and the use of non-monetary measures and indicators of economic activity falls prey to the same illusions as socialism.

In 1945 Neurath responded to these criticisms in unpublished notes and letters to Hayek which Neurath hoped would form the basis for a public exchange.[37] The exchange never happened – Neurath died later that year, and, in any case, Hayek showed little enthusiasm for such an exchange. In his response, Neurath did not deny his commitment to *in natura* calculation (although he took Hayek to mischaracterize the project) but rather denied that he commits the epistemic errors of which Hayek accuses him. He noted that Hayek's criticisms of Cartesian rationalism paralleled his own earlier criticisms of pseudorationalism, and agreed with Hayek that 'pseudorationalism is dangerous and may sometimes support totalitarianism.'[38] Describing himself as the 'arch-enemy' of the 'illusion of complete knowledge', Neurath argued that Hayek had mischaracterized the views of the logical empiricists, and in doing so had

[36] See Hayek, 'Economics and Knowledge', *Economica* 4 (1937), 33–54, reprinted in Hayek, *Individualism and Economic Order* (Chicago: University of Chicago Press, 1948), 33–56; 'The Use of Knowledge in Society', *American Economic Review* 35 (1945), reprinted in Hayek, *Individualism and Economic Order*, 77–91.
[37] See Neurath, 'Physicalism, Planning and the Social Sciences: Bricks Prepared for a Discussion w/Hayek', 26 July 1945, and Neurath–Hayek correspondence, both in *Otto Neurath Nachlass*, Wiener Kreis Archief, Noord-Hollands Archief, Haarlem: The Netherlands.
[38] Neurath to Hayek, 11 January 1945, in *Otto Neurath Nachlass*.

failed to acknowledge their common ground. Neurath's own rejection of pseudorationalism and the illusion of complete knowledge emerged from his version of logical empiricism. In response to Hayek he invoked a series of claims about the sciences that he was in part responsible for placing at the centre of the philosophy and sociology of science. Scientific theory is underdetermined by empirical evidence: 'there are often several systems of hypotheses for the explanation of the same complex of facts.'[39] Evidence itself is uncertain and provisional – observation or protocol statements are open to revision. Theories are a mass of statements that are logically interconnected and confront the world as a whole, not individually. In the metaphor often repeated, we are like sailors who have to patch up their boat at sea. There exist no methods or rules of science that can be employed to definitively confirm or falsify theories. For Neurath, Popper's philosophy of science exemplifies pseudorationalism in the realm of theory: he wondered why Hayek mixes in bad epistemic company.[40]

In Neurath's work these features of science are deployed against the claim that there exists an optimal solution to all economic and social choices.[41] Given the uncertainties and unpredictability involved in the practice of science, the assumptions of optimality look implausible. Correspondingly he rejected the possibility of any technocratic decision-making procedure undertaken by experts. However, in contrast to Hayek, this includes a rejection of the claim that rational choices require decision procedures employing monetary units. Neurath rejected the claim that in-kind calculation is not required in social choices. In doing so he contested Hayek's characterization of in-kind calculation: the units in Neurath's account of in-kind calculations are not simply the physical units, in the sense of material conditions of human activity, but also the social dimensions of life. The inventory of the conditions of life

---

[39] O. Neurath, 'Zur Klassifikation von Hypothesensystemen', *Jahrbuch der Philosophischen Gesellschaft an der Universität Wien 1914 und 1915* (Vienna, 1916), 39–63, translated as 'On the Classification of Systems of Hypotheses', in Neurath, *Philosophical Papers*, 13–31, at 29.

[40] 'You see Logical Empiricism ... is essentially "pluralist" whereas Karl Popper is essentially "absolutist" – remember he thinks that there is <u>one</u> world picture "the best" etc. He thinks we can isolate instances of a negative character and destroy a hypothesis definitively by that etc. ... I am wondering how you the fighter for freedom and toleration feel yourself in full agreement with scholars who are absolutists and not in full agreement with scholars, who like me, destroy the totalitarian outlook with the roots.' Neurath to Hayek, 26 July 1945, in *Otto Neurath Nachlass*. Compare O. Neurath, 'Pseudorationalismus der Falsifikation', *Erkenntnis* 5 (1935), 353–365, translated as 'Pseudorationalism of Falsification', in Neurath, *Philosophical Papers*, 121–131.

[41] O. Neurath, 'After Six Years', *Synthese* 5 (1946), 77–82, reprinted in Neurath, *Economic Writings*, 549–555, at 552.

146   *John O'Neill and Thomas Uebel*

includes data 'concerning work load, morbidity, mortality, food, clothing, housing, educational possibilities, amusement, leisure time etc.'[42] – 'the environment in its broadest sense'.[43] Social and institutional relations come within that characterization: 'a change in a man's food and shelter is of less importance than a change in his state of being bullied or humiliated by certain institutions'.[44] Self-government, freedom and other human relations belong to the 'happiness conditions' of human beings.[45] His complaint against the technocratic movement was not simply that it based its arguments on mistaken epistemic assumptions, but that the measures it considered were too narrow. If Neurath can be understood as a precursor to ecological economics, then his is a version that includes not only the narrowly physical conditions of human well-being, but also its social conditions.[46]

IV.   Horkheimer and the Critique of Instrumental Reason

The influence of the Frankfurt School on modern political ecology is much more widely recognized than that of the Vienna Circle.[47] From Horkheimer and Adorno comes the theme that modern science and the 'enlightenment project' are tied to the domination of both nature and human beings: 'What men want to learn from nature is how to use it to dominate it and other men. That is the only aim.'[48] The subsequent history of this view is well known. Marcuse radicalized this position, by arguing that the liberation of humans and nature requires a new science

---

[42] Neurath, *Economic Writings*, 420.   [43] Neurath, 'Inventory', 149/524.
[44] O. Neurath, 'International Planning for Freedom', *The New Commonwealth Quarterly* (April 1942), 281–292, (July 1942), 23–28, reprinted in Neurath, *Empiricism and Sociology*, 422–440, at 425.
[45] Neurath, *Empiricism and Sociology*, 427.
[46] For a more detailed discussion of these debates between Neurath and Hayek, see O'Neill, 'Ecological Economics and the Politics of Knowledge'. The arguments in this section draw on that discussion. See also: J. O'Neill, 'Knowledge, Planning and Markets: A Missing Chapter in the Socialist Calculation Debates', *Economics and Philosophy* 22 (2006), 1–24; J. O'Neill, *Markets, Deliberation and Environment* (London: Routledge, 2007); J. O'Neill, 'Pluralism and Economic Institutions', in E. Nemeth, S. Schmitz and T. Uebel (eds.), *Neurath's Economics in Context* (Dordrecht: Kluwer, 2007), 77–100; J. O'Neill, 'Austrian Economics and the Limits of Markets'.
[47] See, e.g., A. Biro (ed.), *Critical Ecologies: The Frankfurt School and Contemporary Environmental Crises* (Toronto: University of Toronto Press, 2011); R. Eckersley, *Environmentalism and Political Theory: Towards an Ecocentric Approach* (Albany: SUNY Press, 1992), ch. 5; T. Hayward, *Ecological Thought* (Cambridge: Polity Press, 1994), ch. 1; S. Vogel, *Against Nature: The Concept of Nature in Critical Theory* (Albany: SUNY Press, 1996).
[48] T. Adorno and M. Horkheimer, *Dialektik der Aufklärung* (Amsterdam: Querido, 1947), trans. J. Cumming as *Dialectic of Enlightenment* (New York: Seabury Press, 1972), at 4.

founded on different interests that will employ new concepts and new facts. Habermas was less radical: in his terms, while natural science is constituted by an interest in technical control, there is no problem as such with either this interest or the forms of scientific knowledge within their proper domain in the relation of humans and non-human nature. The problem lies rather in their extension beyond their appropriate domain through the colonization of the life-world by instrumental reason. Varieties of these different themes from the Frankfurt School are to be found in more recent political ecology.

The work of Horkheimer, in particular *The Dialectic of Enlightenment* co-authored with Adorno, is the starting point for this tradition of argument. The central claims of this text were developed after Horkheimer's exchanges with Neurath. However, Horkheimer's 'Latest Attack', which appeared alongside Neurath's 'Inventory' in the *Zeitschrift für Sozialforschung*, was a transitional paper – both in the history of the Frankfurt School and in the subsequent history of political ecology. It marked a shift from the early programme of interdisciplinary materialism typical of the first phase of the work of the Frankfurt School to the articulation of Critical Theory, typical of the second. The exchanges with Neurath, which took place in 1937, and predated the critique of instrumental reason and of the enlightenment project that began around 1940, belong to this transitional stage in Horkheimer's development of critical theory. However, they do anticipate many of the problems which Adorno and Horkheimer would face in their later work.

Horkheimer's criticisms of positivism in the 'Latest Attack' deploy earlier arguments he put forward in 'Materialism and Metaphysics', where he had claimed that positivism denies the possibility of critical reflection on the social and historical context of science itself. Positivism, he had argued, fails to acknowledge the ways in which knowledge is dependent on social action and in consequence 'positivism necessarily understood science itself in an unhistorical way.'[49] In 'Latest Attack' the claim that positivism is necessarily unreflective and ahistorical in its account of the sciences is tied to a failure of positivism to provide a critical perspective on modern society in general and the role of science and instrumental reason in particular. Only by placing science in the context of its history in the 'life process of society' can a critical perspective be sustained.[50] Positivism allows of no such critical stance.[51] The identification of knowledge with the special sciences leaves it unable to

---

[49] M. Horkheimer, 'Materialismus und Metaphysik', *ZfS* 2 (1933), 1–33, translated as 'Materialism and Metaphysics', in Horkheimer, *Critical Theory*, 10–46, at 36.
[50] Horkheimer, 'Latest Attack', 159.   [51] Ibid., 145.

develop a critical stance on the social role of those sciences. Lacking such a perspective, positivism is unable in particular to criticize the role of science in the support of the existing social order: 'In view of the fact that the ruling economic powers use science as well as the whole of society for their special ends, this ideology, this identification of thought with the special sciences, must lead to the perpetuation of the status quo.'[52] Positivism is in this sense necessarily conservative.

In his unpublished rejoinder to Horkheimer's essay, Neurath responded by defending the possibility of critical reflection on the sciences from a naturalistic perspective. He denied that it is possible to pursue reflection from a philosophical stance beyond empirical control. However, while there is no philosophical position beyond science to which the sciences have to answer, rational reflection on the individual sciences is still possible:

Whatever is claimed with one scientific discipline can be criticised by a more comprehensive scientific standpoint, without regard to any divisions between the disciplines, but *we know of no court of appeal beyond the science that judges science and investigates its foundations* . . . Horkheimer makes it sound as if the Unity of Science Movement assigns special authority to isolated individual sciences. Its basic idea, however, is that special importance is granted to the entirety of science and not to take too seriously the often traditional division into single disciplines.[53]

Logical empiricism on this account is compatible with reflection on the sciences of a naturalistic kind – reflection that draws on the wider sciences, where 'science' includes any systematic empirical inquiry, including everyday empirical knowledge, and the history and sociology of science. In this regard it is important to note that the Vienna Circle was not homogenous. It was a conversation, not a set of doctrines, and Neurath's own naturalism diverged from other strands of thought within the Vienna Circle. For example, Neurath's arguments for a more broadly conceived metatheory of science that included history and sociology of science contrasted with Rudolf Carnap's perceived reduction of philosophy to a 'logic of science' characterized by strictly formal methods. From the vantage point of a sociologically informed conception of scientific self-reflection, the possibility of social determination of scientific belief and reflexivity about that fact could be fully acknowledged:

Historical changes do not only alter that which we call 'theoretical formulations' or 'constructions' but also the stock of protocol sentences . . . [W]e must remember that 'constructions' and 'raw materials' cannot be sharply separated.

---

[52] Ibid., 179.
[53] O. Neurath, 'Einheitswissenschaft und logischer Empirismus. Eine Erwiderung', in *Otto Neurath Nachlass*, at 10.

Some of our observations prove themselves to be very stable, but in principle nothing is certain – everything is flux. It is plain that a consistent thinker will seek to apply these considerations, which are based on experience, to his own life and will ask himself how he would act, how he would argue if he would be positioned differently. He will realise that decisive changes in the pursuit of science are not only determined by intensive reflections of a generation of scholars, but also what happens in social life generally, which the scholars are part of.[54]

This naturalistic reflexivity on science itself formed the background of Neurath's own scientifically informed scepticism about the claims made from the special sciences, especially when applied in political decisions. Far from informing a technocratic politics, it provided the grounds for Neurath's scepticism about technocratic politics. What Neurath objected to in Horkheimer's critique was his return to 'certain ideas of German idealism', which assumed a philosophical standpoint outside of the sciences from which criticism can proceed. Neurath rejected the claim that 'there exists a method outside of science which, basing itself on everything that can be stated scientifically, can criticise science, especially by characterising their historical situation in a fashion that is alien to the sciences.'[55] Correspondingly, he distinguished between Horkheimer's reports of the empirical work of the Frankfurt School (in particular his introduction to *Authority and the Family* which employed a language which is 'amenable to empirical control'), and his philosophy, which represented a retreat into idealist metaphysics of 'Hegel, Kant, the neo-Kantians and Husserl'.[56] The problem with the latter is that the criteria for deciding the correctness or otherwise of statements become obscured. 'Horkheimer assumes a vantage point "outside" of science (which works *only* with "*Verstand*") in order to be able to analyse the entire practice of science by means of "*Vernunft*" and to show in a "proper", non-scientific fashion all that lies behind it.'[57]

Neurath's criticisms highlighted a shift within Horkheimer's own relation to the idealist philosophical tradition. The interdisciplinary materialism that marked the first stage of the work of the Frankfurt School had itself been premised on a rejection of a division between the sciences and philosophy:

Materialism requires the unification of philosophy and science. Of course it recognizes that work techniques differ in the more general pursuits of philosophy and the more limited tasks of science, just as it recognizes distinctions of method in research and the presentation of research. But it does not recognize any difference between science and philosophy as such.[58]

---

[54] Ibid., 2.   [55] Ibid., 4.   [56] Ibid., 14.   [57] Ibid., 12.
[58] Horkheimer, *Critical Theory*, 34.

Horkheimer's early account of the possibility of critical reflection on the special sciences parallels that provided by Neurath in his response to Horkheimer's 1937 position.[59] It appealed to the possibility of historical and sociological understanding of the sciences. In response to Max Scheler's criticisms of the materialist demand that philosophy and science be unified, Horkheimer offered the following remark:

The real meaning [of the materialist demand] is the exact opposite of any attempt to absolutize particular scientific doctrines. It requires instead that every piece of knowledge be regarded, not of course as a purely arbitrary creation, but as a representation by particular men in a particular society, context and moment of time ...[60]

Neurath's reply to Horkheimer insisted on a naturalistic reflection of science on itself, and thus involved a restatement of Horkheimer's own earlier materialist concerns in order to challenge the later Horkheimer's idealist arguments about the autonomy of philosophy from science. The shift is not yet fully explicit in 'Latest Attack' and 'Traditional and Critical Theory', but becomes so in the 'Postscript' to 'Traditional and Critical Theory' where Horkheimer responded to Marcuse's 'Philosophy and Critical Theory' in which critical theory is represented as 'the heir not only of German idealism but of philosophy as such'.[61] Within this

---

[59] This is not to say that Neurath and Horkheimer shared the same view of the relationship between philosophy and the sciences. In Horkheimer's early writing and practice, the role of philosophy 'as a theoretical undertaking orientated to the general' was to provide a theoretical unification for the special sciences. See M. Horkheimer, 'Die gegenwärtige Lage der Sozialphilosophie und die Aufgaben eines Instituts für Sozialforschung', in *Frankfurter Universitätsreden* 27 (1931), translated as 'The Present Situation of Social Philosophy and the Tasks of the Institute of Social Research', in M. Horkheimer, *Between Philosophy and Social Science: Selected Early Writings* (Cambridge, MA: MIT Press, 1993), 1–14, at 9. Philosophy integrates the sciences by posing the questions to be addressed by empirical work and organizing the material at a theoretical level, as in the interdisciplinary programme of the Institute from 1931 to 1937. It was comprised of 'investigations stimulated by contemporary philosophical problems in which philosophers, sociologists, economists, historians, and psychologists are brought together in permanent collaboration to undertake in common that which can be carried out individually in the laboratory in other fields' (ibid., 10). By contrast, philosophy had no such special place in Neurath's account. Indeed, it is not clear what space existed at all for philosophy in critical reflection on the sciences: 'Some people ... still wish to separate the discussions of the conceptual foundations of the sciences from the body of scientific work and allow this to continue as "philosophizing". Closer reflexions show that this is not feasible and that the definition of concepts is part and parcel of the work of unified science.' See O. Neurath, 'Physikalismus', *Scientia* 50 (1931), 297–303, translated as 'Physicalism', in Neurath, *Philosophical Papers*, 52–57, at 52.

[60] Horkheimer, *Critical Theory*, 35.

[61] Horkheimer, 'Philosophie und Kritische Theorie', *ZfS* 6 (1937), 625–31, translated as 'Postscript', in *Critical Theory*, 244–252, at 245.

later work, the early interdisciplinary materialism is abandoned. In the *Dialectic of Enlightenment* Horkheimer and Adorno wrote:

Even though we had known for many years that the great discoveries of applied science are paid for with an increasing diminution of theoretical awareness, we still thought that in regard to scientific activity our contribution could be restricted to the criticism or extension of specialist axioms ... However, the fragments united in this volume show that we were forced to abandon this conviction.[62]

Given the 'indefatigable self-destructiveness of enlightenment', philosophical reflection has to forgo 'the affirmative use of scientific and everyday conceptual languages'.[63]

V.   The Legacy of an Unresolved Dispute

The central question that Neurath raised for Horkheimer's position in its shift from his earlier empirically grounded reflection on the social context of the sciences concerns the criterion for determining the acceptability or rejection of competing claims about science and about the social world in which science develops. As Horkheimer noted in his reply to Neurath: 'The weakest point of my piece was pointed out by you, naturally, on page 13 of your reply. "Horkheimer nowhere indicates by means of which control one can determine when a point of view is 'correct' and when it is 'incorrect'."'[64] Having noted it Horkheimer did not reply to this criticism.

The grounds for his critical perspective became even more pressing in his later work. Thus Neurath's critical comment took on increasing significance given the later trajectory of the work of Horkheimer and the Frankfurt School towards the critique of science for which its later influence on environmental thought is best known. In *Eclipse of Reason*, reason as such is taken to be based in an interest in the domination of nature: 'The disease of reason is that reason was born from man's urge to dominate nature, and the "recovery" depends on insight into the nature of the original idea, not on a cure of the latest symptoms.'[65] In developing his critique of reason, Horkheimer wants to avoid irrationalism. His critique aims to remain within the norms of reason itself. The critique is a 'self-critique': 'in such self-critique, reason will at the same time remain

[62] Adorno and Horkheimer, *Dialectic of Enlightenment*, xi.   [63] Ibid., xii.

[64] Horkheimer to Neurath, 29 December 1937, in Horkheimer, *Gesammelte Schriften*, 15, 344–349.

[65] M. Horkheimer, *Eclipse of Reason* (New York: Seabury Press, 1974) [1947], 119.

faithful to itself.'[66] The problem here is how this self-critique can be sustained without undermining itself. As Habermas notes, 'the radical critique of reason proceeds self-referentially; critique cannot simultaneously be radical and leave its own criteria untouched.'[67]

The problem left its own legacy within the Frankfurt School. In the work of Horkheimer it led to the retreat from political engagement that marked his later work. If reason is to avoid being instrumental it is to be divorced from action; the self-critique of reason thus leads to the conservative political quietism of Horkheimer's postwar work. But the legacy is also apparent in the wider work of the Frankfurt School, particularly in the area in which it has been most influential on environmental thought – the critique of science and instrumental reason. As outlined above, this critique subsequently took two different directions, in the work of Marcuse and Habermas. Marcuse maintained the central claim that science is constituted by an interest in the domination of nature: 'science, by virtue of its own method and concepts, has projected and promoted a universe in which the domination of nature has remained linked to the domination of man.'[68] The modern natural sciences project an understanding of nature as 'potential instrumentality, stuff of control and organization'.[69] In the hands of Marcuse this is taken to imply that liberation of both humans and nature requires a new science constituted by different interests, employing new concepts and arriving at new facts. 'Its hypotheses, without losing their rational character, would develop in an essentially different experimental context (that of a pacified world); consequently, science would arrive at essentially different concepts of nature and establish essentially different facts.'[70] However, Marcuse specifies neither the criteria for reasoned choice between theories nor the nature of the new concepts. The idea of a new science with its 'essentially different facts' is left as a utopian promissory note without content.

The other direction of travel is that offered by Habermas. While Habermas also takes science to be constituted by an interest in technical control, he rejects the claim that this can be overcome – that there could be a new natural science constituted by a different interest: 'The idea of a

[66] Ibid., 120.
[67] J. Habermas, 'Bemerkungen zur Entwicklungsgeschichte des Horkheimerschen Werkes', in A. Schmidt and N. Altwicker (eds.), Max Horkheimer heute: Werk und Wirkung (Frankfurt am Main: Fischer, 1986), 163–179, translated as 'Remarks on the Development of Horkheimer's Work', in S. Benhabib, W. Bonss and J. McCole (eds.), On Max Horkheimer (Cambridge, MA: MIT Press, 1993), 49–66, at 57.
[68] H. Marcuse, One-Dimensional Man (New York: Abacus, 1968), 135.
[69] Ibid., 126.   [70] Ibid., 136.

New Science will not stand up to logical scrutiny . . .'[71] The problem is
not that the natural sciences are constituted by an interest in technical
control, but rather the expansion of the sphere of instrumental reason
beyond its proper domain. The problem becomes one of colonization. In
jettisoning the radical criticism of scientific reason and recasting the
problem in these terms, Habermas attempts to provide what is absent
in Horkheimer and Marcuse: his conception of communicative rationality offers an account of which norms of reason apply outside the sphere of
instrumental reason. Dialogue is rational to the extent that it is free from
the exercise of power and strategic action. Participants are equal in their
communicative capacities to state and evaluate arguments, such that the
judgements of participants converge only under the authority of the good
argument. This account of communicative reason, which has its roots in
Kant's account of the enlightenment project, provides the basis of a
deliberative model of democracy that has had particular influence on
environmental political thought.[72] On this view of political deliberation,
the claims of the original Frankfurt critique that have remained important are those that concern the scientization of politics and public opinion
that comes with the extension of instrumental reason beyond its proper
domain. Here, technocratic politics involves the elimination of the practical sphere of public debate about norms, and the subsequent reduction
of political issues to matters of technical reason.[73]

Although this model of a deliberative politics is important in the
environmental sphere, its deployment in practice departs significantly
from the Habermasian account of deliberative democracy. The science
dependence of environmental decisions, problems and politics has meant
that where formal and informal public deliberation has been central to

[71] Habermas, 'Technik und Wissenschaft als Ideologie', in Habermas, *Technik und Wissenschaft als 'Ideologie'* (Frankfurt am Main: Suhrkamp, 1968), 48–103, translated as 'Technology and Science as Ideology', in Habermas, *Towards a Rational Society* (Boston: Beacon Press, 1970), 81–122, at 88.
[72] J. Dryzek, 'Ecology and Discursive Democracy: Beyond Liberal Capitalism and the Administrative State', *Capitalism, Nature and Socialism* 3 (1992), 18–42; J. Dryzek, *Deliberative Democracy and Beyond: Liberals, Critics, Contestations* (Oxford: Oxford University Press, 2000), ch. 6; R. Eckersley, *Environmentalism and Political Theory: Towards an Ecocentric Approach* (Albany: SUNY Press, 1992); R. Eckersley, 'The Discourse Ethic and the Problem of Representing Nature', *Environmental Politics* 8 (1999), 24–49.
[73] This is a constant in Habermas's work ever since his *Theorie und Praxis* (Frankfurt am Main: Suhrkamp, 1963; 2nd ed. 1971), translated as *Theory and Practice* (London: Heineman, 1974); see also his 'Verwissenschaftlichte Politik und öffentliche Meinung', in R. Reich (ed.), *Humanität und politische Verantwortung* (Zürich: Erlenbach, 1964), 54–73, translated as 'The Scientization of Politics and Public Opinion', in Habermas, *Towards a Rational Society*, 62–80.

public life – in areas such as biodiversity loss, genetically modified crops, climate change, pollution and resource depletion – a central issue has been the place of science in that deliberation. Thus, for example, many of the formal experiments in new deliberative institutions such as citizens' juries and citizens' panels have been applied in areas of public policy that involve scientific expertise that is the subject of internal and external controversy. The problem of a decline in public trust in scientific expertise therefore forms the starting point of many practical applications of deliberative institutions, particularly those applied to responding to environmental risks.[74] However, this is precisely the area in which the Habermasian framework seems unable to provide a solution.

As we noted at the outset of this chapter, the tension between science dependence and science scepticism has become a central problem in public life in general, and environmental politics in particular. Public decisions in the modern world rely on claims by experts – the grounds for which are opaque to direct inspection by the citizen and, indeed, by other scientists. Nor is this opacity eliminable. The capacity to make and evaluate particular claims in the special sciences relies on a background of training within particular scientific practices. It relies on particular competences and know-how not all of which is open to explicit articulation. In most matters, both citizen and scientist rely on the competences of others. Habermas's assumption of equality of competence that is built into the model of communicative rationality fails to acknowledge the existence of epistemic inequality, even in the ideal conditions of his non-coercive speech community. Hence Habermas's own position is unable to adequately address one of the central problems of science in modern democratic politics: the tension between science dependence and science scepticism.[75]

It is precisely here that the Neurathian tradition offers insights that are absent in the Frankfurt tradition of criticism of technocratic reason. A myth that has been bequeathed by Horkheimer's and Adorno's criticisms of the logical positivists is that it is necessarily committed to a technocratic politics:

[74] See, for example, O. Renn, T. Webler and P. Wiedemann (eds.), *Fairness and Competence in Citizen Participation: Evaluating New Models for Environmental Discourse* (Dordrecht: Kluwer, 1995), and O. Renn, 'The Challenge of Integrating Deliberation and Expertise: Participation and Discourse in Risk Management', in T. L. MacDaniels and M. J. Small (eds.), *Risk Analysis and Society: An Interdisciplinary Characterization of the Field* (Cambridge: Cambridge University Press, 2004), 289–366.
[75] For an extensive discussion of this claim, see J. O'Neill, 'The Rhetoric of Deliberation: Some Problems in Kantian Theories of Deliberative Democracy', *Res Publica* 8 (2002), 249–268.

Positivist philosophy, which regards the tool 'science' as the automatic champion of progress, is as fallacious as other glorifications of technology. Economic technocracy expects everything from the emancipation of the material means of production. Plato wanted to make philosophers the masters; the technocrats want to make engineers the board of directors of society. Positivism is philosophical technocracy.[76]

This is a myth that is also sustained from a very different perspective by Hayek's criticisms of logical empiricism. Both have defined the subsequent reception of logical empiricism. As we showed at the end of Section III, it is false that the Vienna Circle and Neurath in particular were committed to a technocratic politics. His rejection of technocratic politics is founded on two sets of claims: the absence of a single unit of comparison that could be employed to arrive at a technically optimum outcome for many decisions; and epistemic claims about the limits of scientific expertise which show the technocratic ideal of the discovery of an optimal solution to social decisions to be untenable.

Neurath's naturalistic critical reflection on the sciences is far more sensitive to the tensions between science dependence and science scepticism than the apparently more radical criticisms developed in the first-generation Frankfurt School theorists and the account of colonization in the second. The tension was articulated explicitly in some of Neurath's later works: 'Our life is connected more and more with experts, but on the other hand, we are less prepared to accept other people's judgements, when making decisions.'[77] While unlike Habermas, Neurath does not offer a detailed account of a deliberative theory of democracy, his account of democracy as 'the continual struggle between the expert . . . and the common man'[78] offers much that is absent from Habermas's theory.

The bifurcation of the two traditions of political ecology has a long history. The historical story told in this chapter shows the roots of that bifurcation. Its purpose has not, however, been only historical. In revisiting the conversations of 1937 and their consequences, our aim has also been to show how a partial reconciliation is possible – and suggest what the virtues of such a reconciliation might be. Environmental politics and decision-making cannot avoid science dependence. Understanding the environmental challenges we now face – the physical limits in the capacity of the environment for resource provision, waste assimilation and

---

[76] Horkheimer, *Eclipse of Reason*, 41.
[77] O. Neurath, 'Visual Education: Humanisation vs. Popularisation', unfinished ms., reprinted in E. Nemeth and F. Stadler (eds.), *Encyclopedia and Utopia: The Work of Otto Neurath* (Dordrecht: Kluwer, 1996), 245–335, at 251.
[78] Ibid.

climate regulation – is necessarily science-based. The radical criticisms of the sciences as forms of ideology that are committed to the domination of nature sit uneasily with their role in specifying these challenges. There are, however, significant problems with the role that scientific expertise plays in democratic deliberation, and the conflict between epistemic inequality with democratic equality. But there is reason to believe that the two different traditions of opposition to technocratic politics can be brought together. The kind of naturalist scepticism found in the work of those in the left Vienna Circle speaks centrally to the deliberative environmental politics that has emerged from the Habermasian tradition of the Frankfurt School. Here, at least, there are grounds for reconciliation between the two traditions of political ecology.

8   Uncertainty, Action and Politics
The Problem of Negligibility

Melissa Lane *

Is there any reason for me to reduce my own carbon emissions? That question has notoriously been answered in the negative by Walter Sinnott-Armstrong, who argues that no unit of any individual's emissions is either a necessary or sufficient cause of harm to others, and that in the absence of harm there is no moral reason in this case to reduce one's emissions.[1] His view compares to the converse claim made by Mancur Olson, that 'a man who tried to hold back a flood with a pail would probably be considered more of a crank than a saint',[2] as Richard Tuck discusses in his contribution to this volume. Both theses depend on particular views of causation and its connection to harm, which have been, in each case, much debated, as has an influential way of framing the question in terms of the 'imperceptibility' of the effects in question.[3]

* This chapter grew out of the chapter of *Eco-Republic* that I presented at a conference at Yale University on 'Means and Ends' in April 2011, where Richard Tuck replied to my paper in his own ('What Are Means?: A Response to Melissa Lane, *Against Negligibility*); subsequent versions were presented as a Saul O. Sidore Memorial Lecture at the University of New Hampshire in March 2012, at the Princeton Human Values Forum in April 2012, at the Philomathia Conference on Political Thought and the Environment at the University of Cambridge in May 2012 and in the philosophy seminar of the ANU Research School of Social Sciences in August 2015. For comments and remarks, I am indebted to many people, including especially Christian Barry, Chuck Beitz, Luc Bovens, Geoff Brennan, Corey Brettschneider, Bob Brulle, Mark Budolfson, Ben Cogan, Josh Cohen, John Dunn, Stefan Eich, Ted Fertik, Bob Goodin, Alex Guerrero, Sarah Hannan, Antony Hatzistavrou, Bob Keohane, Jeremy Kessler, Jacob Lipton, Karuna Mantena, Alison McQueen, Lukas Meyer, Tim Mulgan, Craig Murphy, Josh Ober, Michael Oppenheimer, Stephen Pacala, Philip Pettit, Cecilia Ridgeway, Debra Satz, Harold Shapiro, Ken Schultz, Rob Socolow, Adam Tooze, Richard Tuck, and Katja Vogt.
[1] W. Sinnott-Armstrong, 'It's Not *My* Fault: Global Warming and Individual Moral Obligations', in W. Sinnott-Armstrong and Richard B. Howarth (eds.), *Perspectives on Climate Change: Science, Economics, Politics, Ethics*, Advances in the Economics of Environmental Resources, vol. 5 (Amsterdam: Elsevier, 2005), 285–307.
[2] M. Olson, Jr., *The Logic of Collective Action: Public Goods and the Theory of Groups* (Cambridge, MA: Harvard University Press, 1965), 64.
[3] The issues of causation, harm and imperceptibility have spawned overlapping literatures, with an important source in J. Glover, 'It Makes No Difference Whether or Not I Do It',

158   *Melissa Lane*

While the logic of these arguments has been much debated, the tendency to make related rhetorical moves in regard to a very wide range of individual agents (from humans to firms to countries) and contexts of activity (from household choices to market divestment to political initiative) has been less scrutinized. Consider for example how the rhetoric of negligibility has been directly applied to the divestment by individual organizations of stock market holdings in fossil fuel companies. Here is a representative assertion by Drew Faust as president of Harvard University: 'Universities own a very small fraction of the market capitalization of fossil fuel companies. If we and others were to sell our shares, those shares would no doubt find other willing buyers. Divestment is likely to have negligible financial impact on the affected companies.'[4] In this chapter, I diagnose this line of appeal to 'negligibility' as based on a tacit importation of the economic model of perfect competition into a domain – that I label 'political' – where there is no reason to believe that it should apply.

The model of perfect competition that crystallized in twentieth-century welfare economics assumes that others will adjust their behavior in response to whatever an agent might herself do (buy if she sells, sell if she buys) such that a certain equilibrium outcome remains guaranteed.[5] To be sure, individuals or firms can have a localized effect on one another's actions – if Firm A raises its prices, that can lead Firm B to lower its own – but because these actions cancel out to maintain the equilibrium, Firm A's initiative will ultimately have no effect on the overall price of the good, and so each firm must be regarded simply as a price-taker in the market. It is in this sense that I will say that this

Proceedings of the Aristotelian Society, Supplementary Volumes 49 (1975), 171–209. Contributions to these debates by a number of authors are discussed later in this chapter, without claiming to represent the relevant literatures in full. On imperceptibility in particular, see the papers collected in M. J. Almeida (ed.), *Imperceptible Harms and Benefits* (Dordrecht, Boston and London: Kluwer Academic, 2000).

[4] www.harvard.edu/president/news/2013/fossil-fuel-divestment-statement, a reference I owe to Jacob Lipton.

[5] Richard Tuck argued in his book *Free Riding* (Cambridge, MA: Harvard University Press, 2008) that the problem of free riding takes its distinctive shape only in the twentieth century, precisely on the basis of comparing the problem of large group cooperation to the structure of a market model of perfect competition in equilibrium. As Tuck notes also in his contribution to this volume, this is explicit in Mancur Olson's influential mid-century analysis, in which the case of the crank with the pail is paralleled to that of 'a rational farmer' who will not restrict production to help raise prices because he knows that this would be 'a futile and pointless sacrifice', since it would not (by implication) 'have a perceptible effect' on anyone (Olson, *Logic of Collective Action*, 64). I take as my starting point Tuck's argument that equilibrium in a perfectly competitive market underlies Olson's reasoning, while disagreeing with him over the extent to which this paradigm should be extended to political action more generally.

pattern of reasoning takes the actions of others as given. The analysis postulates that actors will collectively act with the effect of maintaining the current equilibrium, such that nothing any individual agent can do can change that equilibrium outcome. On such a model, each player is tempted to let himself or herself or itself off the hook on the grounds that nothing they do can make a real difference. Negligibility in respect of the overall outcome leads to a sense of futility.[6] Why act when one's actions cannot make a meaningful difference?

Yet even allowing for the inevitable differences between models and reality, it is necessary to acknowledge that few domains of human action display the patterning of a perfectly competitive market. I will argue that the application of the theory of negligibility to the domain of individual and political action outside an idealized competitive market has distorted our understanding of action and denuded our understanding of politics. It does so by naturalizing, as given, conditions which even in economic theory are largely idealized (in very few actual real markets are all firms or agents merely price takers), and which are largely inapplicable in real-life political situations. Those who invoke negligibility to assert the futility of individual initiative unjustifiably ignore the uncertainty of the future in relation to both natural processes and human action, stipulatively rule out the possibility of new kinds of individual initiative and collective interaction that could upset the current equilibrium,[7] and fail to consider the relevance of identity and solidarity as intrinsic motivations that can play a part in those new forms of initiative and interaction. In being paralyzed in instrumental and moral reasoning by the defense of the rationality of the free rider in a prisoner's dilemma, or the fear in an assurance game of being a sucker,[8] we lose our grip on the structure of

---

[6] M. Budolfson, 'Collective Action, Climate Change, and the Ethical Significance of Futility', version 4.0, unpublished typescript on file with the author.

[7] R. Hardin, *Indeterminacy and Society* (Princeton, NJ: Princeton University Press, 2003), argues for the importance of interdependence of one person's actions upon those of another person and the indeterminacy that arises from this. While the model of perfect competition allows interdependence, it denies that the outcome will be indeterminate, as the interdependent actions will instead (in the model) maintain the equilibrium.

[8] On 'the fear of being a sucker' by deciding not to free ride on the provision of public goods, see P. Kollock, 'Social Dilemmas: The Anatomy of Cooperation', *Annual Review of Sociology* 24 (1998), 183–214, at 189. In *Eco-Republic*, 64–65, I discuss the same fear (using the term 'patsy') under the heading of fairness, arguing that in the context of voluntary action, 'unfairness seems to reduce to a core of fearing to be taken advantage of,' but that if one has reason to act irrespective of what others do, this objection can be largely defused. See M. Lane, *Eco-Republic: What the Ancients Can Teach Us about Ethics, Virtue, and Sustainable Living* (Princeton, NJ: Princeton University Press, 2012), and *Eco-Republic: Ancient Thinking for a Green Age* (Oxford: Peter Lang, 2011) (the two editions have the same pagination throughout so references will not distinguish between them).

action and of politics itself as a domain of possibility[9] articulated by these
key dimensions of uncertainty, interaction and identity.

In accordance with this diagnosis, this chapter aims not to solve the
problem of negligibility so much as to dissolve it. It will seek to show
where those theories which depend on it are equally dependent on false
and inapt assumptions about the nature of human action and specifically
of politics. I will begin with some basic points about how climate change
should be understood for the purposes of these arguments, and how it is
often misunderstood. I then survey approaches to negligibility in the
rational choice literature on voting and in consequentialist discussions
in moral philosophy of individual action and climate change action more
specifically, seeking not to rebut them in their own terms so much as to
highlight the anti-political (and sometimes factually mistaken) assumptions on which they rely. I will conclude with some brief reflections about
how the eagerness of many current politicians, as well as theorists, to
insist on negligibility contrasts with other ways of conceiving ethics and
politics in the history of political thought.

Two final introductory considerations before undertaking that agenda.
First, in rebutting blanket denials of the potential importance of individual emissions reduction or other forms of an individual agent's actions
relative to some collective of agents, I do not mean to suggest that such
individual action is the sole or even main key to lowering climate
emissions globally. I am interested in defending its possibility as a contribution to change, not its necessity or priority. It is also important to
remember that a seeming alternative to individual emissions reduction –
the call for political action – can itself founder on the same rocks, if the
contribution of individuals towards a not-yet-galvanized political change
is similarly dismissed as inevitably negligible. Finally, the argument
about the non-negligibility of individual action generalizes across levels
of analysis: not only natural human individuals among their kind, but
also individual firms in a market, individual sectors in a complete economy or polity, individual countries within the global order, and so on, are
each vulnerable to having their actions dismissed by invocation of the
rhetoric of negligibility.[10]

---

[9] On the idea of possibility itself, see J. Nefsky, 'How You Can Help, Without Making a
Difference', section 6, unpublished typescript on file with the author.

[10] In M. Lane, *Eco-Republic*, 54–55, I give the examples of the aviation sector within
Merseyside as a region of the United Kingdom and the United Kingdom itself in the
global order, each (on figures available at the time of writing that book) responsible for
not more than some small percentage of a relevant higher-order outcome that could be
readily dismissed as 'negligible'.

Second, the remainder of this chapter will be concerned with the definition of negligibility underlying this equilibrium-analysis claim: to formulate it more crisply, the claim that someone's doing action A makes no difference (or a very small difference, one which is not significant on any relevant measure and so, it is claimed, should be treated as no difference) to bringing about a collective outcome O. This definition bears on how we think about the instrumental rationality of that action, and here we may distinguish two contentions about instrumental rationality that are often derived from negligibility:

(i) *contention of non-instrumentality*: my doing A does not count as a means to bringing about O, and so there is no instrumental reason at all for me to do A in relation to the end of bringing about of O (though there may be some other reason not in the current frame). The imperceptibility of the effects of my doing A is one basis for claiming such non-instrumentality, but there are other ways of construing the claim.

(ii) *contention of cost–benefit failure*: my doing A may contribute a very small amount to bringing about O, but the costs of my doing A outweigh the benefits that my doing A can provide. So it is not instrumentally rational on a cost–benefit analysis for me to do A.

It is contention (i) that states the most drastic challenge that goes under the head of strict negligibility: for if my action is not a means to bringing about the outcome at all, then I have no reason at all of an instrumental kind to take it in relation to that outcome. Contention (ii), by conceding that my action does contribute to bringing about O, stakes its claim in part on empirical cost–benefit analyses.[11] As we consider various rational choice and moral philosophical analyses, we will need to identify which of these two contentions they have in mind.

I. Preliminaries: Climate Change and the Question of Thresholds

Because much of what follows will be concerned with comparisons between individual emissions reduction and voting, it is important to

---

[11] The same is true of a further contention related to (ii), which can be called the claim of global cost–benefit failure and labeled contention (iii): my doing A may contribute a very small amount to bringing about O, and perhaps the cost of my doing so is outweighed by the benefit of my doing so; but as a matter of my overall instrumental rationality, my contribution to O by A is so small as to be outweighed by other rival actions that I might take in relation to all the overall outcomes that I care about. I will return to the global cost–benefit issue in discussing Geoffrey Brennan's thesis of expressive rationality below, but cannot do full justice to it in this chapter.

162   *Melissa Lane*

begin by tackling one apparent disanalogy between these cases: that climate change emissions reduction has no single knowable and salient threshold in the way that voting does. I will argue that climate change in fact shares characteristics with both continuity and threshold functions, although the latter are vague and uncertain. This complex combination of characteristics means that arguments about climate change and its analogy to voting that rely solely on the existence or not of a sharp threshold are misguided.

The most obvious way to draw a parallel between individual reason to act on climate change, and individual reason to vote, would treat the existence of a threshold as crucial.[12] Elections, of course, have a sharp and well-defined threshold defined as X number of votes, such that the X+1th vote (in whatever sequence the votes are counted or identified) is redundant for the purpose of determining who is elected or whether a proposition is passed. Does climate change have a sharp threshold of this kind?

In the case of climate change, identifying a sharp threshold depends on our point of view: a threshold for what? Is it a threshold for degree of harm to humans? To other living beings in the biosphere? A point of no return or of the unleashing of radical climate chaos? The climate system is characterized by many feedback loops and possible tipping points. It may be that climate change processes do have one or more sharp thresholds with respect to one or more of the questions posed above, though we are still uncertain about what they are, and such information as we have is characterized itself by ranges of uncertainty. The Intergovernmental Panel on Climate Change (IPCC) 2014 AR5 Synthesis Report, for example, shows that while '[e]missions scenarios leading to CO_2-equivalent concentrations in 2100 of about 450 ppm or lower are likely to maintain warming below 2°C over the 21st century relative to pre-industrial levels', those scenarios 'reaching concentration levels of about 500 ppm CO_2-eq by 2100' that 'temporarily overshoot concentration levels of roughly 530 ppm CO_2-eq before 2100 ... are *about as likely as not* to achieve that goal'.[13]

---

[12] There is a crucial difference between voting and carbon emissions in another respect: in the case of voting, my vote becomes more efficacious the fewer others vote, so that at the limit, as the sole voter I am decisive; whereas in the case of carbon emissions, my emissions seem to become less efficacious as they are engulfed in more and more emissions from others. I owe this point to Ken Schultz.

[13] IPCC, 2014: *Climate Change 2014: Synthesis Report. Contribution of Working Groups I, II and III to the Fifth Assessment Report of the Intergovernmental Panel on Climate Change*, Core Writing Team, R. K. Pachauri and L. A. Meyer (eds.) (Geneva: IPCC, 2014), 20, 20, 20–21 (emphasis in original), respectively.

Thresholds need not be sharp to be real. Indeed, it has been argued that the sorites paradox (at what point does adding one grain of sand to others constitute a heap?) can be solved only by assuming that all cases of action towards an outcome presuppose a threshold, even if in some cases this threshold is vague.[14] There is some point at which a pile of sand becomes a heap, even though it is only vaguely defined. Likewise, there may well be many thresholds in store within the global climate system with respect to human interests, whether or not they are vague, and whether such vagueness should be construed as ontological or epistemic.[15]

From another perspective, however, it is possible to think about the accumulation of carbon in the atmosphere without focusing on thresholds. For there is a sense in which some of its effects – though not necessarily all of them – are cumulative and continuous. Indeed, the IPCC has premised its principal analyses on the idea of a continuous accumulation, in which the more carbon that is put into the atmosphere, the worse the overall effects (even though there may be specific nonlinear effects and tipping points within that general story).[16] Some moral and political theorists argue that if there is no threshold, then individual contributions that are very small[17] in relation to the whole can be treated as strictly negligible because they count for so little in the overall accumulation. But this is the wrong inference to draw from a continuous accumulation. If more is worse, then every bit more is every bit worse, and so the overall outcome is indeed worse for every bit – however minute – that has been added. No bit is strictly negligible in the sense of making no difference to the badness of the accumulation, although there may still be a question about whether the resulting worseness is itself negligible relative to some specified outcome or concern.

---

[14] Tuck, *Free Riding*; S. Kagan, 'Do I Make a Difference?', *Philosophy & Public Affairs* 39 (2011), 105–141.

[15] If we expect overall emissions to go on increasing indefinitely into the future, however, it is hard to see how any one individual could be held to contribute to any given tipping point, for if she refrained, someone else would simply kick in her mite in the further future. I acknowledge this objection made to me by Mark Budolfson, to which I think the best answer is that – especially with the support of the UNFCC 2015 Paris Agreement – we have reason to expect a collective slowing of emissions to be achieved by the human race at some point in the future.

[16] I owe this point to Stephen Pacala, in his commentary on a paper by L. H. Meyer and P. Sanklecha on 'Individual Expectations and Climate Justice' (a revised and expanded version of a paper in *Analyse & Kritik* 33 (2011), 449–471), which Meyer presented in a meeting of the Princeton PIIRS Communicating Scientific Uncertainty Group on 10 May 2012.

[17] Many discussions of this point use the term 'imperceptible': see the discussion of Parfit below.

The upshot of this section is that we cannot model the climate change problem as a case either of pure threshold or of pure continuity. The carbon we emit will accumulate continuously and may also trigger some thresholds or tipping points – though these may be vague in ways that may be variously construed. It follows that attempts to model the problem of carbon accumulation in the atmosphere in terms of a single well-defined game with a threshold are mistaken, but so are attempts to deny that threshold modeling is relevant at all. With that caution in mind, we can now examine the dominant approaches to individual emissions reduction in rational choice theory, which tend to compare climate change to voting. When we turn to moral philosophy approaches, we will consider some theories which reject the comparison with voting and will be able to assess their broader motivations and implications also.

Comparing Climate Change with Voting: Rational Choice Approaches

Voting, involving a defined threshold, has been seen to raise two versions of non-instrumentality and so negligibility in terms of contention (i). One concern is the justification for casting votes which are redundant in electing a candidate (let us say, those counted, or perhaps with time-zone and write-in ballot effects, even cast, after the threshold of N votes for election has already been reached). Here non-instrumentality appears as what we may call the redundancy problem, which holds that my vote is not in these circumstances a *means* to electing the candidate at all (i). The second concern is the justification for casting votes for unpopular candidates whom one had reason to believe in advance were very unlikely actually to be elected. Here non-instrumentality appears as what we may call the futility problem, which holds again that my vote in these circumstances could not reasonably be considered a *means* to determining the outcome of the election, since it not only made no difference to that outcome but could not reasonably have been expected to do so.[18]

Cutting across these two problems are four general approaches to justifying individual voting: the pivot theory, the mandate theory, redundant causation theory and expressive voting theory. I will outline each of these theories, identifying which problem most concerns each, and

[18] I am using 'instrumental' here as applying only to the votes actually counted in reaching the threshold and not to all those cast in favor of the winning candidate: for discussion of the sequence and very idea of counting, see Tuck, *Free Riding*. Tuck's own more controversial view of instrumentality will be discussed below. Nefsky, 'How You Can Help', also relies on the idea of a temporal sequence.

considering the relevance of each theory both to voting and to individual action on climate change – both reductions in individual carbon emissions and individual political initiatives. In so doing, I will highlight where the dimensions of uncertainty, interaction and identity are either ignored, distorted or partially acknowledged.

The pivot theory is the most intuitively obvious: it holds that one should vote because of the chance that one's vote will be pivotal in crossing the threshold to elect one's preferred candidate. Critics of this view hold that it is a vanishingly small chance that one's vote will be pivotal. Although there are documented cases in which a single vote has proven pivotal,[19] the very low probability of this outcome means that it is not rational to invest even the relatively low effort (costs) needed to vote based on the very low probability of being pivotal (here we see that what is in view is contention (ii), not the more severe contention (i): one's vote could in principle be a means to achieving the outcome, but it is so unlikely a means that the cost–benefit calculation makes voting not worthwhile). In response, others contend that a very low probability times a very significant outcome can still give one significant reason to act on expected value theory. Nevertheless, the pivot theory cannot cope with the redundancy problem. For if the pivot has already been turned, then my subsequent effort to turn it seems pointless on this view (though not knowing in which order votes will be counted might help with this problem from the ex ante point of view). Most think that it cannot cope well with the futility problem either. For if my candidate has no realistic chance of being elected, it is hard to see why I should vote since I am so unlikely to be pivotal (though I will question below whether the realistic standard here should be probability or sheer possibility).

Readers will have noticed that the pivot theory depends precisely on the non-negligibility of my action as potentially determinative of a threshold. The mandate theory, as developed for example by Alexander Guerrero, also offers grounds to think of my action in voting or reducing emissions as non-negligible.[20] For it suggests that the outcome at which I might rationally aim is not merely electing a candidate, but demonstrating the strength of the mandate supporting her party or cause. The advantage of this view is that it applies to both the redundancy and the

---

[19] C. B. Mulligan and C. G. Hunter, 'The Empirical Frequency of a Pivotal Vote', *Public Choice* 116 (2003), 31–54, at 37 with n. 7, note that a single congressional election in the previous 100 years was decided by a single vote (a 1910 race in New York State); they calculate, also at 37, that '41369 votes were cast in that election, or a 0.00002 share of all the votes in the US elections analyzed.' I owe this reference to Benjamin Cogan.

[20] A. A. Guerrero, 'The Paradox of Voting and the Ethics of Political Representation', *Philosophy and Public Affairs* 38 (2010), 272–306.

futility problems: by making the function I care about continuous (an increasing mandate) rather than a single threshold, I have reason to vote even when my candidate will have been elected without my vote and also to vote for a minority party in order to bolster its perceived support and so make its success more likely the next time.

Critics of the mandate theory recall the definition of negligibility in order to argue that there will be no likely discernible difference between the effects of a mandate of M votes, and the effects of a mandate of M+1, where M is reasonably large – as in state or national elections (though local elections may be a different story). Thus, if my vote will make no difference to the effectiveness of the mandate, I have no reason not to free ride on the efforts of others. My vote will not be a means to my end of generating a larger mandate, because the effective mandate would be the same with or without my vote, as per contention (i).

Here we find the holding of the general background constant, which is the first general and distorting view of politics that I wish to highlight. The assumption that a price will remain in equilibrium no matter the perturbations caused by the actions of individual agents holds only so long as one assumes that people or firms are going to go on producing the good, that people are going to continue to want to buy it, and so on. But politics encompasses the possibility of significant changes in such norms and activities, some of which can happen quite quickly – as in the case of political revolution, but also in more mundane cases such as changes in fashion. Thus within the general uncertainty that Hardin argues always inheres insofar as one person's actions depend upon those of another,[21] we can identify an intensified spectrum of what I consider political uncertainty in the special sense of the possibility of sudden and relatively dramatic changes in collective norms or behaviors, in what counts as 'normality'.

The social theory of exactly how such changes can come about is complex and contested; it is less important for our purposes to settle on a single explanation than simply to acknowledge the phenomena. Nevertheless, some relevant factors may be that I am very unlikely to be able to get full information about others' dispositions (the more so in contexts of oppression where falsification of preferences is induced), or indeed about my own; they themselves may well lack knowledge of their own dispositions to act before a certain situation is encountered, as may I; and the chance effects of who happens to encounter whom and so perhaps have a latent disposition triggered, depending on its threshold for triggering, are

[21] Hardin, *Indeterminacy and Society*.

inherently unpredictable. These are the factors, for example, that underlie the explanation given by Timur Kuran of the essential unpredictability of the reaction of millions of diverse agents to the local opening of a few passages to the West out of Hungary that triggered the fall of the Soviet Union.[22] A theory which assumes that it *can* hold the general outcome of others' efforts constant relative to a given equilibrium point is fundamentally apolitical insofar as it fails to grasp the possibility of such sudden shifts.[23] To treat the overall outcome of human interactions as a static given, against which one must assess the negligibility of one's actions, is a form of rationality that takes no account of the ruptures that mark our political history, and indeed, that mark many other aspects of our lives (such as style, dress and demeanor) as well.

Against this backdrop, we can interpret the mandate theory as supporting the rationality of individual action on climate change that is designed not just to make current levels of support visible, but to elicit action from others who may be sensitive to an emerging tipping point. Because a mandate is a signal to others, supporting a stronger mandate would require individual action to have effects that are visible to others. The most obvious cases would be installing solar panels or driving an electric car, but it is possible to bring many less evident actions like insulating one's attic to the attention of others. (Certainly, there is the possible attraction of being induced to appear to be acting rather than really acting, which needs to be taken into account.) The indirect effects of such actions may operate in diverse ways: to enable pure coordination; to stimulate our own and others' preferences; to act as a demonstration effect, updating learning about probabilities; or to provoke a cascade. If it will be rational to contribute if others do so, then contributing to the

---

[22] T. Kuran, 'Now Out of Never: The Element of Surprise in the East European Revolution of 1989', *World Politics* 44 (1991), 7–48, a reference I owe to Josiah Ober. Consider also the January 2013 general election in Israel, in which Yair Lapid's party Yesh Atid won nearly double the number of votes that pre-election polls had predicted. The exit polls on the day of the vote itself tallied with the final result, but the pre-election polls proved wildly misleading – largely because of an unexpectedly high voter turnout: www.timesofisrael.com/exit-polls-netanyahu-allies-narrowly-win-election/.

[23] Richard Tuck's conflation in this volume of '*dirty hands*' (emphasis in original) with 'the situation often faced by people living under unjust political regimes' is overly reductive. By analyzing the latter situation as a case in which 'I may . . . know perfectly well that no one will take any notice of my abstention and there will not be enough citizens like me to bring about political change', he precisely rules out the kinds of cases that interest Kuran (and me) – the justification of individual initiative that may result (though without guarantee) in a broader social transformation. Indeed, Tuck's appeal to '*politics*' (emphasis in original) interprets 'politics' as requiring 'a formal and explicit agreement'. But politics can also be the domain of changing norms and indeed, sometimes, of revolutionary action.

expectations of others about what you will do can be a rational means at the second-order level to affect an outcome.

All of these indirect effects are possible ways in which the mandate theory might apply to individual action on climate change, in the form of both direct emissions reductions and political initiatives. Those who deride individual emissions reductions as ineffective compared with national or international political agreements on climate change need to consider how such agreements might in practice be brought about. For national governments to take action themselves, or to negotiate and then implement such actions together with other governments, concerted political pressure is likely to be required. If politics is presented as the more 'realistic' path to a solution than individual emissions reduction, then the contributions of individuals – made as savvily as possible, whether that means by contributing to lobbying funds or by engaging in civil disobedience – to bringing about those political solutions should be taken seriously, and must themselves be construed as potentially non-negligible.

The third rational choice approach, redundant causation, accepts that my action may be negligible in the sense of making no difference to the outcome. But it argues against contention (i) that such negligible actions can nevertheless count as a means to outcome O. I will focus on the version proposed by Richard Tuck, in which 'counting' is construed as being part of a sufficient cause rather than a necessary one.[24] Tuck's aim is to expand our understanding of instrumentality, by arguing that one need not be a *necessary* cause of an effect in order to be part of what causes it, since *sufficient* causes are also genuine causes (even where they are redundant). (Note that this move could still be challenged by contention (ii), arguing that the costs of being part of a sufficient cause outweigh the benefits it might bring.) In the voting case, even if one's vote proves not to have been *necessary* for the election of one's favored candidate, it may still have been part of the set *sufficient* to elect her and so one still had instrumental reason to vote as a means to the end of her election. The sufficient causation or redundant causation solution applies both to cases with a well-defined threshold, such as an election, and to those with a

---

[24] Tuck, *Free Riding.* The pioneering argument in this area, focusing on overdetermination and partial causation, was offered by A. I. Goldman, 'Why Citizens Should Vote: A Causal Responsibility Approach,' *Social Philosophy and Policy* 16 (1999), 201–217. For a good overview of causation and voting, see G. F. Gaus, *On Philosophy, Politics, and Economics* (Cengage Learning, 2008), 184–191. For an alternative approach to overdetermination in the context of carbon emissions, see C. Barry and G. Øverland, *Individual Responsibility for Carbon Emissions: Is There Anything Wrong with Overdetermining Harm?* (Cambridge: Cambridge University Press, 2015), 168–183.

vague threshold, such as the sorites paradox. By definition, it solves the problem of redundancy; whether or not it solves the problem of futility is harder to determine, resting as it does on the individual's motivation to try to make her own agency count as part of the sufficient set.

Tuck's argument for redundant causation has the advantage of solving the redundancy problem for certain individual actions: for if I can legit-imately see myself as a means even where I am redundant, then the prospect of possible redundancy need not deter my action. The question is, to which actions does it apply? Tuck argues that it does not apply to individual emissions reduction, since I have no reason to expect that others are taking similar actions in enough numbers for us together to constitute (with or without redundancy) a real means to some outcome.[25] Here we find him assuming the same kind of relative certainty about others' actions that we diagnosed in the critics of pivotality and mandate theories previously. But in the case of climate change, how do we know how others will act? This is a case precisely in which we are transitioning from climate change being a minority concern (a 'lone wolf' issue) to being a part of a mainstream movement, and in which we do not know with any certainty when and how this transition will come about.[26]

If we scale up the argument, we can more easily appreciate the irrationality of holding that we have no reason to act unilaterally when it is possible that the future may bring about the necessary support for our action to be maximally effective through the action of others, even if they are not cooperating with us now. Suppose the US Congress decided in, say, 2009 not to act to reduce national emissions, on the grounds if China were not also so to act, the US emissions reduction by itself would not (let's stipulate by 2030) be enough to count as a means to some defined emissions reduction target outcome, one pegged to controlling likely temperature increases to a tolerable level. But Congress was not privy to the internal deliberations or intentions of the Chinese, and it turns out some number of years later that they had indeed brought about significant reductions – enough, had the United States also acted unilaterally in 2009, to have achieved the target outcome.[27]

---

[25] Tuck made this argument in a paper replying to an earlier version of this one (then called 'Against Negligibility'); his paper was called 'What Are Means?: A Response to Melissa Lane, *Against Negligibility*', and the occasion was a conference at Yale University on 'Means and Ends' in April 2011. We had a further iteration of the debate in an exchange of later versions of the same papers at the Cambridge conference in May 2012 from which this volume arises.

[26] Here I echo my formulation in *Eco-Republic*, 63.

[27] The US–China agreement on climate change actions in November 2014 illustrates the kind of framework-changing shifts that are possible but never fully predictable in politics.

Ruling out action on the basis of overly fixed expectations about how others will act is not a requirement of rationality: it can easily become a misguided fatalism.

What about the rationality of individual contribution to a political solution? Tuck himself applies his theory to voting, which is a good place to begin. But we immediately encounter a hitch. For as he acknowledges, his solution works only where the agent has good grounds to believe that others are also going to play their part, so that the desired effect is in fact going to be brought about. Where an isolated voter living in an unsympathetic district votes for a lost cause, she has no good instrumental reason for bothering to vote. (Tuck's example is the British case of the lone Communist in Kensington.) In his contribution to this volume he applies this to individual climate change emissions by arguing that if we had a global treaty to reduce climate change emissions, we would have reason to play our part in reducing our individual emissions even if the treaty failed to be enforced, insofar as a coordination solution has been established that we can now reasonably expect enough others to follow. But, he claims, without such an agreement, we have no instrumental reason to act on our own, because we cannot plausibly see our individually negligible actions as constituting a means to the desired end in any rational sense.[28]

The hard question for Tuck is whether I have reason to support and agitate for the bringing about of such a treaty now, in the absence of a concerted large-scale move to do so. What reason on his view does any individual have to take an initiative in which she may begin isolated, even though there is a chance that she may win fellows to her cause?

Tuck concedes that individuals have reason to *support* the introduction of a global climate change treaty that does not yet exist. But that concession allows that individuals have reason to take action even though most others may not now be actively supporting such a treaty. And this opens the door to the potential rationality of other forms of individual action and political initiative, which may turn out to be effective as a means even though that cannot be guaranteed or estimated as likely in advance. The balance of costs is always an issue, but at least there is a genuine reason lying in the balance against them, as opposed to no reason (as on the negligibility hypothesis) at all.

As with the mandate theory, once one allows the possibility of strategic interaction (a possibility which Tuck excludes in order to stay within the

---

[28] Tuck's paper was finalized before the 2015 UNFCC Paris Agreement; it would be interesting to know his view as to whether the nature of this agreement would count as sufficient reason for individuals and groups to play their parts going forward.

equilibrium market formulation of negligibility, however unrealistic that formulation is of politics), the grounds for supporting individual initiative multiply. This is true in the domains of both individual emissions reduction and individual political action. If I can make my emissions reductions in some form that acts as a signal to others, then I can hope to be a factor in shaping their future behavior in ways that will support and reinforce my own. Not all emissions reductions are equally susceptible to being broadcast in strategic form – it may be hard to convey to others my decision to have shorter showers, but even this has been the subject of newspaper articles that can affect others' perception of a changing social norm.[29] Here we see that uncertainty combined with interaction gives grounds for individual initiatives of all kinds. The fundamental condition of politics is that we do not know whose action will prove effective in galvanizing others, or when, in part because we do not know their dispositions or thresholds for taking action. It follows that we cannot rule out all reason for taking initiatives in the hope of having such galvanizing effects. Cost–benefit calculations may still apply, but the very hope of having an effect on others cannot in the real world (contra the stipulative claims of negligibility drawn from an idealized market model of perfect competition) simply be stipulated away.

So far, I have introduced two of the three key dimensions of the political that I advertised earlier: uncertainty and interaction. It remains to consider identity. This can be done by attending to the fourth theory I promised to survey, namely, the theory of expressive rationality. This approach claims to expand the domain of rationality, not by expanding instrumentality as does Tuck, but rather by offering two distinct accounts of rational action: the one instrumental, the other expressive (hence the term 'two hat' theory of rational choice). On this view, as advanced by Geoffrey Brennan, I vote not because I think my vote is causally related to the outcome (regardless of whether regarded as pivotally or as a mandate, and regardless of whether regarded as causally necessary or sufficient). Rather, I vote because I care about expressing my values. Expressive rationality is on this view properly construed as a form of rationality – for why should I not be allowed to adopt the end of expressing my values, as opposed to other ends I might adopt? It is simply distinct from instrumental rationality.[30]

Brennan has himself applied his view to climate change regulation, arguing that citizens' interests will counsel against it (it will cost them

---

[29] Again, there is the possibility of faking one's actions, which must be factored in.
[30] Compare Max Weber's distinction between *Zweckrationalität* and *Wertrationalität*.

money), but their values may lead them nevertheless to endorse it.[31] We might equally apply this view to individual emissions reduction: in which case, individuals' interests will counsel against such a reduction (as it will impose costs on them) but their values may lead them to pursue it nonetheless. Brennan addresses the problems of both redundancy and futility: I need not worry that my action may be either instrumentally redundant or futile, if I have separate expressive grounds for taking it anyway. And he does so by focusing on the individual's identity and values. On his view, I have reason to act to express my identity and my values.

There is a stronger way and a weaker way of interpreting Brennan. The stronger way is to read him as conceding in advance that an action is not instrumentally rational, hence explaining it instead as expressively rational. That is subject to the criticisms I have made above on the basis of uncertainty: for how can we be certain that actions of the kind that concern me (individual emissions reduction or individual political initiatives on climate change) are not instrumentally rational? On the weaker interpretation, we can see expressive rationality as a potentially independent but also potentially supplemental ground for action. The advantage of the weaker interpretation is that it allows for political actions which blend expressiveness and the prospect for strategic influencing of others and of political outcomes – which is a characteristic of many political actions.

Those who most defiantly declare their expressive commitment – the Luthers who proclaim 'here I stand; I can do no other' – are often those who in fact have the greatest effect in moving others to act. Perhaps some are genuinely indifferent to that prospect, but others will be aware of the potential force that lies in becoming an exemplar. One cannot make oneself an exemplar – that depends on others' responses – but one can make oneself available to be adopted as an exemplar, even if one's primary motive is expressive.[32] Nor need we conceive of responses to

---

[31] G. Brennan, 'Climate Change: A Rational Choice Politics View', *Australian Journal of Agricultural and Resource Economics* 53 (2009), 309–326; Brennan has responded to Tuck and Goldman on the case of voting in G. Brennan and G. Sayre-McCord, 'Voting and Causal Responsibility', in D. Sobel, P. Vallentyne and S. Wall (eds.), *Oxford Studies in Political Philosophy* (Oxford: Oxford University Press, 2015), 36–59.

[32] For discussion of exemplarity, see *Eco-Republic*, and also M. Lane, 'Constraint, Freedom, and Exemplar: History and Theory without Teleology,' in J. Floyd and M. Stears (eds.), *Political Philosophy versus History? Contextualism and Real Politics in Contemporary Political Thought* (Cambridge: Cambridge University Press, 2011), 128–150. See also A. Ferrara, *The Force of the Example: Explorations in the Paradigm of Judgment* (New York: Columbia University Press, 2008). I have benefited from discussion with Karuna Mantena of exemplarity in Gandhi, as identified by A. Bilgrami, 'Gandhi, the Philosopher', *Economic and Political Weekly* 38 (2003), 4159–4165, though she is more skeptically sensitive to its limits as an interpretation of his ideas.

exemplarity as occurring only in a piecemeal, linear fashion, as if people line up one by one to follow. Rather, it is much more likely that a sudden shift in imaginative conceptions and/or in social norms may take place, galvanized by an exemplar whose model is found to speak to aspirations latent in the hearts of many (as in Kuran's model also).

Conversely, we should note that most expressive actions defended by Brennan take the form of actions that *could be* instrumentally effective.[33] We are unlikely to think that a good way to express concern about climate change would be to drive very quickly up and down the motorway (though ironic protests could qualify). Expression is an act of communication, which must be understood by others in order to count as expression.[34] The most straightforward way to express my concern about climate change in a way that will be intelligible to others is either visibly to reduce my emissions or to support political initiatives that would help reduce it. I act in ways that I see as instrumental (this Brennan does not deny, since he focuses his argument on contention (ii) about cost–benefit failure rather than on contention (i) denying instrumentality at all). And this expression may potentially lead to greater instrumental effects through interaction with others. Contrary to the 'two hat' theory, I can wear more than one hat at a time. There is no sharp divide between expressive actions and instrumental effects.

II.   Consequentialist Approaches to the Rationality and Morality of Seemingly Negligible Individual Action

Rational choice is concerned with the consequences of my action for my own goals: consequentialism, with the general consequences of my action on goodness of the state of the world as a whole according to some measure (call this utility, without restricting it to hedonism). So in moving from rational choice theory to ethical consequentialism, we move from instrumental rationality for my individual ends to instrumental rationality for collective ends (however one defines the relevant collective, whether at a local, national or global level). Therefore consequentialists face the same question as rational choice theorists of whether a given action can be understood as an instrumental means to some outcome, or

---

[33] I owe this point to Bob Goodin at the 'Political Thought and the Environment' conference, May 2012, Cambridge University, from which this volume emerged.

[34] N. C. Manson and O. O'Neill, *Rethinking Informed Consent in Bioethics* (Cambridge and New York: Cambridge University Press, 2007). The framework for understanding communication in this work is further discussed in R. O. Keohane, M. Lane and M. Oppenheimer, 'The Ethics of Scientific Communication under Uncertainty', *Politics, Philosophy & Economics* 13 (2014), 343–368.

more broadly as having consequences for that outcome, which is why this section focuses primarily on consequentialist ethicists: for it is they who most directly have confronted the problem of negligibility. (Of course, if one deems an action to be an instrumental means to some outcome, so defeating contention (i), one must still confront contention (ii) in order to complete a consequentialist analysis. For the overall question of costs and benefits may make a difference to whether my taking an action, even one that is not strictly negligible, is morally required.)

One influential line of consequentialist analysis, well expressed by Derek Parfit, has challenged the assessment of actions bringing about only very small benefit as negligible altogether (and so serves as one line of refutation, avant la lettre in its original formulation, of Sinnott-Armstrong's position invoked at the outset of this chapter). Parfit argued in *Reasons and Persons* that actions whose effects are imperceptible can nevertheless make a small difference to an outcome.[35] In making a threshold argument, Parfit's analysis takes seriously the uncertainty of the future. He holds that if an action A has an effect – albeit an imperceptible and very small one – on outcome O, A has a very small chance of being pivotal in the outcome. Such a small chance should be multiplied by the overall benefit of O, which in many contexts will result in a large number and so support the consequentialist value of doing A.

Parfit's framing of the question in terms of perceptibility risks confusing the issue somewhat, as the real issue is not whether and to whom an effect is perceptible, but how it is or is not related to a given outcome. Nevertheless, the issue of imperceptibility has been widely discussed. It has recently been explored by Shelly Kagan in the course of taking a different view of uncertainty and its implications from that of Parfit.[36] Kagan argues that all cases of seeming imperceptibility have thresholds which may be triggered by some event. Hence it is always possible, however unlikely, that my causing that event may cause the overall (bad) outcome. But he moves away from the probability calculation advised by Parfit in refusing to hold the world and the actions of others as fixed – even as probabilistically determined – in assessing the consequences of a single individual's actions. Instead he adopts a more chaotic view of historical causation and so identifies the sheer possibility of

---

[35] D. Parfit, *Reasons and Persons* (Oxford: Clarendon Press, 1984), 67–86. Parfit was building on an earlier article by J. Glover, 'It Makes No Difference Whether or Not I Do It', 180.

[36] Kagan, 'Do I Make a Difference?'. For a commentary on Kagan focusing primarily on the understanding of 'imperceptibility', see J. Nefsky, 'Consequentialism and the Problem of Collective Harm: A Reply to Kagan,' *Philosophy & Public Affairs* 39 (2011), 364–395.

affecting an outcome – as opposed to any particular level of probability – as the appropriate standard in judging whether or not my action should be counted in the consequentialist calculus.

While Broome joins Parfit and Kagan in holding that there is some sense in which I can consider actions of this kind as capable of bringing about harm, he largely abandons the language of 'imperceptibility' in favor of that of 'negligibility' (though he still refers to 'imperceptibility' at times) and offers a distinct line of analysis.[37] Broome argues that the effects of individual carbon emissions are, precisely, *not* 'negligible', even though they are 'so minute' in comparison with global emissions.[38] He points out that the effects on those who are harmed by emissions are unchanged regardless of whether those emissions come from a single source or from billions of distributed sources.[39] Thus, while accepting Parfit's basic structure of reasoning about expected utility, Broome focuses not on the reasons I have to act so as to bring about a global solution to climate change, but on the immediate reasons I have to act so as to stop harming others by putting my contribution of carbon (however small) into the atmosphere. He argues on that basis that each person has a moral obligation on grounds of justice to reduce her emissions to zero by reducing and offsetting.[40] Finally, he adds there that such individual reductions may also have beneficial side effects in encouraging others to act similarly, as well as indirect political effects in giving politicians the sense that the public cares about climate change. On our present terms, this is a recognition of the possibility of interaction.[41]

To these concerns with uncertainty and interaction, other consequentialists add an appeal to the identity of the moral agent. Philip Pettit and Geoffrey Brennan have argued that the consequentialist may have to tie her hands – adopting a strict rule of action – in order to avoid undermining a goal by the rational incentive to free ride, and instead to develop the requisite sense of identity necessary to achieving her goals.[42] They take the example of individual goals such as dental health, in which a person 'will be tempted at each moment to free ride on future efforts' because a calculation of whether adherence to a tooth-brushing maxim at any given

[37] J. Broome, *Climate Matters: Ethics in a Warming World*, Amnesty International Global Ethics Series (New York: W. W. Norton, 2012), 76.
[38] Ibid., 74.   [39] Ibid., 75–76.   [40] Ibid., 78–81.
[41] Ibid., 81. For an alternative way of calculating the harms that individual emissions cause to future people, see J. Nolt, 'Greenhouse Gas Emission and the Domination of Posterity', in D. G. Arnold (ed.), *The Ethics of Global Climate Change* (Cambridge: Cambridge University Press, 2011).
[42] P. Pettit and G. Brennan, 'Restrictive Consequentialism', *Australasian Journal of Philosophy* 64 (1986), 438–455.

moment will give a negative result.[43] This temptation arises in cases where an outcome (a 'good') has the following characteristics: 'it emerges over a period from independent actions; each of those actions is relatively burdensome; and none of the actions makes the difference between the appearance and non-appearance of the good.'[44] Their third condition bespeaks the negligibility problem in the form of the sorites or heap; their first condition, the independence on which the formulation of negligibility depends.

If we ask to what extent their reasoning could be applied to political free riding – to free riding on others' present and future selves, as opposed to my own future self merely – we can see that the independence condition plays a complex role. On the one hand, it is the assurance that even if I do not brush my teeth today, I can simply start tomorrow, that gives me the rational incentive to free ride on my future self today. But is brushing my teeth today really independent of brushing my teeth tomorrow? Many psychological and ethical analyses would say no: if I brush today, I make it more likely that I will brush tomorrow by coming to think of myself as the kind of person who brushes (identity); whereas the opposite will be true if I do not brush today. The Pettit–Brennan solution is not just a reformulation of consequentialism to fit this vexing category of goods; it is also a prescription for the habit forming and hence the identity forming of the virtuous person.

In a paper focused on why consequentialists should be virtue theorists, Dale Jamieson moves from a distinct view about uncertainty to an appeal to the identity of the virtuous agent as such. He argues that the right approach for consequentialists to uncertainty is a principle of 'noncontingency', meaning that one's actions (specifically, the action of minimizing our contribution to the harm of carbon emissions) should generally not be contingent on one's beliefs about the behavior of others.[45] This is because such contingency would require calculation of innumerable effects, the impossibility of which would risk leading to a 'downward spiral of noncooperation' which could be avoided if each individual took noncontingent initiative.[46] Such noncontingent initiative is best supported by the development of environmental virtues, Jamieson argues.[47]

---

[43] Ibid., 453.   [44] Ibid., 452–453.

[45] D. Jamieson, 'Why Utilitarians Should Be Virtue Theorists', in S. M. Gardiner, S. Caney, D. Jamieson and H. Shue (eds.), *Climate Ethics: Essential Readings* (Oxford: Oxford University Press, 2010) 315–331, at 318 (first published in *Utilitas* 19 (2007), 160–183).

[46] Jamieson, 'Why Utilitarians', 318. The term 'spiral' was also analyzed by Glover, 'It Makes No Difference Whether or Not I Do It', 180.

[47] I develop a similar view in *Eco-Republic*.

In light of the argument of this paper, we can appreciate that the virtues should be understood as developing our identity, not simply as instrumental to interactive effects on others, though they are that also. And so we can further conclude that concern with our identity is not just a matter of expressing it, as in expressive rationality; it must also be a concern with cultivating it appropriately. While the theorists we have been discussing have acknowledged this point within reformulations of consequentialism, it may lead others to adopt non-consequentialist approaches altogether, in which one's identity and concern with acting virtuously (perhaps with being a virtuous agent, but not a moral saint) become the primary explanations of why one would take the initiative of individual action even when others do not.

III.   Conclusion: The Parameters of Power and Agency

I argued in *Eco-Republic* that negligibility 'purchases impunity with powerlessness'.[48] We might reflect further on why so many people who otherwise seek and revel in power are so attracted to the rhetorical claim that human action is negligible in driving climate change. Vladimir Putin in 2012 pressed a leading Russian climate scientist on this point: when the scientist rejected such denial of the significance of the human contribution, Putin eagerly objected to him, saying, 'There are experts who believe that the changes in the climate are unrelated to human activity, that human activity has just a minimal, tiny effect, within the margin of error.'[49] Putin is not someone likely to downplay his power in many contexts. Why should he be so eager to do so in this one?

My answer is that with power comes responsibility. If one admits one's power to affect greenhouse gases, both as an individual and as a member of human collectivities, one is thereby responsible.[50] Yet the rhetoric of many negligibility arguments – not perhaps in the case of Putin, but in the case of Drew Faust and of many others like her – portray individual

[48] Lane, *Eco-Republic*, 51–52.

[49] As quoted in K. Gessen, 'Polar Express', *The New Yorker* (24 and 31 December 2012), 98–117, at 111. The scientist was Vladimir Lipenkov of the Arctic and Antarctic Research Institute of St. Petersburg.

[50] Negligibility is of course not the only argument of what Robert Brulle calls the 'counter-movement' against mandatory restrictions on carbon emissions; some argue that carbon emissions do not do harm, or that if they do there is no alternative, or take up other variants of these positions. See Robert J. Brulle, 'Institutionalizing Delay: Foundation Funding and the Creation of U.S. Climate Change Counter-Movement Organizations', *Climatic Change* 122 (2014). My interest here is in diagnosing the special attractiveness of the negligibility view.

agents as powerless to effect change because of the inexorable logic of an idealized market. Return to Drew Faust's assertion as quoted at the outset of this chapter. It depends on the assumption that the actual market in the shares of what she calls 'fossil fuel companies' is well conceived as involving perfect competition which has arrived at a stable equilibrium, and that the future actions of others can be fully expected to contribute to maintaining that equilibrium. But this rules out precisely the kind of shift in identities and interactions that make future choices of real-world agents, including their market choices, uncertain. In this case, the aim of the divestment movement is to act in public, to exemplify and so to encourage a shift in social values that would make the stocks of these companies less desirable and so ultimately drive down their price, as a signal to the companies that alternative energy sources might be a better investment strategy. While the immediate context is a market, the agents in question are acting not only within the market but also and simultaneously within the broader domain of politics, with potential to shift the terms of the equilibrium on which market participants settle and not simply to reproduce them as previously given. It is the very symbolic and expressive effects of divestment that can potentially shift the instrumental calculations of market participants and so change the terms of the market equilibrium that emerges. Even action in a market is not – in real life, as opposed to a model of perfect competition – insulated from the broader domain of uncertainty, interaction and identity that characterizes politics.

Once we reject negligibility as a false freezing of the fundamental conditions of politics – the conditions of uncertainty, interaction and identity – we can recognize once again a much wider array of political possibility. Indeed, if one takes a longer view of the history of political thought, the grip of negligibility will seem surprising. For it is seldom that the efficacy of the individual as a political agent has genuinely been challenged. Even the ring of Gyges story in Plato's *Republic* allows that unjust actions hidden by an invisibility ring have consequences – after all, they can help to make the ring wearer into a tyrant. The ring does not make actions negligible; it merely shields their doer from punishment for them.[51] The same is true of the structure of Rousseau's stag hunt: if a group has staked out a stag hunt the success of which depends on each sticking to her post, then if I secretly abandon my post to chase after a

---

[51] I have changed my view on this from previous work (Lane, *Eco-Republic*, 48) in which I compared the 'invisibility' of actions by someone with the ring of Gyges with the 'ignorability' of putatively negligible actions. The ring wearer's actions may be invisible, but their effects will be visible and consequential.

hare, I will have harmed my companions by making it the case that their hunt (for want of my participation) fails.[52]

In these classic pre-modern accounts, individual actions have real consequences for oneself or others, good or bad. These thinkers recognized that people disagree about how to weigh those consequences and choose among them; they did not anticipate the appeal of a model stipulating that one's actions could make no difference to an overall outcome at all. Hence the concern that hands might in politics be dirtied – indeed, the problem of dirty hands was primarily a problem about the effects of outsized political initiative, not about the lack of any incentive to take it. It is especially (if not only) in the grip of the twentieth-century market model of perfect competition that we have come to conclude too readily that our hands are necessarily dirty – at the price of conceding that they are impotent. Once we loosen the grip of that model and so give up on the stipulative presumption that our actions are necessarily negligible, we can return to the much richer set of concerns in the history of political thought about how we use the potential sources of power that we cannot rule out possessing.

---

[52] Jean-Jacques Rousseau, *Discourse on the Origins of Inequality*, in Rousseau, *The Discourses and Other Early Political Writings*, ed. Victor Gourevitch (Cambridge: Cambridge University Press, 1997), 'Second Discourse', 163. For discussion, see B. Skyrms, 'The Stag Hunt', *Proceedings and Addresses of the American Philosophical Association* 75 (2001), 31–41, a paper which he develops further in B. Skyrms, *The Stag Hunt and the Evolution of Social Structure* (Cambridge: Cambridge University Press, 2004).

9 What Kind of Problem Is Negligibility?
A Response to Melissa Lane

Richard Tuck

Melissa Lane has now produced two powerful and important essays (one is a chapter in this volume and one is a paper presented at a conference at Yale which we both attended) which have prompted me to revisit the arguments I put forward in *Free Riding*,[1] and to draw some conclusions from them which I think I did not make as clear as they might have been. They have also led me to try to develop in more detail some thoughts about instrumentality which I sketched in the book, but to which I did not assign their full weight. In the end, Lane and I still differ about what should count as instrumental rationality, though we are closer to one another than either of us is to the standard account of instrumentally rational action which is found for example in economics textbooks. The issue Lane is concerned with, climate change, is an example I too began to think about towards the end of writing *Free Riding*, though I did not in the event use it in the book; it is clearly a vivid and apposite case to which issues of instrumentality, and in particular the question of negligible contributions, are central, and this is true whether or not one thinks that combating climate change is possible or, indeed, desirable. I will for the purposes of this chapter simply assume that it is both.

First, I want to clarify the terminology. As Lane observes, the literature in this area tends to use interchangeably the terms 'negligible' and 'imperceptible' to describe those small increments to cumulative activities which seem to make no appreciable difference to the outcome. But we should be clear that the words 'imperceptible' or 'negligible' apply properly to the *effect* of a given increment, not the increment itself. To see this, we can consider the most famous case of negligibility, the ancient sorites paradox, which I dealt with extensively in *Free Riding*, and which Lane also cites in her chapter. According to the sorites argument, any one stone added to a group of stones will make no difference to whether

---

[1] R. Tuck, *Free Riding* (Cambridge, MA: Harvard University Press, 2008).

the group is a 'heap' or not: there is no precise threshold at which the set of stones becomes a heap, and consequently, on the face of it, the stone has no effect on the outcome. But the stone itself is of course not imperceptible, and each set of stones can be precisely distinguished from the others by inspection – we can count them. The problem is that our perception of the set as a 'heap' is – so to speak – coarse-grained. This is not at all unusual: many of our perceptions are coarse-grained, in the sense that I can fail to see the incremental changes whereby one state of affairs changes into another.[2] For many things this does not matter, but for a wide variety of things where our interest in the outcome *depends* on how it is perceived, the coarse-grained character of perception is critical. For example, we care about having a headache (leaving aside any evidentiary character it may possess about hidden dangers) only because of the pain it causes us, and our perception of pain like many other perceptions is coarse-grained: a slight addition to whatever the chemicals are in the brain (say) which are causing the headache will not change the level of the pain we experience. So it is perfectly reasonable to say that the additional chemicals are 'negligible' or 'imperceptible', in the sense that the change they make in our brain is imperceptible in terms of our *pain*, though not imperceptible in terms of a chemical assay.[3] The relevance of this to the question of climate change is of course that in the end the adverse consequences of climate change are differences made to human lives, not to the mere level of gases in the atmosphere, and individual contributions to the reduction of greenhouse gases are like the slight

---

[2] For a graphic demonstration of this, see the videos illustrating 'change-blindness' on the website of the experimental psychologist Kevin O'Regan, at http://nivea.psycho.univ-paris5.fr/Slowchanges/index.html.

[3] In a noteworthy passage in *Reasons and Persons* (Oxford: Oxford University Press, 1984), Derek Parfit denied this, in order (he believed) to avoid being caught out in sorites-like arguments: 'I believe that someone's pain can become less painful, or less bad, by an amount too small to be noticed. Someone's pain is worse, in the sense that has moral relevance, if this person minds the pain more, or has a stronger desire that the pain cease. I believe that someone can mind his pain slightly less, or have a slightly weaker desire that his pain cease, even though he cannot notice any difference' (79). But this is no answer to the sorites. As the way Parfit puts it makes clear, there are two components to the mental state of this person. One is what we might term brute pain, and the other is an attitude to it; the two are not the same, since on Parfit's own showing at a particular moment one can be slightly less than it was (the desire that the pain cease) while the other stays the same (the pain). But suppose that as a matter of fact at that moment the person's attitude to the pain undergoes no change, and neither does his pain: there can then be a sorites-like problem, since there can be a measurable change in whatever the underlying physical conditions are, and the accumulation of such measurable changes, each one imperceptible with regard to its effects, can alter both the pain *and* the attitude to it. So the fact that (in Parfit's sense) a pain can become less bad without this being noticed does not mean that we cannot have a sorites problem about pain.

additions to the chemicals in the brain: they necessarily have a loose fit to the changes which matter to us.

How then should we think about this problem, at least as a problem in the first instance for *instrumental* rationality, that is, choosing means to a specifiable end in order to bring it about? It is this kind of rationality on which I want to concentrate; Lane also deals with what has been termed *expressive* rationality, in which we choose an action because it expresses in some way our values or commitments, but in which its causal relationship to a desired outcome is irrelevant. She makes some extremely cogent points about the degree to which there is usually some kind of instrumentality built into it, and if there is not there should be. I agree with her on this, but insofar as it does involve instrumental rationality it shares in whatever difficulties we find over negligibility, and insofar as it does not, it is not a solution to the puzzles but an alternative way of thinking about one's life. I could perhaps add that – at least in the area of electoral politics – I think that a concentration on expressive rationality has done substantial harm, since it tends to reduce politics to a kind of theatre, and directs attention away from the real consequences of mass action. In the last part of her chapter Lane turns to specifically *moral* reasons for restricting our emissions; I will have much less to say about this, though I suspect that instrumentality also plays more of a part in moral thinking about these issues than we might initially suppose.

The first way of thinking about the problem is the commonest, both in economics and in the areas of the other social sciences which look to economics as their model. This is the position whose history I tried to uncover in *Free Riding*, and which I concluded there has a surprisingly recent history. It is very well put in Mancur Olson's 1965 book, *The Logic of Collective Action*:

Even if the member of a large group[4] were to neglect his own interests entirely, he still would not rationally contribute towards the provision of any collective or public good, since his own contribution would not be perceptible. A farmer who placed the interests of other farmers above his own would not necessarily restrict his production to raise farm prices, since he would know that his sacrifice would not bring a noticeable benefit to anyone. Such a rational farmer, however unselfish, would not make such a futile and pointless sacrifice, but he would allocate his philanthropy in order to have a perceptible effect on someone. Selfless behavior that has no perceptible effect is sometimes not even considered praiseworthy. A man who tried to hold back a flood with a pail would probably be considered more of a crank than a saint, even by those he was trying to help.

---

[4] For Olson, a 'large group' is defined as a group where no one member can alter the character of a collective enterprise.

It is no doubt possible infinitesimally to lower the level of a river in flood with a pail, just as it is possible for a single farmer infinitesimally to raise prices by limiting his production, but in both cases the effect is imperceptible, and those who sacrifice themselves in the interest of imperceptible improvements may not even receive the praise normally due selfless behavior.[5]

Olson's use of a farmer as an instance reminds us that this argument began in economics, with the North American grain market being a prime example of a perfectly competitive market in which no producer had any effect on the price of grain, as no farmer produced enough to make any appreciable difference to the overall quantities of grain traded. Though Olson used the farmer in this passage, his preferred example throughout his book was trades unionism: he repeatedly stressed that unions could not work on a wholly voluntary basis, and required mechanisms such as the closed shop to force rational workers into collaborating in their unions.

However, if we take the essence of the modern economists' theory of perfect competition to be that it is *rational* for small producers (including the producers of labour) to compete with one another in this fashion, then, as I said, its history is much more recent than is usually supposed. From Adam Smith down to the early twentieth century, most economists believed instead that it was rational for producers (and consumers) to form *cartels* and to collaborate in improving their bargaining position vis-à-vis the individuals or groups with which they traded. Perhaps the most striking example of this is provided by an economist who is usually regarded as one of the creators of the modern subject, Francis Ysidro Edgeworth. In his *Mathematical Psychics* of 1881 Edgeworth argued (against the expectations of most of his modern readers) that such things as trades unions or the Irish tenants' Land League[6] were a rational attempt by workers or tenant farmers to extract more from their employers or landlords than they would achieve by competing against one another: as he said, 'in the matter of *unionism*, as well as in that of the predeterminate *wage-fund*, the 'untutored mind' of the workman had gone more straight to the point than economic intelligence *misled by a bad method*, reasoning without mathematics upon

---

[5] M. Olsen, *The Logic of Collective Action* (Cambridge, MA: Harvard University Press, 1965), 64.

[6] This was even more important as an example, as far as he was concerned, than trade unions: Edgeworth came from an Anglo-Irish landowning family and grew up in Edgworthstown in County Longford. He was a supporter of Gladstone's solution to the Irish Question, which was the imposition of a system of fair rents upon both landlords and tenants, rather than let the market decide the outcome.

mathematical subjects.'[7] And unlike his successors, Edgeworth assumed that if a trade union provided extra bargaining power to its members, there was a good reason for them to join it.

In this respect Edgeworth was standing in a long line of broadly consequentialist theorists who believed that it was a *failure* of rationality not to collaborate, rather than (as the modern rational choice theorist has it) a *triumph* of rationality. There is a famous passage in Hume's *Treatise*, for example, which has often been cited by modern rational choice theorists as an example of their view of collaboration, but which in fact says the opposite:

> *There is no quality in human nature, which causes more fatal errors in our conduct, than that which leads us to prefer whatever is present to the distant and remote, and makes us desire objects more according to their situation than their intrinsic value.* Two neighbours may agree to drain a meadow, which they possess in common; because 'tis easy for them to know each others mind; and each must perceive, that the immediate consequence of his failing in his part, is, the abandoning the whole project. But 'tis very difficult, and indeed impossible, that a thousand persons should agree in any such action; it being difficult for them to concert so complicated a design, and still more difficult for them to execute it; while each seeks a pretext to free himself of the trouble and expence, and wou'd lay the whole burden on others.[8]

But as the opening sentence of this passage makes clear, for Hume this inability to collaborate in a large-scale project is like our inability to be prudent about the future: it is a 'fatal error', and not the paradoxical consequence of our basic rationality (though, like imprudence, it may have to be overcome by coercive structures such as, he went on to say, 'political society'). And as *Mathematical Psychics* illustrates, this continued to be the natural assumption well into the formative years of modern economics.[9]

---

[7] F. Y. Edgeworth, *Mathematical Psychics* (London: C. K. Paul, 1881), 43–45. Edgeworth understood very well that a perfectly competitive market would generate more production than a cartelized or monopolized market; but unlike the 'New' Welfare Economists of the 1930s, he did not suppose that it was at all likely that cartels obliged to move into a competitive market would in fact be compensated for doing so. More realistic than his successors, he thought that there was no reason for a cartel to prefer the competitive equilibrium to one in which their bargaining power gained for them a higher level of utility than they would receive under competition without compensation.

[8] D. Hume, *A Treatise of Human Nature*, ed. D. F. Norton and M. J. Norton (Oxford: Oxford University Press, 2000), III.II.8.8, emphasis added.

[9] See for example Henry Sidgwick's *The Principles of Political Economy* (much admired by Edgeworth) on why an element of enforcement might be needed in socially beneficial cooperative action such as the protection of land from flooding. 'In a perfectly ideal community of economic men all the persons concerned would no doubt voluntarily

And yet it came to believed, first by economists and then by political scientists, in the middle of the twentieth century, that collaboration in large groups was not rational but almost paradigmatically irrational. The shift is most visible in Edward Chamberlain's *The Theory of Monopolistic Competition*, in which he gave a succinct statement of his general theory of perfect competition. If one assumes that each seller in a market 'seeks independently to maximize his profit', then there will be

a monopoly price for any fairly small number of sellers. No one will cut from the monopoly figure because he would force others to follow him, and thereby work his own undoing. As their numbers increase, it is impossible to say at just what point this consideration ceases to be a factor. If there were 100 sellers, a cut by any one which doubled his sales would, if his gains were taken equally from each of his competitors, reduce the sales of each of them by only 1/99, and this might be so small as not to force them, because of the cut, to do anything which they would not do without it. At whatever point this becomes true, the barrier to the downward movement of price from the point which will maximize the joint profits of all is removed. No one seller will look upon himself as causing the dislodgement, since he secures his gains with comparatively little disturbance to any of his rivals. Under these circumstances there is no reason for him to withold a shading of his price which is to his advantage, and which has no repercussions. Nor is there any reason for the others not to do likewise, and the price becomes the purely competitive one.[10]

Here we have – I believe – for the very first time a clear and unequivocal version of the modern theory, resting squarely on the idea of negligibility, which Olson thirty years later thought to be so obvious that its truth could simply be taken for granted. There are a number of possible reasons for the change, among them a terror of what mass collaborative action had been able to do to the world, but I do not want here to go over the historical ground which I covered extensively in *Free Riding*. The important point to make for my present purposes is simply that, as one might say, rationality has a history: what seems self-evidently rational to one age can seem the exact opposite to another, to such a degree that it

---

agree to take the measures required to ward off such common dangers: but in any community of human beings that we can hope to see, the most that we can reasonably expect is that the great majority of any industrial class will be adequately enlightened, vigilant, and careful in protecting their own interests; and where the efforts and sacrifice of a great majority are liable to be rendered almost useless by the neglect of one or two individuals, it will always be dangerous to trust to voluntary association.' H. Sidgwick, *The Principles of Political Economy*, 2nd ed. (London: Macmillan 1887), 410. Note how for Sidgwick the mark of 'economic men' is precisely that they cooperate. And note also how the theme of flooding seems to recur in this literature!

[10] E. Chamberlain, *The Theory of Monopolistic Competition* (Cambridge, MA: Harvard University Press, 1933), 49.

becomes very difficult for people now to see the real character of (for example) Hume's remarks on collaboration.

It is however not enough simply to point to the historically protean character of the idea of rationality: the standard modern theory acquires its force from a seemingly simple and obvious thought, and if earlier theorists did not see its force (so the argument would go) then so much the worse for them. After all, the way Olson formulated his position is straightforward. An action has either perceptible or imperceptible effects on a situation. If the effect is imperceptible, then no one can be said to benefit from it, and the action cannot be thought of as standing in a causal relationship to the outcome. There is no difference in this respect between an action which is part of a set of similar actions (like the farmer's), and one which stands alone (like the solitary crank's): exactly the same considerations apply, and if the effects are imperceptible then the action should not be performed, at least not for instrumental reasons.

Olson raised an interesting and potentially important point with his remark that 'Selfless behavior that has no perceptible effect is sometimes not even considered praiseworthy.' In general, a view like Olson's is perfectly compatible with the belief that we are under a *moral*, but not a prudential or instrumental, obligation to perform an action with imperceptible effects. Indeed, it is often assumed (though I have some hesitations myself about saying this) that Kant's idea of the categorical imperative was designed precisely to capture the fact that we might have a moral duty to act in such a way that if everyone were to do likewise there would be a clear good, even if we know perfectly well that not everyone, and indeed not anyone, is going to act like us. Some people have even supposed that this is the point of moral thinking: that it gets us to do things which narrow instrumental considerations may not permit. (This supposition is oddly like evolutionary explanations of altruism, in which we are alleged to be 'hard-wired' to do things which instrumental reasoning would lead us to reject.) In principle, I accept (like Lane) that there can be moral reasons for action which are not dependent on the acts of other people, and in situations where my action may not by itself make an appreciable difference, but Olson's remark reminds us that this is a more complicated matter than we might initially suppose. Some actions which, if everyone did likewise, would collectively produce a clearly desirable – and morally important – outcome, like preventing a devastating flood, may indeed not seem intuitively praiseworthy when performed in isolation. Contrast this with the man who stands up to protest against a cruel tyrant, but who finds himself alone: such a man has often seemed highly praiseworthy, though his effect on the tyrant's conduct is no greater than the crank's effect on the flood. I will return to consider this issue later in the chapter.

One common and intuitively plausible response to Olson (in line with the views of the theorists a century ago) is simply that there seems something very odd about it. As Brian Barry expostulated on reading this passage of Olson's book, 'this is surely absurd. If each contribution is literally "imperceptible" how can all the contributions together add up to anything?'[11] And if they do add up to something, why do we not think that our contribution is contributing to the outcome? However, Barry did not address the question of the crank, and indeed few people have done so, since it seems equally absurd (on the face of it) that anyone should suppose that the crank was acting rationally. But if that is so, Olson's argument is not self-evidently false. Another commonly observed difficulty about Olson's idea is that the mechanisms Olson proposed to solve the problem of imperceptibility, such as, in particular, coercive arrangements like a union closed shop, seem to face the same difficulties as the original voluntary agreements – if there is no reason to perform an action which has imperceptible results, then there is no reason to enforce a coercive arrangement on an individual when doing so has an imperceptible effect on the success with which a coercive mechanism is enforced. We all know that one or two burglaries in a neighbourhood do not suddenly call into question the presence of an effective police force; if there is a good reason to catch and punish those burglars, then there would seem to be an equally good reason for the criminals not to burgle in the first place (assuming – and this is of course a large assumption – that burglary is a kind of free riding, in the sense that the burglar too does not want to see the collapse of a stable property system from which he also benefits). So Olson's argument seems to be extraordinarily far-reaching, and most people (outside hard-line rational choice circles) have resisted it. But it is surprisingly hard to spell out just what is wrong with Olson.

Lane suggests another way of addressing the issue, with her remark that the pointlessness of a negligible contribution

is the wrong inference to draw from a continuous accumulation. If more is worse, then every bit more is every bit worse, and so the overall outcome is indeed worse for every bit – however minute – that has been added. No bit is strictly negligible in the sense of making no difference to the badness of the accumulation, although there may still be a question about whether the resulting worseness is itself negligible relative to some specified outcome or concern.[12]

---

[11] B. Barry, *Sociologists, Economists and Democracy* (London: Collier-Macmillan, 1970).
[12] Chapter 8 in this volume.

But if she means by this that *taken wholly in isolation from other contributions* each bit makes a difference, then that seems very implausible. On this account, Olson's crank is justified in what he is doing: if many bucketfuls would stem the flood, one bucketful by itself must make the situation better, however slightly. But common sense tells us that the damage a flood can do is extremely coarse-grained with regard to minute quantities of water, and a single bucketful cannot limit the damage to the slightest degree, though it can reduce the flood by some measurable amount – the difference between these two things is precisely what makes these situations puzzling, as I have said. If, on the other hand, Lane means that *taken in conjunction with other contributions* the crank's bucketful makes a difference, then I agree, for reasons I will turn to later. But that is slight consolation for the argument she is interested in, as she wishes to show how an isolated action such as our unilaterally reducing our carbon emissions can be justified in instrumental terms.

A third way of thinking about the problem, which Lane also wants to use to show that an isolated action can make sense, is represented by the position taken up by, among others, Derek Parfit and – with particular reference to climate change – John Broome. They have applied more widely an argument which applied initially to voting in elections, and which goes as follows. It is often thought that there is no reason to vote unless I have good reason to think that my vote will be pivotal, that is, change the result of the election, and in elections within large modern groups the chances of there being a pivotal vote is very small; in the modern United States the chance has been calculated at 1 in 60 million.[13] The difference which a particular result in the presidential election makes to me is likely to be fairly small, so on a self-interested calculation I should not vote (this is known to political scientists as 'the problem of turnout'). But Parfit argued that even a small increase in utility for each individual distributed across an entire population will come to a large number, and if I care about aggregate utility I may well conclude that – on the principle of maximizing the expected utility of my action – there is a reason for me to vote.[14] It should be observed that this is true only if one is interested in maximizing *aggregate* utility rather than *average* utility, itself a contentious issue; average utility comes out, of course, close to one's own utility. If, however, one can apply this kind of argument to climate change, as

---

[13] A. Gelman, N. Silver and A. Edlin, 'What Is the Probability Your Vote Will Make a Difference?', *Economic Inquiry* 50 (2012), 321–326.

[14] This has also become a standard view among political scientists, without (I believe) any awareness of Parfit's argument. See e.g. A. Edlin, A. Gelman and N. Kaplan, 'Voting as a Rational Choice: Why and How People Vote to Improve the Well-Being of Others', *Rationality and Society* 19 (2007), 293–314.

Broome does, a self-interested agent should be as keen to reduce his emissions as an altruistic one, since the catastrophic effects of global warming will greatly damage each one of us. Though Lane treats Broome's arguments as an example of moral reasoning, it can equally be an example of self-interested rational choice.

But even if we accept that this is a good argument when applied to voting, is it equally applicable to the issue of climate change? There are a number of issues here: for example, if I think I will be the only person to turn out for an election, I have an extremely good reason to do so, but that is patently not true of reducing my emissions to bring about a global reduction of carbon dioxide. The analogy in the case of climate change is therefore not simply with voting as such, but voting for a particular candidate knowing that there will be a large number (a flood) of votes for his rival; in this situation is there any point in being the lone voter? Will he not in fact look like Olson's crank? The answer to these questions is, on this view, given by the fact that there is a tiny but measurable probability of *any* vote having an affect on the outcome, and that therefore even a lone voter may have a reason to vote. Correspondingly there is a tiny but measurable probability that a single individual might bring about some alteration in the climate, and this is the conclusion Lane wants to reach. But there is a major problem about this argument. An election of the standard kind contains a determinate threshold: this is, after all, how it is possible in the first place for a vote to be *pivotal*. One vote *can* be enough to make the difference between victory and a tie. Can this be true of sorites-like problems such as climate change, which on the face of it do not exhibit anything like a threshold?

In *Free Riding* I argued that at least one plausible way to think about the sorites is along the lines urged by Timothy Williamson in his book on *Vagueness*,[15] that is, that we may imagine that embedded in any sorites is a threshold at which one state turns into another, but we cannot know where that threshold is. And Lane uses this idea in part to justify treating our contribution even to a sorites as potentially pivotal.[16] But this is to misunderstand the implications of the idea that a sorites contains a

---

[15] T. Williamson, *Vagueness* (London: Routledge, 1994).

[16] Chapter 8 in this volume: '[I]t has been argued that the sorites paradox (at what point does adding one grain of sand to others constitute a heap?) can be solved only by assuming that all cases of action toward an outcome presuppose a threshold, even if in some cases this threshold is vague. There is some point at which a pile of sand becomes a heap, even though it is only vaguely defined. Likewise, there may well be many thresholds in store within the global climate system with respect to human interests, whether or not they are vague, and whether such vagueness should be construed as ontological or epistemic.'

radically unknowable threshold: the possible existence of a threshold of this peculiar kind does *not* mean that my action can then be thought of as in principle pivotal. Take the original paradox of the heap: even if there is some embedded threshold at which a set of stones turns into a heap, we know that for any particular instance of a heap we must necessarily have overshot the threshold, since otherwise we could say precisely where the threshold is to be found. But then whatever contribution I make to a successful accumulation is unnecessary, since by definition it must be part of a redundant set of contributions, and therefore cannot be pivotal. Every instance of a sorites, I argued in *Free Riding*, is thus analogous to a serial vote in which long after the precise threshold is reached for the election of a candidate the voters continue to cast their ballots. If at the start of a roll-call vote we knew for certain that this would be the case, then we would be in exactly the same position as we are when faced with a sorites, despite the fact that as with all ballots there is precise information about where the threshold is to be found, since we would *also* know that the threshold will be overshot and that our own vote will be unnecessary. What a sorites adds to a situation like this is simply *certain knowledge* that if the threshold is reached then it will be overshot, rather than the mere *possibility* that it might be which is a feature of an ordinary serial vote. So the presumption that there is a threshold somewhere in the sorites does not permit the conclusion that my action might be pivotal; the fact that it is a sorites continues to imply, as it always did, that no contribution can be thought of as necessary to bring about the outcome. If this is correct, we cannot straightforwardly take existing theories about the instrumental rationality of voting and transfer them to the question of climate change.

Lane has one more argument to establish that we have instrumental reasons for unilateral action to reduce emissions, and it is by far her strongest; it is also the argument which seems to feature most extensively in public discussions of the question. It is the claim that unilateral action can be *exemplary*, and that it can start a kind of cascade of actions which in the end are enough to bring about change. But despite the obvious plausibility of this, I think exemplarity is a trickier notion than is often thought. Take again the case of Olson's crank. As Olson said, it is perfectly possible that his actions would be seen by his neighbours not as inspiring but as derisory. What would make the action derisory would in general be a strong sense on the part of the neighbours that – for whatever reason – not enough people are going to follow the example to give it a point. That illustrates the fact that exemplarity is not – so to speak – an inherent property of an action. An action can be exemplary in a context in which it can *for other reasons* prompt action; it is a little like the way that a supersaturated solution (to continue with liquid metaphors) can crystallize out when it is disturbed, though with the critical difference that it is not usually a sudden step-change but an accumulation of exemplary actions of various kinds which brings about the change. And that points up the problem with exemplarity in this context: to some extent we have simply transposed the problem away from its original setting to a new one. In this respect it resembles Olson's own solution to his problem, namely coercive structures, which as I suggested earlier merely transposed the problem of free riding away from its original location such as wage-bargaining to a new location, the organization of an effective collective against the free rider. I can be exemplary only if enough other people are willing to follow my example, and if that is the case it is likely that there will be a reasonable number of people already willing to step forward and act as examples: so why should I do so? (Again, we are talking purely about *instrumental* reasons.) Exemplarity turns easily into another case of free riding, and if we can explain why we should not free ride, we may not need examples – though of course they may in practice be useful as coordinating devices. But we will still need to explain why we should not free ride if we are to explain why *we* rather than other people should act in an exemplary fashion.

There may of course be other reasons of a broadly instrumental kind for unilateral action. In *Free Riding* I gave the instance of a lone Communist voting in Kensington, an instance Lane naturally picked up. The Communist knows his candidate cannot come close to winning the election, but he might reasonably want his fellow voters to know that Communism remains a political option. But these kinds of reason are not what we are concerned with, since once we admit them we are straying into a very different area. We want to know whether *from the point of view of affecting the electoral outcome* there is any reason for the Communist to vote, and the answer to that must be no. There may be many other broadly instrumental reasons for voting, and they may turn out in practice (by chance) to affect the outcome (like the many proposals by political scientists to affect turnout, such as bake sales at the polling stations), but they are irrelevant to the original question of what relationship our vote (or other contribution) is to the collective outcome we desire.

So how should we think about these things? Was Olson right after all? To answer these questions we need to return to the issue of redundancy, which (I claimed) is necessarily built in to examples of sorites.[17]

---

[17] The first person to argue this was Alvin Goldman in his path-breaking 'Why Citizens Should Vote: A Causal Responsibility Approach', *Social Philosophy and Policy* 16 (1999), 201–217, though he did not apply it to sorites cases.

Although it is seldom recognized – largely because it raises formidable philosophical difficulties – the fact that my action is rendered redundant by other people's actions does not mean that I have no causal influence on the outcome. The standard account of causation is that an event or action causes an outcome if the outcome would not have occurred without the prior event. But this is not always true. For example, two armed policemen pursue a bank robber, and one of them shoots and kills him. There can be no doubt that the policeman whose bullet hits the robber is causally responsible for the robber's death, but equally there can be no doubt that if he had not fired the other policeman would have done, with the same result. So we cannot say that the shot caused the death in the sense that if it had not occurred, the death would not have occurred. The policeman's shot was *sufficient* (in the ordinary language of causality) but not *necessary*. Redundancy has proven to be one of the most intractable problems in the current analysis of causation, but we do not need at the moment to provide a solution to the problem; all we need to do is to recognize that redundant causation is genuine *causation*, and that a redundant act stands in a straightforward causal relationship to its outcome. (This is after all why it is a problem).

This fact about redundant causation means that it can be rational on narrowly instrumental grounds to, say, cast a ballot in a serial vote, where by 'narrow' grounds I mean that the action stands in a genuine causal relationship to the outcome. But this comes with an important proviso: I must want to be someone who has a role in bringing about the state of affairs I wish to see. On the ordinary, 'pivotal' view of collective action, this is not something which needs to be independently specified, since by definition the state of affairs can be secured only by my action. But when we admit redundancy we have to separately specify my desire to see the outcome and my desire to bring it about. To see how this works, consider the roll-call vote, in which voters cast their ballots serially. An early voter might well know that there enough people in his camp to guarantee the result he wishes, and that if he abstains it will make no difference to the outcome. But that does not mean that if he *does* vote, he will not have been responsible for bringing about the result. In a straightforward first-past-the-post election, the people concerned can if they wish so engineer their participation in the vote that exactly the number necessary to secure the result they want will turn out, and then the puzzle of redundancy will not arise. But as I said, that will never be the case with a vague threshold – here, I know that if there *are* enough contributions to bring about a significant change, there must always be *more than enough* to do so, and my own contribution will not be necessary. But that does not mean it has no causal relationship to the outcome.[18]

One point to clarify: while this seems clearly true of an early voter, or an early contributor to a vaguely specified collective enterprise, in a serial process like a roll-call vote or the sequential piling-on of stones to make a heap, it will not be true of a late voter or contributor; by the time they do their bit, the result has already been decided. What of the usual situation, where we all go to the polls or make our contribution in a non-serial fashion, and do not usually know when we do so whether enough people have already participated to make our contribution irrelevant? (This, incidentally, may not be an anxiety in the case of climate change, since we can receive regular reports about the level of carbon dioxide in the atmosphere – structurally, climate change is more like a roll-call vote than a normal election.) In the case of a normal ballot, I argued in *Free Riding* that the *process of counting* is essentially serial. Our votes are (so to speak) arranged in a series once the counting process begins, and there is a large probability (in an election where our candidate has a reasonable chance of winning) that my vote will find its way into the series before the result is determined. This is concretely the case in British elections, where the paper ballots are literally sorted into piles for each candidate once the process of counting the votes begins, but it is implicit in the mechanical counting used in US elections. The same general argument would apply to cases where there is some mechanism other than counting which produces the result. Imagine people throwing stones over a wall with the intention of creating a heap on the other side (this seems to me pretty comparable to the psychology we bring to an election). They do not know as they throw their stones what the accumulation looks like, but at some (unspecifiable) point a heap will come into being, and there may be quite a large probability that any particular stone thrown over the wall contributed to the result). So if (say) in an election 10,000 votes were cast

---

[18] 'Enough' and 'sufficient' are revealing terms: in every sorites there is a point where we have 'enough', but the judgement of where that point is varies all the time. 'Enough', interestingly, was one of the central ancient examples of the sorites paradox. Galen listed 'satiety' among the things eliminated from the world if we took the sorites at its face value, among 'a heap of grain', 'a mass', 'a mountain', 'strong love' (the Syriac translator of the relevant text observed that this was οἶστρος, overwhelming desire – when does tepid affection become overmastering passion?), 'a row' (of objects), 'strong wind', 'a city', 'a wave', 'the open sea', 'a flock of sheep', 'a herd of cattle', 'a nation', 'a crowd', 'youth', 'manhood' and 'baldness'. Galen, *On Medical Experience*, ed. and trans. R. Walzer (Oxford: Oxford University Press, 1944), 114, 123–125. This is a text which was discovered in Istanbul in 1931, in the form of an Arabic translation of a Syriac translation of the Greek original. But it is a remarkably accurate translation, as was seen when it was compared with some existing fragments of the original.

for candidate A and 3,999 for candidate B, what I termed in *Free Riding* the 'efficacious set' must have consisted of 4,000 of the 10,000 votes cast for A, and if we voted for A there would be a 2 in 5 chance that our ballot was part of it. The smaller the majority, the larger the probability that our vote was part of the efficacious set, but even with a sizable majority (as in this example) the probability is still quite high that the efficacious set contained our ballot, and that our vote thereby brought about the result. Certainly it is high enough to make action worthwhile if we care about the outcome and care about our own agency in bringing it about.

But *should* we care about our own agency? This is an issue which has seldom been discussed in a focussed fashion, largely because, as I said, on a standard counter-factual account of causation the question does not arise. But with redundant causation we are faced with the possibility that if I act I can bring about the outcome – I can play a genuine causal role in the process – but my action is not necessary. At this point most economists (in particular) would say that despite the instrumental character of the action, and despite its causal relationship to a goal I might passionately wish for, it is not rational to perform the action, since rationality consists not merely in a successful choice of means to bring about an end, but in the efficient allocation of *all* our resources. If one solely considers one's budget of time or effort, one should not expend resources on actions that are not necessary.[19] There are a number of things to say about this.

The first is that the requirement that we should expend resources only on things that are necessary may be impossibly stringent. On the view of some major philosophers, we cannot say confidently that *any* prior event is *necessary* to bring about an outcome. The world is a complex place, and the possibility of over-determination is ever-present. Necessity, on this view, inheres in the relationship between the event and the outcome in the sense that if an event specified in the appropriate fashion occurs, then (by the general laws of physics etc.) the outcome necessarily follows. (If the first policeman pulls the trigger, the outcome is necessarily, given the prior state of the world, that the bullet kills the robber.)[20]

---

[19] See e.g. A. Downs, *An Economic Theory of Democracy* (New York: Harper and Row, 1957) p. 5: 'the economic definition [of rationality] refers solely to a man who moves towards his goals in a way which, to the best of his knowledge, uses the least possible input of scarce resources per unit of valued output.'

[20] The most well-known of these philosophers is J. S. Mill, who wrote in his *System of Logic* that 'the cause, philosophically speaking, is the sum total of the conditions, positive and negative taken together; the whole of the contingencies of every description, which being realized, the consequent invariably follows'. J. S. Mill, *A System of Logic Ratiocinative and Inductive, Being a Connected View of the Principles of Evidence and the Methods of Scientific*

But this is not the same as saying that the event was necessary for the outcome to occur, and it is this necessity which matters to the economist. The best we can do (on the view of these philosophers about causation) might be to choose among actions which are causally sufficient, and if that means that we have to abandon the picture of precise and rational budgeting, so be it. Even if we concede that some of our actions may be necessary to bring about a desired outcome, it does not follow that we should choose them over actions which are merely sufficient. In *Free Riding* I gave as an example an imaginary episode in which I am taking my dog for a walk on the beach, and I see a swimmer in difficulties. Someone else on the beach has also seen the swimmer. Only I can make sure that my dog does not run away and get into trouble; while if I do not help the swimmer, the other person will do so. But it is unlikely that I would decide that the best course of action for me must therefore be to hold tightly onto the dog's leash and not go to the help of the drowning man: the importance of the sufficient action trumps the necessity of the unimportant one.

The second thing to say is that there may be a rather deep puzzle about wanting outcomes and not wanting to bring them about. This is a puzzle which is concealed by the conventional language of 'rational choice', according to which the subject matter of rationality is choice – in other words, it is already presumed that agents are choosing to do things. But on the strict account of rationality which one finds for example in economics, action is a secondary consideration: rationality consists

Investigation, in J. M. Robson (ed.), *The Collected Works of John Stuart Mill*, vol. VII (London: Routledge and Kegan Paul, 1974), III.v.3. He meant by this, it is clear from his subsequent discussion, that we should strictly speaking term a 'cause' any antecedent condition to an event whose occurrence, given the other conditions in place, was 'invariably' associated with the outcome, and in whose absence the other conditions would not be so associated. (Mill's whole project was intended to avoid using the idea of 'necessity', the doctrine of which, he remarked, 'weighed on my existence like an incubus'.) But rather surprisingly, Hobbes may have thought something similar: in his *Of Liberty and Necessity* he remarked, 'I hold that to be a *sufficient cause*, to which nothing is wanting that is needful to the producing of the *effect*. The same also is a *necessary* cause. For if it be possible that a <u>sufficient</u> cause shall not bring forth the <u>effect</u>, then there wanteth somewhat which was needful to the producing of it, and so <u>the</u> cause was not *sufficient*: but if it be impossible that a *sufficient* cause should not produce the *effect*, then is a *sufficient* cause a *necessary* cause, for that is said to produce an effect *necessarily* that cannot but produce it.' T. Hobbes, *The English Works*, ed. W. Molesworth, 11 vols. (London: John Bohn, 1840), vol. 4, 274–275. When Hobbes talks about necessity, therefore, he may often have meant the kind of necessary relations which are part of sufficiency, rather than the necessity which is implied by counter-factual causation. Hart and Honoré, in H. L. A. Hart and T. Honoré, *Causation in the Law* (Oxford: Oxford University Press, 1985), also suggested that this account is closest in spirit to the idea of causation implicit in our legal system.

(as e.g. Frank Hahn put it)[21] simply in having 'an orderly personality', that is, having a consistent set of preferences over states of the world. Given that on the standard modern view a person's preferences do not have to be at all self-regarding in a crude fashion, that is, in a fashion in which his own self-regarding interests are involved, there is no reason why the set should not include all possible states, including ones in which he takes no part. (It is not even clear, at least to me, that they exclude *past* states – if I am simply ranking states of the world in terms of how I value them, why can't (say) the Terror be part of the ranking?). On this view, an agent's own activity figures as a detachable aspect of his preferences – he might have an independent desire to bring something about himself, but this is not integral to having a preference (he might simply like DIY).

But is it reasonable for me to want something, and – all other things being equal – not to want to bring it about? Suppose that there was a state of affairs which I wanted, and which I could bring about *with no cost to myself whatsoever* (say, I could do it in some magical fashion simply by thinking 'let it be'). Does it make sense for me to want this state of affairs and not to want to think 'let it be'? We would be inclined to say that there was something very odd about wanting something but not wanting to bring it about, if one could do so in this costless fashion. And if this is so, then situations where I want the outcome but do not want to bring it about have to be understood merely in the familiar terms of trade-offs between my costs and my benefits, where 'benefit' means the coming into being of a desired state of affairs. One might go further, if one agreed with Bob Goodin. He has argued about the idea of so-called pure altruism[22] that 'it depicts as charitable paradigmatically someone who not only would *let* others help instead, but, on balance, would *prefer* that others help instead. But that is just not what it is to *care* about someone else . . .'[23] In the case at least of altruistic wants, the desire to do something oneself for the other person seems to be integral to the altruistic

---

[21] See his remark in the Introduction to F. Hahn and M. Hollis (eds.), *Philosophy and Economic Theory* (Oxford: Oxford University Press, 1979), 12.

[22] A 'pure' altruist is interested only in the provision of a particular public good, and does not care whether it is provided through his own action or through that of someone else. See J. Andreoni, 'Giving with Impure Altruism: Applications to Charity and Ricardian Equivalence', *The Journal of Political Economy* 97 (1989), 1447–1458; J. Andreoni, 'Impure Altruism and Donations to Public Goods: A Theory of Warm-Glow Giving', *The Economic Journal* 100 (1990), 464–477; K. J. Arrow, 'Gifts and Exchanges', in E. S. Phelps (ed.), *Altruism, Morality, and Economic Theory* (New York: Russell Sage Foundation, 1975), 13–28, at 17–18; T. Nagel, 'Comment', in *Altruism, Morality, and Economic Theory*, 63–70, at 65.

[23] R. Goodin, *Reasons for Welfare* (Princeton, NJ: Princeton University Press, 1988), 157. He went on to observe that actual patterns of charitable giving suggest strongly that people do care about their own agency.

desire itself. One might also say, with regard to climate change, that at least at the governmental level there can be a democratic mandate from the electorate for their state to *act*, so that if we treat states as agents trying to decide whether or not to reduce their emissions in order to lower global levels of carbon dioxide, a desire for agency is – so to speak – built into their psychologies.

It is also true that from the point of view of some kinds of theories about democracy, agency is a key feature of what it is to be a democrat. Downs's argument famously presupposed that to be a voter is to be like a consumer in a market, so that if democracy could be defended as a political system it could be only on the grounds that it is an efficient means of allocating public goods. And on this view, it is true, agency is a puzzle – though as I have just argued, it *may* make sense even in this setting. But Downs's view is notoriously thin, and most modern democrats have repudiated it, insisting instead that there is some sort of *value* to democratic institutions (for example, the view I myself find most convincing, that we are in some fashion *self-legislators* only in democracies). But at the same time they have often accepted what I have called the 'economists' model' of rational behaviour, according to which we have no reason to vote; the combination of these two commitments has produced many of the distinctive features of modern democratic theory, including above all its tendency to downgrade voting and elevate such things as deliberation. This is true even of Jeremy Waldron, who is the most inclined of all modern theorists to give full weight to voting.[24] By stressing *equality* as the prime feature of majoritarianism, he has laid himself open to the reasonable response that a lottery is even more egalitarian, and his principal answer to this has been that 'majority-decision differs from the coin-tossing method in giving positive decisional weight to the fact that a given individual member of the group holds a certain view' (p. 113). But in part he was forced to say this because he too believes that a vote cast in a large group 'may be said to carry no weight at all' (p. 114), though he was avowedly troubled by the implications of this for majoritarianism. If one adds to Waldron's insistence on equality an insistence on *agency* – that the point of voting is that we can *bring about* the outcome – one has, I think, an appropriate defence of actual democratic institutions. And if this is true, a committed democrat should *eo ipso* believe that he should vote even when his vote may be redundant.[25]

---

[24] See in particular his defence of majoritarianism in J. Waldron, *Law and Disagreement* (Oxford: Oxford University Press, 1999), esp. 101–118.

[25] For more, see R. Tuck, *The Sleeping Sovereign* (Cambridge: Cambridge University Press, 2016).

So my view is that if at the very least we care about an outcome and wish ourselves to bring it about (something which is assumed in Lane's chapter), it can make sense to make a negligible contribution to a collective enterprise if enough other people are going to do so, but not if they are not. When I have presented this argument, I have often been met by disbelief that my contribution in some enormous collective enterprise can possibly be taken to have a causal efficacy with regard to the outcome. To make this point myself, for the purposes of argument, I have sometimes quoted the title of Spike Milligan's wartime autobiography, *Adolf Hitler: My Part in His Downfall* – the joke being precisely that Milligan did nothing exceptional in his time as a soldier. Did Milligan really bring about Hitler's downfall? I think the answer has to be yes. There is no reason why great events should have to have strenuous causes: one of the remarkable things about collective human endeavour is that it makes it easy to do things which an individual would find virtually impossible. If ten of us gather round a car and lift it, the fact that each exerts rather little energy in doing so does not mean that somehow we are not really responsible for lifting it; it just means that it has made it very easy for us to do so. Each individual is still as responsible (conditional upon the others' actions) as he would be if he were alone and using an efficient jack. In the case of Hitler's war, the fact that some people did exert enormous energy, and indeed gave their lives, and others did not, does not alter the account of causal responsibility – the men who survived and did rather little were as responsible for Hitler's downfall as those who died in battle. It does not follow that we should not praise those who died far more than those who survived; if one of us, while lifting the car, collapsed and died from his exertions, and if it was tremendously important to shift the car, he would be remembered with more honour, but no one would change the causal story of the event. And of course it is right to say that it was the sacrifice of the dead soldiers which made it possible for the living soldiers to bring about the outcome.

However, in the case of climate change I am afraid that the immediate conclusion to draw from what I have been arguing is that the popular idea is correct: if the Chinese (or some sufficiently large section of the human race) do not introduce appropriate measures to reduce emissions, then there is indeed no *instrumental* point in our doing so, in the sense that our individual actions will in truth have no causal power over any improvement in the climate. But there are two important further implications of my general view which offer a degree of consolation to a climate activist. First, on this view it is rational to stick to an agreed target even in cases like global warming where there is no precisely defined threshold, since one will wish to be part of the efficacious set. The knowledge that there is this reason for contributing ought then to make such an agreement easier to reach, as the participants should understand that each one of them has a reason not to defect. Though it should of course be acknowledged that human beings are often not rational, and that mechanisms of enforcement are often desirable – just as they are in (what I would regard as) the comparable case of making sure that we do something in the future that we know will benefit us. In each case there is a good reason to perform the action, but ordinary human imprudence may intervene unless our good intentions are bolstered by something like an enforceable commitment. This is one of the key differences between my position and Olson's, as Olson believed that there is no good reason to perform the action until a mechanism of enforcement has been put in place, whereas I (like most people before the mid-twentieth century) believe that there is a good reason to collaborate, and that enforcement mechanisms are there in the event of failure. So ordinary politics offers a degree of hope which on the economists' model of rationality it should not, particularly in the international sphere where effective coercive mechanisms are always likely to be lacking.

The more interesting consolation is something to which I gave insufficient thought in *Free Riding*, and which I have taken more seriously as a result of my conversations with Lane. If I am producing carbon emissions, I am contributing to the overproduction of carbon dioxide, even though if I were unilaterally to stop I would not contribute to the diminution of carbon dioxide in the atmosphere. This sounds paradoxical at first hearing, but it simply follows from an account of our actions as causally efficacious *conditional upon the actions of other people* and from the vagueness of the goal. If enough other people are putting carbon into the air, by joining them I am contributing to the existing levels of carbon, but if not enough people refrain, my own refraining will not contribute to an appreciable diminution in the levels. What this means is that essentially the problem for an isolated agent faced with something like climate change is the old problem of *dirty hands*, and it resembles the situation often faced by people living under unjust political regimes. By refusing to take part in political activity I can reassure myself that I am not contributing to the unjust politics of my society, even though I may also know perfectly well that no one will take any notice of my abstention and there will not be enough citizens like me to bring about political change. Put in this way, we can see that this is not at all a paradoxical situation, but one which is entirely psychologically familiar.

But if we take this argument seriously in the case of climate change, it may lay a very stringent requirement on our actions. From the perspective of a view like Lane's, as she says explicitly, every little counts, so that even a small reduction in our own carbon footprint is worth making as a contribution to a better outcome. But if we turn this around, and say that everything I am currently emitting, even if in very small quantities, is a contribution to a bad outcome, and if we believe that a small reduction cannot be justified as a contribution to a good outcome, then it looks as if the correct conclusion is that I should eliminate *any* action of mine which can be taken to contribute, in however small a degree, to the accumulation of carbon dioxide in the atmosphere, and that half-measures are pointless. If Milligan could feel that in making his contribution, however small, to the war against Hitler he brought about Hitler's downfall, then one of Hitler's soldiers must correspondingly have felt that however small his role in the German Army, he was fully responsible for what that Army did. Though I believe this to be a correct conclusion, I am not quite sure how to respond to it, since it seems potentially to put a heavy load of guilt on all of us. I suspect the appropriate response is, once again, *politics*, in the sense that above everything we should try to reach a formal and explicit agreement which would *inter alia* determine the levels of emissions which collectively we should try to reach, and we should not try to follow Lane into the sphere of unilateral action.

In conclusion, I want very briefly to touch on the subject of *purely moral*, non-instrumental reasons for action in this area. First, if one is a moral consequentialist, then one's moral reasons for action cannot be non-instrumental. They may differ from the reasons of the wholly self-interested agent, as we saw above in the case of Parfit, but many of the same problems will apply (possibly, as comes out with the idea of the 'pure' altruist, even the problem of *agency*). One might be a non-consequentialist and hold that for some reason there is a moral duty to limit one's carbon output, but it is not clear on anything other than non-consequentialist grounds what actually *matters* about increasing levels of carbon dioxide. On the kind of account which (as I said earlier in the chapter) often seems to lurk behind a version of Kantianism, actions acquire their 'moral' significance precisely at the point at which instrumental reasons somehow ought to apply but do not. It is not that instrumental reasons belong to a wholly different domain from moral ones, when we are thinking about these cases, but rather that we 'ought' to perform an action which (so to speak) mimics instrumentality: if enough people do what is right, out comes the desirable result, and that is *why* we should do what is right. This is very far removed from the terrifying glamour of *fiat justicia ruat coelum*. (J. S. Mill had this in mind in his well-known remarks in chapter 1 of *Utilitarianism* about Kant's concealed consequentialism.) A non-consequentialist moral view may be relevant if we restate the problem of free riding as one of *unfairness*: if other people contribute to the common enterprise, why should I free ride on them? But, first, this familiar and often reasonable thought will apply only to situations where enough other people are contributing so that I can benefit from their actions: unless I am benefitted by your action, I cannot be said to be unfair to you in not reciprocating. Are his neighbours being *unfair* when they do not join in with Olson's crank? We may well say that someone is being unfair if they do not contribute when others do; but on my view, in those situations there is also an instrumental reason for contributing. Second – and rather hesitantly – I find these kinds of claim about reciprocity more puzzling than is often thought. Suppose other people take the view that simply as a human being I am entitled to their care, for example through a National Health Service (which in the United Kingdom is non-contributory) Does that create a new set of obligations on me, for example to moderate my lifestyle? People often talk as if it does, but why should it? And if the rest of the world works to diminish climate change, why is that not like setting up a National Health Service from which I, a non-contributor, am going to benefit? The moral arguments in this area seem on inspection to be no more straightforward than the purely instrumental ones.

10 Optimism, Pessimism and Fatalism

David Runciman

There often appears to be a close relationship between environmental politics and a sense of fatalism. Environmental threats can leave people feeling powerless. It is a small step from feelings of powerlessness to shoulder-shrugging resignation: if we believe there is little we can do to remedy a situation, then there is little point in trying to remedy it. Two features of environmental politics combine to inspire a sense of fatalism. One is the complexity of the problem: environmental science is not easy to understand and its models contain sufficient caveats and contingencies to confuse non-experts about what is really at stake (experts can be confused as well). The other is the scale of the challenge: putative fixes require large-scale collective action whose effects will take many years or even decades to play out. Anything we do collectively will not achieve results for a long time. Anything we do as individuals has little impact on collective outcomes. Of course, these difficulties of complexity and scale are hardly unique to environmental politics: collective action problems are rife in modern politics.[1] But they are particularly acute in the face of an unfolding crisis like climate change. The gap between the lived experience of individuals and the knowledge and the patience required to make a real difference leaves the door open to widespread resignation: what will be, will be.

So far, so gloomy. Just as it is commonplace to associate environmental politics with fatalism, it is equally commonplace to associate fatalism with pessimism. A future we cannot control is one in which we are powerless to stop the worst from happening. However, in this chapter I want to question the second link – between fatalism and pessimism – as a way of reflecting on the first – between fatalism and environmental politics. The history of political thought provides a resource for doing both. It shows

---

[1] M. Olson, *The Logic of Collective Action* (Cambridge, MA: Harvard University Press, 1965); J. S. Coleman, *Individual Interests and Collective Action: Studies in Rationality and Social Change* (Cambridge: Cambridge University Press, 1986). For an alternative view, see R. Tuck, *Free Riding* (Cambridge, MA: Harvard University Press, 2008).

that fatalism does not have to be pessimistic. It can also be optimistic, though that orientation is rarer and easy to miss. As Andrew Gamble writes in *Politics and Fate*:

Fate as destiny has acquired a sombre association with death, destruction and ruin . . . To be fatalistic is to believe that events are unfolding in such a way that no other outcome is even possible; it is to be without hope that any change could be brought about by human agency. This does not mean that the outcomes are necessarily bad. It is possible to be a fatalist and an optimist. In religious ideas of providence, for example, the world is working in a pre-ordained way but the consequences are benign. It is more usual, however, to find fatalism linked to pessimism . . . The word fate is rarely used to describe something which happens to an individual which is good; it is much more common to find it applied to events and outcomes which are regarded as bad.[2]

Fatalism leaves little room for human agency to make a difference, but whether you consider that a good or bad thing depends on what sort of difference you believe human agency capable of making. It does not follow that human life will turn out badly just because human beings are not masters of their own fate. For those with limited faith in human nature that might be one reason to suppose it could still turn out well. So to be without hope that human agency can be responsible for meaningful change is not necessarily to be without hope altogether. However, hopelessness is often how it turns out.

Gamble identifies optimistic fatalism with religious ideas of providence, which implies a contrast between pre-modern (and perhaps non-Western) notions of fate and more modern, secular modes of thinking about the same idea. If you believe in a benign divinity who controls your fate and the fate of the universe, then it can make sense treat the impotence of human agency with relative cheerfulness. Thank God it's not just down to us! By contrast, if you believe in democracy and the power of the state (as many moderns do), then the inability of human beings to master their fate is much more alarming. It implies a failure of the whole project of modernity, which valorizes the capacity of individual and collective human agency to take on the future and make of it what we want and need it to be. Of course, many moderns, from Machiavelli on, have understood the capacity of chance to wreck the best-laid plans. It does not follow that human beings are therefore powerless in the face of the future (Machiavelli certainly didn't think so). But chance is not the same as fate. To be a fatalist is to assume not merely that the future is unpredictable but that it will take care of itself. We won't make something of it. It will make something of us. As Gamble puts it: 'This is a very

---

[2] A. Gamble, *Politics and Fate* (Cambridge: Polity Press, 2000), 12.

modern fatalism which regards the end of politics, the end of history, the end of the nation-state, the end of authority and the end of the public domain as marking the end of the ambition of human beings to be the controllers of their own fate. Instead they have been enslaved by the forces that modernity has unleashed on the world.'[3]

It is not hard to see how this kind of fatalism might translate to environmental politics: the forces that modernity has unleashed stand ready to overwhelm us in ways that we no longer have the capacity to control. No benign divinity exists to remedy the situation. However, a contrast of this kind – between pre-modern and modern conceptions of fate, between religion and democracy, between fatalism and anti-fatalism – is too crude. One of the things that the history of modern political thought can teach us is that the lines between an understanding of chance and of fate, and between optimistic and pessimistic fatalism, are blurry and easily crossed. It is possible to believe that free-thinking citizens are powerless to control their destiny while believing that the future is on their side. It is equally possible to believe in democracy and also to have a strongly developed sense of providence. For that reason anti-fatalism and fatalism can sometimes be very hard to tell apart. In this chapter I want to explore these possibilities through the ideas of two modern thinkers who thought deeply about the varieties of fatalism and the limitations of human agency: Tocqueville and Hayek. I then want to apply some of their insights to the challenge of environmental politics in order to highlight the risks that optimistic fatalism poses alongside the more pessimistic kind.

Tocqueville thought that a pervading sense of fatalism – what he called 'the doctrine of *fatalité*' – represented one of the most serious threats to modern, democratic societies. This fatalism was closely tied to an idea of providence. Democracy was, as Tocqueville depicted it, God's providential plan for the universe, so that to oppose its inexorable spread 'would then appear to be a struggle against God himself'.[4] However, democratic fatalism was not simply, or even primarily, a religious phenomenon. The evidence for the inevitable coming of the democratic age was supplied by social science: it was a conclusion that could be drawn from a scientific study of the 'pattern of events' and by tracing their historical causes and effects. Democratic fatalism was not spread by preachers. Rather, it was the preserve of historians and political scientists, who treated the future as explicable only in terms of the patterns of the past. 'It is not enough for

---

[3] Ibid., 13–14.
[4] A. de Tocqueville, *Democracy in America*, ed. H. C. Mansfied and D. Winthrop (Chicago: Chicago University Press, 2000), 617.

them to show how the facts have come about,' Tocqueville wrote. 'They also take pleasure in making one see that it could not have happened in any other way.'[5] Tocqueville did not believe that democratic social science could foretell the future in such a way as to serve as a guide to human action: it did not perform an overtly predictive function. Rather, it provided the backdrop to human decision-making and it pervaded those decisions by inculcating a general sense that human agency was subject to forces beyond its immediate power to control. Democratic fatalism arose out of a belief that the future belonged to democracy, in contrast to a belief that the future lay open for any democracy to shape to its own ends.

Fatalism in this sense has a number of distinctive features. First, it is not far removed from the essential sense of confidence in democracy that Tocqueville believed was required for its successful functioning, especially as he had encountered it in the United States.[6] Democracy in America worked because Americans believed in their democracy. Their faith enabled them to persevere with a form of politics that appeared from day to day to be dysfunctional, divisive and superficial. It was a long-run bet on a system that suffered from a widespread set of short-term weaknesses (including a pre-occupation with elections and electoral cycles at the expense of more far-sighted decision-making). The strengths of democracy, Tocqueville believed, reveal themselves only over time (which is one reason why they are eventually perceived by historians and political scientists). Yet faith in long-run advantages that are not visible from moment to moment can slide into a fatalistic assumption that the future will take care of itself. The line between essential confidence and unwarranted faith is a fine one. It can be very difficult to tell when it has been crossed.

Second, not only is this kind of faith a secular extension of religious ideas of providence, it may also come to stand in opposition to forms of religious faith. Tocqueville thought that American confidence in the democratic future needed to be undercut by American religiosity in regard to personal experience and personal responsibility, in order to give individuals a sense that their destiny was not simply bound up in their collective fate. This was primarily a Protestant sensibility and it was one of the advantages of American society that its democratic citizens were often also individualists in a religious sense. Such individualism

---

[5] Ibid., 472.
[6] For a fuller version of this argument, see D. Runciman, *The Confidence Trap: A History of Democracy in Crisis from World War I to the Present* (Princeton, NJ: Princeton University Press, 2013), 'Introduction'.

does not map in a straightforward way onto democratic habits of mind; in many cases, it confounds them, by making individuals personally responsible for their ultimate fate. So, from Tocqueville's perspective, it was not a case of democracy countering religious fatalism; it was a case of religion countering democratic fatalism. One of the future challenges for democracy, Tocqueville believed, was whether it could achieve the same results in predominantly Catholic countries, including his own, France.

Finally, democratic fatalism does not simply engender a passive mode of politics. Fatalism is usually described, as I described it in the opening paragraph of this chapter, as a form of resignation: the fatalist, knowing there is nothing to be done about the future, does nothing. Tocqueville, by contrast, noticed that democratic fatalism was consistent with the restless and impatient quality of American political life. One of the reasons that American democracy delivered results in the long run was that it was so adaptable: the energy that ran through American society generated a changeable, erratic, impatient political culture that rarely stopped to reflect on what it was doing. American democracy, as Tocqueville remarked, makes more mistakes than other systems of government but it corrects more mistakes as well. To put it another way, its changeability meant that it rarely got stuck with the mistakes that it made. At any given moment it might look like it was not working, but if you persisted with it, something else would come along soon (as they say about the weather in various parts of the United States: if you don't like it, just stick around for a few hours). So faith in the future might not merely be consistent with, but in large part derive its security from the mindless energy of the present.

Furthermore, faith in the future is consistent with recklessness as well as restlessness. That is one of the hallmarks of optimistic fatalism: if the future can be left to take care of itself, then it liberates the inhabitants of the present to take risks, since their mistakes will not have lasting consequences. This is a form of moral hazard. Of course, it is not simply an American or a democratic mode of thought. Many moderns have embraced restlessness and recklessness of this kind. Lenin, for instance, was an optimistic fatalist in this sense: he believed that the revelations of Marxist social science had liberated enlightened political agents in the present to take their chances, since they could hardly wreck the future; all they could do was either hinder or accelerate it.[7] Lenin's faith in the future was ideological and his perspective was a grandiose and self-aggrandizing one. Tocqueville observed a reckless fatalism that was far

[7] See, for example, V. I. Lenin, *Two Tactics of Social Democracy in the Democratic Revolution* (Geneva, 1905): www.marxists.org/archive/lenin/works/1905/tactics/.

more pragmatic and prosaic. He gave an example of what he had in mind when he told the story of his encounter with some steamboat builders during his travels around the United States.[8] American steamboats of the period (the early 1830s) were notoriously rickety and unreliable; Tocqueville nearly drowned when one he was travelling on sank during a trip down the Ohio River. Why weren't they sturdier, he wanted to know. He was told by the people who built them that the speed of technological progress in the United States meant it was not worth their while updating the existing crafts when new, improved models were always just around the corner. Better to take their chances in the present than to try to second-guess the future.

But is this sort of recklessness really a form of fatalism? No, if fatalism entails a belief that the future has been mapped out in advance, so that there is a pre-determined pattern to unfolding events. Blind faith in technological progress does not suppose that future developments can be known before they happen: they are often the products of chance, even if their cumulative effect is to reconcile democracy with God's providential plan for the universe. Nonetheless, this kind of faith in progress shares with more conventional fatalism a sense that the future has a momentum of its own that curtails the capacity of human beings to shape their own destiny. Our destiny is not within our power to control even though we can be confident that it will ultimately serve our interests. Of course, this mindset would be entirely self-defeating if everyone was conditioned by it in the same way: a nation of shipbuilders who each persisted with their rickety vessels while waiting for someone else to come up with something better would make no progress at all. But it would not take much to entice a few of them to tinker with their own crafts if no one else was doing it, and a little tinkering can generate a lot of change. As Tocqueville said: the condition of democratic life is that more mistakes get made and more mistakes get corrected. What is significant is that a move from waiting for others to do the tinkering to doing the tinkering yourself does not require a huge shift in outlook. Faith in progress can make you passive or it can make you twitchy; depending on your circumstances (both of temperament and of opportunity) it might make you move from one state of mind to the other quite quickly. Each can be a manifestation of a form of fatalistic recklessness.

In a series of exchanges with his friend John Stuart Mill, Tocqueville discussed the varieties of fatalism. Mill distinguished between what he called 'pure' fatalism and what he described as the prevailing 'modified'

---

[8] This episode is recounted in G. W. Pierson, *Tocqueville in America* (Baltimore: Johns Hopkins University Press, 1996), 645.

version.[9] Pure fatalism was a belief that the future had already been decided. It made its adherents either stupefied or serene; in either case they were accepting of the path that was chosen for them. It was almost always a manifestation of a set of religious or traditional beliefs and Mill associated it with the philosophy of the Far East. Modified fatalism was a more modern and Western phenomenon. It derived from an understanding that individuals are the product of social and economic forces beyond their power to control; it could be reinforced by social science (including the new science of psychology). Modified fatalists might be passive and resigned as a result of a sense of their powerlessness. But just as likely they would become impatient, complaining, dissatisfied. The impersonal forces that conditioned their fate might be a provocation to rail against it. Equally they might become complacent, happy to count their blessings. But complacency could also make modified fatalists wilful and reckless, believing that their fate gave them license to abdicate personal responsibility for their actions. Modified fatalism, Mill thought, was an essentially childish state of mind.

Democratic fatalism was far closer to the modified than the pure version. It was not serene. It was alternately impatient and complacent, or as Tocqueville put it, 'ardent and resigned'. Indeed, one of the distinguishing characteristics of a democratic society was how nearly related to each other these states of mind were. Passivity and activity in the face of the future were not necessarily opposed to each other. They were, if anything, two sides of the same coin, the twin conditions of a social state that both enabled and encouraged its inhabitants to see themselves as being swept along by the rapid tide of historical progress.[10] Active modern citizens were not the tide itself; they were simply riding it, some with pleasure, some with abandon, some with fear and some with

---

[9] J. S. Mill, The Collected Works of John Stuart Mill, *vol. VII:* A System of Logic Ratiocinative and Inductive (Toronto: University of Toronto Press, 1974), 'Of Liberty and Necessity'; see also J. S. Mill, *The Earlier Letters of John Stuart Mill 1812–1848* (London: Routledge & Kegan Paul, 1963), and A. de Tocqueville, *Selected Letters on Politics and Society*, ed. R. Boesche (Berkeley: University of California Press, 1985).

[10] There is a contemporary medical analogy here: anxiety and depression are often viewed as very different conditions, one twitchy and reactive, the other listless and passive. But they are in fact very closely related to each other. As Louis Menand writes, summarizing the current medical consensus: 'Anxiety is hard to distinguish clinically from depression. We picture anxious people as hyper and over-reactive, and depressed people as lethargic and indifferent. But depression, too, can be understood as a response to a perceived or imagined threat, and antidepressants like Prozac and Effexor also alleviate anxiety. Medically, anxiety and depression appear to be two related symptom clusters arising from (or causing) the same underlying neurological condition.' L. Menand, 'The Prisoner of Stress', *New Yorker* (January 27, 2014): www.newyorker.com/magazine/2014/01/27/the-prisoner-of-stress.

indifference. Democracy promoted modified fatalism because it made individuals feel small in the face of the crowd, because it encouraged them to discount the short-term failings of their political system for the sake of a future that would ameliorate them, because it made them impatient for rewards that were always somewhere out of reach. The result was that democratic citizens had a tendency to relapse into a condition of childishness, sometimes blithely cheerful, sometimes sullenly resentful, sometimes wildly angry, but rarely if ever believing that the future was theirs to make for themselves. Someone or something else would take care of it for them.

Neither Tocqueville nor Mill believed that this characterization of democracy was either inevitable or universal. They were both anti-fatalists. They hoped that democratic societies, starting with the United States, might learn to dispense with modified fatalism: it ought to be possible for them to grow up and thereby grow out of it. This would be achieved by political education, by the accumulation of experience and above all by the knowledge that comes with making and learning from mistakes. Children grow up when they discover that that their actions have consequences; the same, both Mill and Tocqueville hoped, would be true of democracies, as their inhabitants discovered that the future is made out of their accumulated actions in the present. Although we cannot choose the future we want we can be sure that the future we get will be the result of the routine choices we make. That ought to be enough to make us take our choices seriously. However, the risk remained that problems of complexity and scale would overwhelm democracies and leave them trapped in their fatalism. One reason this risk was real was that such fatalism can be hard to distinguish from the energetic impulses that are required to counter it. A lot of activity in the present, far from safeguarding against fatalism, can mask a slide into it.

Contemporary environmental politics in Western democracies seems to chime with many of these fears. It has no single face. It appears intermittently frightened, indifferent and blithely optimistic. It chops and changes, responding to short-term triggers and avoiding long-term commitments. Political arguments about climate change rarely arrive at the question of our shared responsibility. More often they are about apportioning blame and identifying culprits, whether these are countries or individuals, corporations or pressure groups, politicians or the public. The impatience manifests itself as an intolerance of complexity; the recklessness as an assumption that time is on our side. It is not, of course, all passivity and resignation. There is a lot of frenetic activity, from activists on the one hand and from innovators and techno-enthusiasts on the other. Few of these people think of themselves as fatalists, or if they do they are also doing their best to resist the passivity that is often assumed to accompany that state of mind (some environmental campaigners perhaps believe that what they are doing is futile in the face of overwhelming odds but persist anyway in order to position themselves against the prevailing fatalism of the age). So much is evident in the case of environmental activists who are working frenetically to wake democracies up to the scale of the problem. But it is equally true of those who believe that the best bet for finding a way out is to pin our faith on the ingenuity and adaptability of open societies. From this perspective it is always a mistake to try to second-guess the future, because we can have no idea what resources will be available to us in the future to meet the challenges we will face. After all, who saw the Internet coming?

This kind of faith in technological progress often presents itself as explicitly anti-fatalistic. It is the doomsters (including the environmental activists) who are derided as the prisoners of fatalism, seeking to bind our political choices in the present to a future whose imperatives they believe they can judge in advance. Techno-optimism can present itself as anti-fatalistic in two respects. First, it presupposes a future that remains open to human input: how it will turn out depends on what we come up with. Second, it goes along with a series of active political commitments in the present. If innovation depends on free markets and the free exchange of ideas, then we need to hold our nerve and limit our impulse to use the power of the state to interfere with these innately creative forces. A 'green' politics that takes the present state of knowledge as the best guide to the future and utilizes the power of the state to control it, through taxation, market regulation and injunctions to personal behaviour, will, according to its critics, result in the inevitable curtailment of our future options. Better to curtail our present impulse to interfere in order to leave the future open. That means a political choice to set limits to political interference. The impulse to tie the hands of politicians can paint itself as anti-fatalistic because it imagines two possible futures: one in which we hold our nerve and ride the wave of innovation; one in which we lose our nerve and stifle it. Which future we get is down to us.

A significant intellectual source for this line of thinking is Hayek. In this context Hayek is revered both as an anti-fatalist and as an optimist who understood that the human potential for creative innovation always outstrips the capacity of human beings to wreck their future, so long as we have the courage to embrace the uncertainty of the future in the choices we make in the present. Hayek is celebrated as the thinker who identified spontaneity, not pre-emption, as our best hope for a safe and prosperous continuation of the species. That, for instance, is the role he plays in Matt Ridley's *The Rational Optimist*, a book that largely dismisses the threat posed by climate change and captures this line of thinking. Ridley believes that the real threat comes from present anxieties producing pre-emptive political action that stifles innovation and the free exchange of ideas ('When I look at the politics of emission reduction', he writes, 'my optimism wobbles').[11] However, Hayek himself is a more complex figure, grappling with a more ambivalent intellectual heritage, than the enthusiasm of his present champions would indicate. Hayek does not simply stand for optimistic anti-fatalism over pessimistic fatalism and for spontaneity over pre-emption. He also reveals the ways in which fatalism and anti-fatalism can slide into each other, with the result that creative activity and passive indifference become hard to tell apart. The roots of these ambivalences and uncertainties lie in the ideas of Tocqueville.

Tocqueville was one of Hayek's intellectual heroes. The gathering of economists and political thinkers that Hayek initiated in 1947 to discuss the threat posed by state planning and majoritarian politics to human creativity and freedom was originally to be called the 'Tocqueville-Acton Society', after the two thinkers Hayek considered the greatest nineteenth-century defenders of the freedom of the individual in the face of the coming age of democracy. (The group eventually got named after its meeting place and became what it is today the 'Mont Pelerin Society' – too many participants thought Hayek's preferred title made it sound like a Catholic debating society.) Tocqueville, in Hayek's eyes, understood better than anyone the risk posed to modern democracy by a putative 'tyranny of the majority', which would sacrifice spontaneity for the false security of government control. Hayek took the title of his 1944 book *The Road to Serfdom* from the closing pages of Tocqueville's *Democracy in America*, where Tocqueville had mapped out the possibility of a democratic future in which ordinary citizens, fearful of uncertain and unpredictable outcomes, hand over power to tutelary states that promise to control the future for them. In the aftermath of the Second World War, Hayek's fear was that the battle-scarred citizens of Europe, tired of the privations they had endured, would demand a safer future in which much less was left to chance. Worse, their politicians would give it to them, in the form of extensive welfare states, high taxation and nationalized industries. The result would be the death of freedom. Hayek saw all this as a form of democratic fatalism: politicians, in thrall to the idea that they were powerless to resist what the majority wanted, were drifting along with their fate. Letting the people choose the future they preferred

---

[11] M. Ridley, *The Rational Optimist: How Prosperity Evolves* (London: Fourth Estate, 2010), 347.

ultimately meant stripping them of the capacity to make meaningful choices. This was the road to serfdom.

Hayek regarded the Mont Pelerin Society as a vanguard attempt to inculcate the virtues of anti-fatalism in a fatalistic age. He wanted everyone, voters and intellectuals alike, to understand that state control was not the only future available and there was no reason to suppose that politicians were powerless in the face of the demands of the present. But it would take courage and determination to resist those demands. The defence of freedom required faith in a future that was beyond anyone's capacity to control. Hayek saw a pressing need to defend a way of thinking that 'regards with reverence those spontaneous social forces though which the individual creates things greater than he knows', as he put it in a speech marking the launch of his new society.[12] There were various institutional measures that could be adopted to preserve spontaneity and Hayek spent much of the rest of his life promoting them through his political writings.[13] These included constitutional limits on the power of the majority to control political decision-making, robust protection for an independent judiciary, reform of electoral processes to limit the influence of interest groups and the promotion of market reforms across areas of creeping governmental control. But he never deviated from his central aim in the mid- to late 1940s: to defend and celebrate a conception of the future that was reliably resistant to political interference, and to encourage humans beings to put their trust in it.

This is certainly optimistic. But is it anti-fatalistic? Not entirely. It is a mode of thought that has links, both temperamentally and intellectually, to some of the forms of fatalism that Tocqueville identified. A commitment to an open future is not simply an embrace of adaptability over constraint. It is also a form of binding: it requires that we limit our impulse in the present to guard against the worst that might happen in the future and in doing so we rule out our ability to pre-empt it. Ruling out pre-emption ties the present to the idea of an open future in such a way as to ensure that the future is impervious to our best guesses in the present about what it might contain. It makes precautionary thinking impossible. To put it another way, it is a form of faith, not simply a form of rationalism. This is a faith that has its basis in rationalism, as Tocqueville recognized. It is a secular product of modern social science: the study of cause and effect and the expectation that the future will

---

[12] Quoted in Gamble, *Politics and Fate*, 196.

[13] See F. A. Hayek, *The Constitution of Liberty* (London: Routledge & Kegan Paul, 1960); F. A. Hayek, *Law, Legislation and Liberty: A New Statement of the Liberal Principles of Justice and Political Economy* (London: Routledge & Kegan Paul, 1979).

continue to follow the patterns of the past. Hayek was a Catholic but he was primarily speaking as an economist. Having confidence in the creative capacity of spontaneous social forces may be a reasonable expectation. But it still requires a leap of faith (or 'reverence', as Hayek puts it).

Trusting in a future that we cannot control is consistent with the full range of fatalistic inclinations that Tocqueville identified, from resignation to reckless energy. A lot of social and economic activity might look like the sort of energetic and ingenious experimentation that is needed to counter the assumption that the world is drifting towards a miserable fate (for instance, that it is drifting towards runaway climate change whose effects we will be unable to deal with). But it is hard to tell apart from the sort of mindless activity that imagines something will always come along to rescue us in the end so long as we keep moving. How can we be sure that something will come along in time? The truth is that we can't. We just have to put our faith in it. Rationally speaking it must be possible that pre-emption is sometimes a better bet than experimentation, if we are to assume that the future truly lies open. Why rule out the option that acting on our present fears will prevent the worst from happening? If it is because experimentation has been the better bet up until now – Ridley's book, for example, makes a lot of play of the wolf-crying features of past environmental scares, from population explosions to global cooling, which had they been heeded would have left us far worse off than we are now – then this looks like a more conventional kind of determinism that treats the future as pre-determined by the patterns of the past. In the case of environmental scare stories, thinking that the future will be like the past is certainly optimistic but it is not obviously rational. There is no reason to suppose that acting on our present fears is always wrong just because it has tended to be wrong in the past. This time may be different (because some time is bound to be different). Rational optimism has an inherent tendency to slide into optimistic fatalism.

It is also a mistake to assume that majoritarian tyranny invariably comes down on the side of security and governmental control. That was Hayek's assumption and he thought he had warrant for it from Tocqueville. But Tocqueville understood that there was more than one way the tyranny of the majority could play out. Majoritarian politics can certainly be passive and risk averse, resulting in what he called the 'mild despotism' of public opinion, which stifles innovation and generates a cautious political culture that defers to state control. But it can also be wild and reckless, resulting in impatience with all forms of officialdom and contempt for expert opinion. Alongside the road to serfdom runs the road to anarchic populism, which is fuelled by an impatience that discounts caution for the sake of immediate pay-offs. When Tocqueville talks about the tyranny of the majority he describes lynching and race riots, war fever and witch hunts, not just sheep-like acquiescence in the death of freedom. Of course lynching and race riots, war fever and witch hunts are destructive of freedom as well, but they reflect the chaotic and untutored side of democratic life, where blind frustration collides with state control. Democratic publics, as well as wanting to control the future, intensely dislike anyone who makes them wait for it to arrive. Anger bubbles over and violence ensues.

Hayek was fixated on only one side of democratic fatalism as Tocqueville had understood it: the drift into servility. He did not take enough account of the other side: the wilfulness of the present. Wilfulness does not look like fatalism because it is active and energetic. But the sort of wilful energy that disregards the future consequences of present actions in favour of momentary satisfactions is entirely consistent with a belief that the future will take care of itself. Indeed, such a belief can fuel much of the anger and irritation, which gets directed at those who appear to be standing in the way of the unfolding future and holding it up. Hayek saw little risk of this in 1947. He was far more worried that after a generation of wild and reckless politics – from the First World War through the Great Depression and then on to the Second World War – the instincts of the majority would all be the other way. Voters would be shepherded into the grip of politicians who promised to nail down the future so that it could not break free and wreak more havoc. Hayek wanted them to know they had a choice. They could choose to leave the future open. If they did not, they would end up trapped in a future they could not control because their freedom of choice would have been lost to them.

Hayek thought that the desire to control the future produced blinkered politics and constrained options. But so does the impulse to leave the future open. It makes for a cramped and bitty politics, in which most political energy is directed against short-term provocations. Arguments go round in circles since no one is in a position to nail anything down. The possibility of meaningful discussion about long-term choices is dramatically curtailed. This is a recognizable description of democratic politics, both in Tocqueville's time and in our own. It is democracy in frenetic, irritable mode, frothing over with surface activity that serves as an outlet for political frustrations that have nowhere else to go. It does not look fatalistic because it is so full of sound and noise. But it is fatalistic, because most of it is just noise.

2017 is not 1947. The balance of risk has changed. If we are trapped, it is not by servile instincts towards governments that know best. It is by a relentless and reckless scepticism directed against governments that are assumed not to know what they are doing and against forms of expert authority that presume to know better than we do what the future has in store. This anarchic populism is more pronounced in some places that others – more pronounced in America than in some parts of Western Europe, more pronounced on the right than on the left. But it is present everywhere – on the left as well as on the right – and it is spreading. Its spread has been greatly accelerated by the new information technology, which makes it far easier for irritations and frustrations to find an outlet. It also makes it easier for witch-hunts and other forms of mob rule to gather a head of steam. Ours is a far less violent world than it was in the last century, never mind in the century before that. But the tyranny of the majority in the twenty-first century has more in common with the intemperate passions of Tocqueville's America of the early 1830s than with the exhausted fears of Hayek's Europe of the late 1940s. It is ardent, not resigned, and it makes it very hard for elected politicians to do anything that might rouse its anger.

If the balance of risk has changed, then the choice before us is not as Hayek described it. He thought we needed to defeat fatalism by choosing to put our faith in an open future. If we think that by leaving the future open we have shrugged off fatalism, then we are mistaken. It risks leaving us stuck with a politics that lacks the resources to move out of frenetic, resentful mode and into something more durable and reflective. So it is not a straight choice between fatalism and freedom. We need to find a way between the fatalism that gives up on personal freedom and the fatalism that can't give up on it even when it needs to. The reason that Hayekian confidence in an open future is fatalistic is that it precludes the possibility of a future in which this turns out to be the wrong approach because the risk of disaster is too great. A truly open future must include the possibility of circumstances in which failure to plan for the future proves catastrophic. Indeed, it moves from a possibility to a probability to a racing certainty the longer the future lasts: at some point pre-emption will turn out to be a better bet than innovation, if only because nothing lasts forever. The fact that it is very hard to know when that point has been reached is not sufficient reason to stop looking for it. Techno-optimism is not self-fulfilling. It is ultimately self-defeating, because it locks us in to a mindset that becomes blind to its own shrunken horizons.

The trouble with all fatalisms – optimistic and pessimistic, ardent and resigned – is that they preclude alternative futures. The particular trouble with optimistic fatalists like Hayek and Ridley is that they tend to reject this characterization of themselves, because they think of themselves as anti-fatalists. Pure fatalists of the kind described by Mill – people who believe their future has already been mapped out for them and that what looks like freedom of choice is merely going through the motions – do not tend to mistake what they are. They know that they have given up on personal autonomy. But modified fatalists can be self-deceived, just as irresponsible children can sometimes think that because they are taking their own decisions they have suddenly become adults. One of the fundamental difficulties of environmental politics is that the sceptics have come to see themselves as free-thinking and open-minded, breaking the chains of conventional wisdom and group think. They have bought into the Hayekian contrast between freedom and fatalism. But if that is a false choice – as I believe it is – then the self-perception of the Hayekians is also wrong. This kind of open-mindedness is its own form of close-mindedness, because a commitment to an open future closes down our options in the present. It is insufficiently sensitive to the full range of future possibilities. It is also insufficiently sensitive to the ways that contrarian scepticism does not confront the tyranny of the majority so much as feed off it.

In the case of climate change, there is some contemporary evidence that epistemological scepticism and optimistic fatalism go together. One striking feature of the current political debate about climate change is the extent to which sceptics have come to impugn the motives of climate scientists and others, supposing that where the scientists posit a consensus there is in fact a conspiracy at work to push a political agenda. The 'climategate' affair, following the emergence of emails from the University of East Anglia in 2009 that appeared to show that researchers had cherry-picked evidence and suppressed dissent, helped to fuel the conviction of sceptics that conspiratorial forces were at work. The scientists involved were subject to widespread censure and abuse, although the scale of their indiscretions was minor and better explained as corner-cutting carelessness than criminal conspiracy (subsequent inquiries found no evidence of scientific misconduct). Newspapers lined up to cast doubt on the entire global warming 'industry' and public opinion concerning the threat posed by climate change was at best left confused and at worst violently antagonistic by the revelations.

Two features stand out about stories like these. First, sceptics are not bravely fighting against the fatalistic and fearful tide of majoritarian opinion, as Hayek believed he was doing in 1947; if anything, they are riding it, in its active rather than passive mode. The politics of climate change stokes the resentful and angry side of democracy, through which public opinion acts as an easily roused vehicle of irritation and impatience. It is much harder to build a majority in favour of concerted political action based on scientific opinion than it is to find a majority willing to discount scientific opinion because of the resentment that comes with being told what to do. It is relatively easy for the majority to shrug off difficult truths, because expert opinion can always be painted as elitist. Sometimes the shrugging off turns ugly: witch hunts and personal assaults (online if not in person) are rife in the world of climate politics, where ad hominem and ad feminam attacks are the norm, not the exception. Environmental politics in contemporary democracies is not as violent as nineteenth-century American politics, but it is just as confrontational.

Second, researchers in the psychology of climate scepticism have found a strong correlation between suspicion of scientific consensus and faith in free market ideology: in the words of one study, 'rejection of climate science is strongly associated with the endorsement of a laissez-faire view of unregulated free markets.'[14] The same study noted a similar correlation between mistrust of the scientific consensus and what it called 'conspiracist ideation': climate sceptics tend to think that warnings about the risk of future environmental catastrophe are best explained as attempts to capture and manipulate the political process for personal or ideological gain. Conspiracism – the tendency to posit conspiracies as the best explanation for complex or chance events – is often seen as a negative and broadly pessimistic state of mind; conspiracy theories are viewed as the preserve of the angry, the embittered and the dysfunctional, the 'losers' of modern society.[15] But in this case conspiracist ideation goes along with a form of optimistic fatalism. Faith in free markets gives us reasons for supposing that no technical or environmental challenge is as dangerous as it looks, so long as we let the market do its work of experimentation and innovation. Any attempt to interfere with the market can be explained only by nefarious motives. Pessimism is revealed as a marker for the desire to manipulate the future. The optimists are the ones who want to let it run its course.

In his 1956 book *The Power Elite*, C. Wright Mills identified two ways in which democratic publics tend to misunderstand the way that power is exercised in their societies. Some people, he says, become fatalists, and put their faith in providence and fortune. Theirs is a politics of drift. Others become conspiracists, supposing that history is in the grip of manipulative elites. Theirs is a politics of resentment. On this account, fatalists are passive and withdrawn, seeing in the complexity of political affairs only a reflection of their own impotence, as a result of which they often choose to avoid political engagement altogether. Conspiracists are

---

[14] S. Lewandowsky, K. Oberauer and G. Gignac, 'NASA Faked the Moon Landing – Therefore (Climate) Science Is a Hoax: An Anatomy of the Motivated Rejection of Science', *Psychological Science* 24 (2013), 622–633.

[15] For a wider discussion of attitudes to conspiracism, see A. Moore, 'Conspiracy and Conspiracy Theory in Democratic Politics', *Critical Review* 28 (2016), 1–23.

active and angry, railing against a politics that has been stolen from them by a tiny few and wanting to grab it back. Mills wrote: 'To accept either view – of all history as conspiracy or of all history as drift – is to relax the effort to understand the facts of power and the ways of the powerful.'[16] There is much truth in this. But Mills was wrong to suppose that these two views of the world are opposed to each other: that passive fatalism stands in contrast to active resentment. They often go together, as they do in contemporary climate politics. Climate scepticism is not anti-fatalistic. It is an expression of one kind of fatalism, in which faith in markets goes along with resentment at political control and optimism about an open future produces a blind suspicion of anyone who pushes an alternative. Fatalism does not have to be pessimistic and it does not have to be passive. Yet even when it is active and hopeful, it is still blinkered, with all the ugliness that blinkered politics invariably pro-duces. It is hard to imagine a politics of climate change that does not have some ugly features. In that sense, democratic politics is always blinkered: it is utopian to suppose there could ever be full transparency and full disclosure of what is at stake. But there is still a difference between politicians who are alive to the risks of getting trapped in optimism and the ones who believe that optimism is its own guarantee of a secure future.

Tocqueville was right to think that one of the fundamental challenges of democracy is to find a way between these competing fatalisms. It is possible to get trapped in myopic and relentless activity just as it is in cowed and risk-averse passivity. Tocqueville also saw that one of the perennial temptations of democratic life is to suppose that non-democracies do it better. For those who want decisive action on climate change – including extensive government investment in green technolo-gies – autocratic regimes can appear to offer a solution. The present rulers of China, for instance, appear far better equipped to override public indifference to long-term risks, simply by dint of their ability to impose their will through centralized state power. If Chinese technocrats want to 'green' a city, they can, without public inquiries and planning rounds and local elections and all the other noise and clutter of demo-cratic politics getting in the way. But this is a false hope: autocratic politics, for all its decisiveness, is less adaptable in the long run than messy and mindless democracy.[17] Non-democratic regimes might make fewer mistakes than democracies, but they tend to get stuck with the mistakes they make. Their decisiveness tempts them down blind alleys

---

[16] C. Wright Mills, *The Power Elite* (Oxford: Oxford University Press, 2000), 27.

[17] For a fuller account of this argument, see Runciman, *The Confidence Trap*.

and their intolerance of dissent keeps them stuck there. Here a Hayekian scepticism about governmental attempts to second-guess the future is warranted. As Ridley likes to point out, the record of autocratic regimes in taking decisive action to tackle long-term threats is pretty disastrous. Exhibit number one is China's 'one-child' policy of the 1970s, a cruel and self-defeating attempt to curtail one form of growth for the sake of a sustainable future. Lasting demographic shifts are far more efficiently driven by the prosperity and freedom of choice that comes from relatively open societies – as women acquire the capacity to make their own reproductive choices – than from dirigiste ones.

Yet the fact that autocratic regimes make a mess of trying to control the future does not mean that democratic regimes should avoid all attempts to do the same. Ridley argues that China's one-child policy was an outcrop of Western environmentalism, which exported its inflated Malthusian fears to the one society politically desperate enough to implement them.[18] But it would be absurd to argue that because you can draw a line from environmentalism to botched experiments in population control you can also draw a line the other way, i.e. to suggest that all environmental planning will end up as oppressive and counter-productive as China's attempts to manage its population. Precisely because democracies are more adaptable than autocracies they are better able to experiment with pre-emptive long-term solutions as well as experimental short-term ones. They are far less likely to get trapped with the ones that don't work. To rule out all planning for the long term in favour of endless experimentalism is unnecessarily restrictive. It is also potentially self-defeating. It reinforces the angry and irritable side of democratic politics which comes to operate as a barrier to the adaptability on which its long-term viability depends.

To be an anti-fatalist is to be alive to the risks that come from the full range of fatalisms, optimistic and pessimistic, experimental and pre-emptive. For both Mill and Tocqueville the surest way to discover these risks was through the widest possible range of lived experience and above all the experience of making mistakes: that was how human beings learned that the future, for all its imperviousness to human control, still depended on the choices that they make in the present. The difficulty with that model of anti-fatalism when it comes to the environmental challenges of the twenty-first century is the familiar one of their complexity and scale. It is far harder to learn from your mistakes when individual mistakes get lost in the morass of collective action and collective mistakes

---

[18] M. Ridley, 'The Western Environment Movement's Role in China's One-Child Policy', *The Times* (7 November 2015), www.rationaloptimist.com/blog/one-child-policy/.

take years or even decades to reveal themselves. Under those circumstances, some planning for an uncertain future is required if we are not to get trapped in the mindset that assumes the free exchange of ideas will always produce the resources we need when we need them. Optimistic fatalists imagine that there is no mistake that cannot be corrected in time so long as we leave the future open. One reason for pessimism in the present is that the optimistic fatalists appear to have the upper hand. In this respect, their fatalism might yet be self-fulfilling. Climate change raises the risk of getting trapped in a future whose effects, while presently unknown, will be bad enough to trump the capacity of human ingenuity to ameliorate them. This is what makes the politics of environmental catastrophe different and it is the reason why all forms of fatalism are worth resisting while we can.

Afterword
Climate Change in the Light of the Past

Quentin Skinner

I begin with some information about climate change that is readily available to anyone with access to the Internet. The accuracy of the information is of course disputed by many who have an interest in disputing it. (Science is always enmeshed in politics, as several chapters in this volume vividly illustrate.) But the claims in question seem by now to be generally accepted by those with any competence to judge. During the past century, global surface temperatures have risen by an average of approximately 0.8°C, with two-thirds of that increase occurring since 1980. Between 1950 and 2009, global sea levels rose at an average annual rate of approximately 1.5 millimetres, although for unknown reasons this rate almost doubled between 1993 and 2009. Meanwhile arctic summer ice has been in continuous retreat since the end of the 1970s, with a downward slope of 13 percent during that period, resulting in an estimated loss of half a million square miles per decade.

We may in part be witnessing the unfolding of a natural and cyclical process. But there are elementary theoretical grounds for concluding that our own behaviour must be making things worse. Suppose you wanted to warm the planet's lands and seas, what would be a rational strategy to pursue? One method would be to consume carbon-based fuels at a colossal rate, since carbon dioxide absorbs heat emitted from the earth's surface, thereby preventing its escape and raising surface temperatures. But this of course is what we are currently doing. According to the US Department of Energy's figures for 2010, the global emission of carbon dioxide during that year amounted to over thirty billion tonnes, and the figure continues to rise. A scarcely less effective method would be to deforest on a huge scale, since trees absorb carbon dioxide, thereby inhibiting its warming of the earth's surface. Again, this is what we are currently doing. The World Wildlife fund estimates that 130,000 square kilometres of forest are currently being lost every year. A further method would be to raise livestock as a staple source of food, since cattle produce methane, and methane has a warming effect more than twenty times greater than that of carbon dioxide. Once again, this is what we are currently doing. According to the UN News Centre, the rearing of cattle currently occupies 30 percent of the earth's land surface, giving rise to almost 40 percent of all human-related methane in the atmosphere. We have strong theoretical grounds for concluding that the climate changes we are already experiencing must in part – perhaps in large part – be anthropogenic in character.

We know the risks: more intense heat waves, increased coastal flooding, decreased availability of fresh water. We also know how to mitigate these effects: we must change our diet, halt deforestation and above all reduce our dependence on fossil fuels. The problems seem so grave, and the solutions so obvious, that one might have expected some massive precautionary action to have been taken by now at state or even global level. But so far nothing has been done to slow the pace of these changes on anything like a massive or even a discernibly effective scale.

Why not? One reason that is likely to strike any reader of the present volume is that we are ill-equipped by our inherited traditions of thinking about the natural world to deal adequately with our current predicament. Among the developed nations of the West, these traditions have been largely Judaeo-Christian in origin, and the Old Testament account of the relationship between God, mankind and nature is one in which man is given dominion 'over every living thing' and 'over all the earth'.[1] God's act of creation is initially described simply as an exercise of his power to produce abundance and fruitfulness. But as the story unfolds Adam is told to subdue the earth, and Noah is assured that 'all that moveth' has been delivered into his hands for his use.[2] This is not to say that nature is viewed solely as a resource to be exploited. God intends Adam to act as an improver and 'keeper', and admonishes him not merely to be fruitful but to replenish the earth.[3] But nature is never viewed as sacred. To say that mankind has dominion over the earth is to affirm that he has the right to dispose of it at will, and this is to imply that nature cannot be divine.[4] As Annabel Brett points out in Chapter 2, we are left with little sense that the relationship between mankind and the natural world is governed by any clear moral principles. Within this tradition of thinking, such principles are generally seen as applying exclusively to the interconnections between human beings, not between human beings and anything else.

The tradition of which I am speaking is complex, however, and one strand of Christian thinking has always interpreted the claim that God

---

[1] Genesis I:26 and 28.   [2] Genesis I:28 and IX:2.   [3] Genesis I:28 and II:15.
[4] See J. Passmore, *Man's Responsibility for Nature* (London: Duckworth, 1974), 6–12.

designed nature for human use in a more conservative (and conservationist) way.[5] If we are speaking of God's design, some have argued, then
it can only be impious to suggest that we can hope to improve on it.
Malcolm Bull quotes fascinatingly in Chapter 5 from John Muir, the late
nineteenth-century pioneer of American environmentalism, who
declared that nature is 'God's first temple', and thus that the existing
state of the natural world must be preserved not merely without alteration but with reverence and awe. As the editors point out in their
Introduction, some writers on 'green' political theory have recently written in similar terms, pointing to a supposed decline from a golden age in
which nature was treated with due respect to our modern era of exploitation and waste.

These lines of thought were never dominant in the Christian tradition,
however, and in the early modern period of European history the idea of
nature as a resource to be exploited entirely for human benefit gained
a prominence that it has never subsequently lost. One reason for this
development – a reason not often emphasized – is singled out by
Malcolm Bull in Chapter 5. During the era of the Renaissance, the
valuing of *otium*, the life of contemplative leisure, came to be associated
with the vice of idleness, and in particular with the avoidance of our civic
and religious obligation to promote the common good. But as Bull notes,
uncultivated nature could similarly be regarded as idle and unproductive,
with the result that the preservation of forests and wildernesses easily
came to seem a positively immoral commitment.

Of far wider influence was the view of nature that accompanied and
helped to legitimize the scientific revolution of the seventeenth century.
According to the programme outlined by Francis Bacon in his *Novum
Organum*, the chief value of scientific enquiry stems from its capacity to
procure 'the relief of man's estate and the increase of his power over
Nature'.[6] Bacon acknowledges that 'Man by the Fall declined both from
his state of innocence and his lordship over creation.'[7] But the promise
he holds out is that 'this loss can be repaired by the Arts and Sciences.'[8]
'By means of many labours, the created world will at last be subjected to

---

[5] See the discussion in K. Thomas, *Man and the Natural World* (Oxford: Oxford University
    Press, 1983), esp. 24–25.
[6] F. Bacon, *Instauratio Magna, pars secunda: Novum Organum* (London, 1620), book II,
    aphorism LII, 359: 'emendationem Status hominis, & Ampli[fic]ationem potestatis eius
    super Naturam'.
[7] Ibid., 360: 'Homo enim per lapsum & de Statu Innocentiae decidit, & de Regno in
    Creaturas'.
[8] Ibid., 'reparari potest … per Artes & Scientias'.

the providing of bread to mankind, that is, to the uses of human life.'[9] From this perspective, to think of nature as chiefly in need of care and protection came to be regarded as a benighted attempt to prevent the increase of human prosperity and happiness. As Robert Boyle was to complain in his *Free Enquiry into the Vulgarly Receiv'd Notion of Nature* in 1686, 'the veneration, wherewith Men are imbued for what they call *Nature*' has proved to be nothing more than 'a discouraging impediment to the Empire of Man over the inferior Creatures of God'.[10] Boyle fears that, while men continue to look upon nature 'as such a venerable thing', they will 'make a kind of scruple of Conscience to endeavour so to emulate any of her Works, as to excel them'.[11] But he retorts that, in the name of human improvement, these scruples must now be overcome, and with the rise of modern science in the West they were indeed largely set aside.

More recently, we have been further discouraged from worrying about our destructive proclivities by a range of arguments about rational social behaviour that have enjoyed wide currency since the Second World War.[12] As Melissa Lane and Richard Tuck both note in their chapters in this volume, these arguments originally derived in large part from the investigation of voting behaviour in democracies. The effect of anyone's particular vote, it was observed, will generally be of negligible significance in relation to any electoral outcome. But if the effects of an action are imperceptible, there can be no instrumental reason for performing it. These contentions have recently been applied to the debate about climate change as a means of assuring us that anything we may attempt to do at the individual level to alleviate global warming will have an outcome so negligible as to make it irrational to undertake such actions at all.[13] With this assurance has come the claim that individual citizens cannot therefore be said to have any moral obligation to alter their current behaviour, especially if others continue to act as before. The implication is that, if any precautionary action is to be envisaged, it will make sense only if it takes the form of national and preferably global initiatives.

---

[9] Ibid., 'Creatura ... per labores varios ... tandem ex parte ad panem homini praebendum, id est, ad usus vitae humanae subigitur.' For a full account of this theme in Bacon's philosophy, see C. Webster, *The Great Instauration* (London, 1975), 324–342.

[10] R. Boyle, *A Free Enquiry into the Vulgarly Receiv'd Notion of Nature* (London, 1686), 18–19.

[11] Boyle, *Free Enquiry*, 19. Cf. Passmore, *Man's Responsibility for Nature*, 11.

[12] On the remarkably recent development of this understanding of rational action, see R. Tuck, *Free Riding* (Cambridge, MA: Harvard University Press, 2008), esp. 1–15.

[13] On this view of negligibility, see M. Lane, *Eco-Republic: Ancient Thinking for a Green Age* (Oxford: Peter Lang, 2011), esp. 51–76.

Unfortunately, as John O'Neill and Thomas Uebel mention in Chapter 7, and as David Runciman particularly emphasizes in Chapter 10, this orthodoxy has been flourishing at a time when a related analysis of rational behaviour has led to the suggestion that any actions taken at national or global level may be likely to do more harm than good. Runciman traces this conviction back to the bromides issued by Friedrich von Hayek and his followers during and after the Second World War, which have lately been applied to the debate about climate change by such commentators as Matt Ridley in his book *The Rational Optimist* of 2010. Drawing on the work of Alexis de Tocqueville, as Runciman shows, Hayek assailed the preference for improved social security that so many governments voiced in the aftermath of war. The surest means of increasing prosperity, Hayek retorted, will always be to minimize state interference, to put our trust in competitive markets, and thereby give free rein to the ingenuity and innovation that such systems can best promote. Applied to the debate about climate change, the main effect of this optimistic fatalism, as Runciman nicely labels it, has been to make its exponents critical of any tendency to act on our current fears. Once again we are being urged to leave the future open and trust to human ingenuity to find solutions once the need for them becomes imperative. Meanwhile we should leave things alone.

Of all the reasons for our present inaction, perhaps the most significant is that climate change is such a very inconvenient truth. It is glaringly inconvenient to many powerful interest groups, including airlines, car manufacturers and the suppliers of gas and oil. These industries and their backers are regularly accused not merely of ruthless lobbying, but of deliberately spreading doubt and confusion about the findings of climate science, and many opinion polls suggest that their tactics may be enjoying widespread success. But it is probably of more importance that the truths about climate change are no less inconvenient to ordinary citizens. Many have taken up the cry that whatever we do as individuals will make no appreciable difference, and have also made it clear that they are not prepared to alter their way of life, and will vote out of office any elected politicians who try to make them do so. The danger is the opposite of the one diagnosed by Hayek: people are not asking for greater security; they are asking for greater freedom to live their lives as they currently desire. The outcome has been that policies which may already be scientifically indispensable remain impossible to implement in any democratic state.

The dusk may be gathering, but this is the moment, we are told, when the owl of Minerva can be expected to spread her wings. So where is wisdom to be found? What intellectual resources can we hope to mobilize? Here the contributors to the present volume have some provocative suggestions to make, and in putting them forward they strike out across some new terrain. By contrast with the narrow and technical way in which environmental issues are sometimes debated, they seek to connect our immediate concerns about our ecosystem with a number of broader topics in the history of Western political thought.

What, first of all, should we say to those who insist, in Hayekian vein, that governments ought not to take any strong precautionary measures at the present time? David Runciman's chapter offers a powerful response, focusing on the refusal of those who hold this view to recognize that climate change may have altered the terms of the entire debate. The optimistic fatalist believes that taking arms against an unknown future will always be less sensible than leaving things to work themselves out. But it is a mere leap of faith to suppose that this will always be the rational policy to adopt. If, as Runciman puts it, the future is genuinely open, it must contain the possibility of a catastrophe for which it would be irrational not to prepare ourselves. Moreover, is it really true that what is to come is still unknown? The possibility of catastrophe seems to be looming with frightening credibility, and it may soon be too late even to act on our present fears.

Next, what should we say to those fellow-citizens who contend that, since there is nothing that anyone can do to make an appreciable difference, there is little point in doing anything at all? Melissa Lane seeks in Chapter 8 to meet this objection head-on, insisting that it may be instrumentally rational even at the individual level for each one of us to alter our behaviour. Richard Tuck picks up her suggestion in Chapter 9, although he remains unconvinced by some of her arguments. Lane and Tuck are in agreement, however, that some compelling normative considerations can be invoked, and it seems to me that this is the juncture at which our inherited traditions of moral and political thinking may be capable of offering us the most direct and effective support.

As Lane emphasizes, one promising line of argument, well-known to students of classical and Renaissance philosophy, centres on the concept of exemplarity.[14] To the educational theorists of the Renaissance it seemed obvious that, as Thomas Elyot wrote in his *Boke named the Governour* of 1531, the reason why there is no science of greater 'commodity and pleasure' than the study of history is that it affords us so many

---

[14] On this element in Renaissance thought, see T. Hampton, *Writing from History: The Rhetoric of Exemplarity in Renaissance Literature* (Ithaca, NY: Cornell University Press, 1990). See also the symposium on exemplarity in *The Journal of the History of Ideas* 59 (1998).

striking and memorable examples of virtues to be emulated and vices to be eschewed.[15] It is true that, if we look to our classical sources for such *exempla*, they tend to offer us images of heroic virtue that might seem doubtfully relevant to the present time. But if we turn to the revision of the classical tradition initiated by Christianity, we find the ancient virtues of courage and heroism largely transmuted into an ideal of fortitude, an ideal of courage to suffer and heroic willingness to endure. Nietzsche was to excoriate this transformation as the triumph of a slave morality, but it had the effect of bringing to prominence a value that may yet prove to be of crucial significance in our current predicament: the value of self-sacrifice, the belief that we should be willing to incur personal loss in the name of securing a greater or future good.

The relevance of this ideal to the debate about climate change seems direct and obvious. Some people undoubtedly feel a strong desire to limit their engagement with the carbon-based economy, and in many instances this involves them in considerable sacrifices of their immediate interests. It is true that – as Tuck objects to Lane – it may be hard to make the case that such people are acting in an instrumentally rational style. Their behaviour is in a sense rational, since their goal is evidently to bear witness to the importance of self-sacrifice and their conduct undoubtedly conduces to that end. But they can hardly fail to acknowledge that their individual efforts will have little effect, and cannot in consequence be said to be acting with full instrumental rationality. The same applies to those who fall under the influence of such role models; they appear less as instrumentally rational agents and more as persons who have experienced an epiphany that has changed their outlook on life.

As a number of commentators have begun to point out, however, such exemplars may nevertheless be of increasing importance in relation to the politics of climate change.[16] The value of self-sacrifice retains a powerful resonance even in the secularized cultures of the modern West, and it is plausible to suppose that such principled and altruistic persons may sometimes exert a disproportionate influence. Moreover, there is evidence that large numbers of young people may be willing, even in the absence of such exemplars, to make spontaneous changes to their standard of living in the name of securing a better future. One recent survey of over 6500 students from 34 countries found that, at least in the prosperous nations of the developed world,

[15] Thomas Elyot, *The boke named the Governour* (London, 1531), fol. 38v; cf. also fols. 36r-v.

[16] See M. Lane, *Eco-Republic*, esp. 179–182, and M. Maniates and J. Meyer (eds.), *The Environmental Politics of Sacrifice* (Cambridge, MA: Harvard University Press, 2010).

there was a high and consistent willingness to envisage such sacrifices in the name of future good.[17]

Of all the lines of moral argument we have inherited, the one with the strongest power to make us reconsider our individual duties in relation to climate change is probably the so-called harm principle. As classically formulated by John Stuart Mill in the opening chapter of *On Liberty*, the principle states that 'the only purpose for which power can be rightfully exercised over any member of a civilized community, against his will, is to prevent harm to others.'[18] But the principle can equally well be stated in negative terms. If some action of mine is directly causing harm to others, then that action must be contrary to justice and ought not to be performed. But the carbon emissions for which each one of us is responsible – however negligible they may seem when measured against the total – undoubtedly cause harm to others. According to the World Health Organization's report on air pollution of March 2014, 3.7 million people died prematurely in 2012 as a result of outdoor air pollution, one of the main causes of which is carbon emissions from transport and industry. Everyone who drives a car contributed to those deaths.

Richard Tuck ends his chapter by suggesting that this argument places upon us such a heavy load of guilt that the appropriate response must surely be to aim for collective agreements rather than following individual initiatives. But this is perhaps to let ourselves off too lightly. If I know that what I am doing is having harmful consequences, then I have good reason to take avoiding action, even if no one else follows my example and it consequently has no appreciable effect. It is arguable, in other words, that the current fashion for emphasizing negligibility misses the moral point, and that we need to face the fact that each one of us is responsible for doing harm, some of which could easily have been avoided.

We could go further, as Deborah Coen does in Chapter 6, and argue that the phenomenon of climate change is imposing a new understanding of responsibility itself. When John Passmore published his classic book, *Man's Responsibility for Nature* in 1974, his title referred exclusively to our moral responsibility for ensuring that the world of nature was not further polluted and debased.[19] Nowadays, by contrast, we stand not merely in a

---

[17] J. H. Liu and C. G. Sibley, 'Hope for the Future? Understanding Self-Sacrifice among Young Citizens of the World in the Face of Global Warming', *Analyses of Social Issues and Public Policy* 12 (2012), 190–203.

[18] J. S. Mill, *On Liberty*, ed. Stefan Collini (Cambridge: Cambridge University Press, 1989), 13.

[19] For my own attempt to assess Passmore's contribution, see Q. Skinner, 'Reasonable Prospects', *Times Literary Supplement* (14 June 1974), 638–639.

moral but a causal relationship to many events that, as recently as a generation ago, would have been classified as wholly natural occurrences. Consider the case of hurricanes. With the rise of surface sea temperatures, more energy is being stored in the oceans that, in storm conditions, gives rise to higher winds. But surface temperatures are rising in part because of the increased storage of carbon dioxide, and this increased storage is in part the result of human activity. We cannot evade the conclusion that we are in part causally responsible, and hence in part to blame, for the harm that hurricanes cause. The onset of climate change has forced us to reconsider the very category of the natural by contrast with the man-made.

To say that each of us bears some responsibility is not to imply that we can hope to resolve our environmental problems at the level of individual action by bringing about a change of heart. One reason is that too many people, at least at the present time, seem unwilling to acknowledge the threats we face. But the main reason is that, even if each of us were to do as much as possible on our own account, this would still leave us with the levels of industrial and agricultural pollution that are currently doing most of the damage and need above all to be curbed.

This in turn is to admit that, if our problems are to be adequately addressed, any action will have to take the form of massive coercive interference by international agencies and individual states. The chapters in this volume by Deborah Coen and by John O'Neill and Thomas Uebel unambiguously and depressingly spell out the politics that will inevitably be involved. O'Neill and Uebel raise some particularly cogent doubts about the assumption of equality of competence built into Habermas's influential model of communicative rationality. We cannot expect the decisions that need to be made about climate change to be democratically taken. They will be based on the expert findings of climate scientists, and we shall be asked to act on their assessment of the risks. Nor will it be possible for the resulting policies to be democratically implemented. The sometimes hectoring interventions of climate scientists have already caused widespread resentment, further fuelled by populist demagogues who control much of our free (that is, capitalist rather than state-owned) newspapers and other media, in consequence of which there is little prospect that the necessary policies will be willingly embraced.

Does this mean that democratic politics will become discredited? Or that the final act of democratic politics may be to refuse to implement changes that have become indispensable? If one reflects on how the debate is currently being conducted in the media and the political arena, the latter alternative begins to look a genuine and terrifying possibility. Perhaps the only circumstances in which we shall eventually do what

230   *Quentin Skinner*

needs to be done is when we are struck by some enormous catastrophe that can unambiguously be attributed to climate change. If and when this happens, then surely everyone will agree to do what rationality demands should be done. But by then it will probably be too late. The more one contemplates the disjunction between what is scientifically necessary and what is politically possible, the more it seems hard to end on anything but a deeply pessimistic note.

Index

Adolf Hitler: My Part in his Downfall
    (Milligan) 198
Adorno, Theodor 137, 146, 151, 154–155
agency
    and democracy 197
    failure of, and fatalism 203–204
    of nature and non-humans 9
agriculture
    improvement of 79–80
    and soil formation theories 76, 80–82
alchemy, and modern science 24
Althusius, Johannes 27
altruism 196–197
animal rights 26–27
    in Catholic scholastic law 33–34
    Hobbes on 35–36
    in natural law 30–33
Anthropocene 5, 90–91
anti-fatalism 209, 211–212, 215, 219
    in environmental politics 210, 215–216,
    218–220
anti-statism, environmentalist 5
anxieties
    and depression 208
    environmental 4–5, 9, 131–132
    see also fear
apocalypse
    and corruption 109
    environmental predictions of 110
Appian 39
Arnisaeus, Henning 40–41
Ascham, Antony 34
autocracy 218–219
    see also tyranny

Bacon, Francis 24, 29, 38, 223–224
Bailey, John 85–86
Barry, Brian 187
Baudrillard, Jean 115–116
Beck, Ulrich 9
Beckmann, Johann 63, 68
bees, politicality of 26

Benson, Ezra Taft 97
Bible, human dominion over nature in 33,
    37–38, 222
Blith, Walter 37–38
Boyle, Robert 224
Branner, John Casper 123
Brennan, Geoffrey 161, 171–172, 175–176
Brett, Annabel 12–13
Bridgewater treatise on the natural history
    of the Earth (Buckland) 88–89
Broome, John 175, 188–189
Brulle, Robert 177
Brundtland Commission Report (*Our
    Common Future*) 5
Bruno, Giordano 31
Büchting, Johann Jacob 59
Buckland, William 70–71, 73, 88–89,
    92–93
Buckle, Henry Thomas 126
Buddle, John 88
Budolfson, Mark 163
Buffon, George-Louis Leclerc, Comte de
    73, 92
Bull, Malcolm 15, 222–223

cameralist writings
    on government 47–52, 67–68
    on sustainability 13–14, 44–45, 47,
    52–54, 57–58, 65–69
Canguilhem, Georges 127
capability-rights 34
Carlowitz, Hans Carl von 45–46, 57, 63,
    65–66
Carnap, Rudolf 148–149
Carson, Rachel 4
Carthage, Roman conquest of 39–41
Catholic scholastic natural law, on animal
    rights 33–34
causation
    and harm 157
    Hobbes on 195
    Mill on 194–195

causation (cont.)
  and necessity 194–197
  redundant *see* redundant causation theory
Chakrabarty, Dipesh 90
Chamberlain, Edward 185
change
  political 166–167, 169
  see also climate change
Charleston earthquake (1884) 125–126
Chase, Stuart 97
China
  agreement with US on climate change
    actions (2014) 169
  one-child policy of 219
Christianity, on humans and nature 33,
    37–38, 222–223
citizenship, early modern 27
civil order 116–122
civil society 29
civitas, and *urbs* 39–41
classical texts
  on humans and nature 24–25
  on natural law 30
  on political community 39
Clerk, John 74–75
Cliff, Edward P. 109–110
climate, Hutton's theory on 78–79
climate change 1, 5, 162, 221–222
  as disaster 132
  as inconvenient truth 225–226
  individual action on 18–19, 160
    and harm principle 228
    and negligibility theory 18–19, 175,
      177–178, 181–182, 188–189,
      198–200
    rationality of 167–173, 190–191, 224
    and self-sacrifice ideal 227–228
    thresholds for 162–164
  Paris Agreement on 170
  and politics *see* environmental politics
  responsibility for 228–229
  scepticism 177
    fatalism of 216–218
  scientific knowledge on 162–163
Club of Rome, *The Limits to Growth*
    Report 4–5
coal
  reserves
    exhaustion of 53, 73–74, 82–89, 92
    geological models of 70–72
    revolutionary powers of 73
Coen, Deborah 16–17, 228
Cold War period, disaster studies in
    128–129
commonwealth concept 38, 51–52

communities
  early modern political thought on 12–13,
    26, 36–37, 41–42
  political communities 39–41
competition, perfect, rationality in
    economic models of 182–185
consequentialism 173–177
conspiracism 217
  and fatalism 217–218
cooperation, rationality of 183–186
cornucopianism
  alternatives to 15
  and economic growth 14–15, 72
corruption
  and the apocalypse 109
  and idleness 109–110
  Machiavelli on 94–95, 103–104, 109
cost–benefit analyses 161
Cotta, Heinrich 66–67
Creation story (Genesis), and geological
    time 88
critical theory 134–135, 147, 150
Crutzen, Paul 90
Cujas, Jacques 30
Culley, George 85–86
curiosity 119
Cursory Remarks on Bread and Coal
    (anonymous) 84
Cyert, Richard M. 101–102

Darwin, Erasmus 73
Daston, Lorraine 119, 121
Davis, Mike 127
Davison, Charles 125–126
Däzel, G.U. 64
De Republica (Arnisaeus) 40
*The Death of Nature: Women, Ecology and the
    Scientific Revolution* (Merchant) 24
decadence
  conservation as a form of 110
  and renewal 107–109
decision-making
  autocratic 218–219
  intergenerational 140
  rational
    in economics 139, 142, 145, 194
    see also rational choice theory
deep time 88
deforestation, in Scotland 80
deliberative democracy 153–155
democracy 219
  and agency 197
  angry side of 216–217, 219
  deliberative 153–155
  short-termism of 18

democratic fatalism 204–206, 208–209,
     213–214
depression, and anxiety 208
Dialectic of Enlightenment (Horkheimer and
     Adorno) 151
diplomacy, environmental 4
disaster science 17
  history of 116
     and Lisbon earthquake 122–128
     modern 128–132
  predictions based on 115–116, 123
disasters, fear of, and civil order 116–122
distributional justice 68
Dithmar, Christoph 58
dominium (dominion) 27–28
  in Catholic scholastic law 33–34
  Hobbes on 35
  of humans over nature 33, 35–39, 41,
     222
double time 110
Douglas, Mary 131
Downs, A. 194, 197

Earth Day (1970) 4
Earthquake of Charleston (1884) 125–126
Earthquake of Lisbon (1755) 122–128
East Anglia, floods in 77
Eclipse of Reason (Horkheimer) 151–152
ecology 46
  economic 141–142, 145–146
  political 134, 155–156
     of Frankfurt School 133, 146–147,
        152–154
     of Vienna Circle/physicalists 133
economic ecology 141–142, 145–146
economic growth
  alternatives to 15
  and cornucopianism 14–15, 72
  criticism of 14
economic planning, science-based 143
economics
  cooperation incentives in 183–186
  perfect competition models in 182–185
  political 60–61, 93
  rational decision-making in 139, 142,
     145, 194
economy
  slack/idleness in 99–101
  socialist 138–140
     calculation debates on 138–141
Edgeworth, Francis Ysidro 183–184
Edington, Robert 86
Elements of Agriculture (Hutton) 79–83
Elyot, Thomas 226–227
Emerson, Ralph Waldo 6

emissions reduction, individual 18, 160
  effectiveness of 168
  and negligibility theory 18–19, 175
  and rational choice theory 171–172
emotions 130
  see also fear
empiricism, logical 145, 148
England *see* Great Britain
Enlightenment/early modern science
     13–14, 44, 58–59, 64
  of coal exhaustion 82–86, 92
  geological time conceptions of 74–76,
     83–84, 91–93
  and security 121
  of soil fertility 73, 80–82, 91–92
environment 3–4
  anxieties about 4–5, 9, 131–132
  and industrialism 43
  scientific knowledge of 131, 223–224
environmental history 2–3, 6–7
environmental political thought *see* political
     thought
environmental politics 3–4, 7–10, 169
  fatalism in 19, 202, 204, 209–210, 220,
     225
     anti-fatalism 210, 215–216, 218–220
     of climate change scepticism 17,
        216–218
     optimistic fatalism 217–218, 225–226
  and fear 131–132
  and history of political thought 19–20
  necessity of 200, 229–230
  science scepticism and science dependency
     in 16–18, 154–156, 229
environmentalism
  anti-statism in 5
  contemporary 5
  democratic scepticism of 16
  democratic 17
  and ethics 6–8
  and religion 110
  and resource use 94
     slack as useful concept in 102,
        109–111
  and science 133–134
  in United States 95–97
ethical consequentialism 173–177
ethics, environmental 6–8
  see also morality
expert knowledge *see* science/scientific
     knowledge
expressive rationality theory 182
  on individual climate change action
     171–173, 190–191
  on voting 171

families 27–28
famine
    causes of 53–54
    fear of 53
    studies of 127
fatalism
    and conspiracism 217–218
    democratic 204–206, 208–209, 213–214
    in environmental politics 19, 202, 204,
        209–210, 220, 225
    of climate change scepticism 216–218
    history of political thought on 202–204
        Hayek 210–215, 225
        Tocqueville 204–209, 211–214, 218
    and pessimism 202–203
    and politics 202–203, 209, 211–212,
        217–218
    see also anti-fatalism; optimistic fatalism
Faust, Drew 158, 178
fear
    environmental 131–132
    politics of 116–122
    and science/scientific knowledge
        119–120, 124–127, 129–130,
        132
    see also anxieties
fertility, of soil 45, 60, 73, 80–82, 91–92
floods, in East Anglia 77
Florence 108
Forest of Dean geological model (Sopwith)
    70–72
forestry
    management of, in Germany 56–59,
        62–63, 66–68
    scientific 46–47, 63–65
    see also deforestation
fossil fuels, Victorian views of 73
Foucault, Michel 29, 57
Frankfurt School
    political ecology of 133, 146–147, 152–154
    science/reason criticism of 134–135, 137,
        151–153
    and Vienna Circle 135–137
free riding problem 158, 176, 191, 201
Free Riding (Tuck) 180
future
    early modern thought on 13
    faith/trust in 212–213, 215
    predictions of, and scientific expertise 17

Galen 193
Gamble, Andrew 203–204
The General View of the Agriculture of the
        County of Northumberland (Bailey
        and Culley) 85–86

Genesis 33
    Creation story in, and geological time
        88
Gentili, Alberico 31–33, 40–41
geological models, of Sopwith 70–72
geological time 73–76, 83–84, 91–93
geology, and political economy 93
Geology and Mineralogy considered with
        reference to Natural Theology
        (Buckland) 88–89
Germany
    early modern political thought in
        (cameralist)
        on government role 47–52, 67–68
        on sustainability 13–14, 44–45, 47,
            52–54, 57–58, 65–69
    forestry management/scientific forestry in
        46–47, 56–59, 62–68
Giddens, Anthony 9
Glen Tilt (Scotland), Hutton's geological
        explorations of 74–76
global justice 8–9
    and environmental issues 9–10
global warming see climate change
God's will/purpose
    of human conservation of nature
        222–223
    of human dominion over nature/animals
        33, 37–38, 222
Goldman, Alvin 191
Goodin, Bob 196–197
government
    happiness of people as goal of 50–51, 58
    role of
        early modern political thought on 44,
            47–52, 67–68
        in environmental issues 67–68, 81
    see also states
Great Britain
    coal resources of 70–72, 82–86
    farming systems in 38
    political economists in 60–61
Grotius, Hugo 30–31

Habermas, Jürgen 147, 152–153
    on deliberative democracy 153–154
Haeckel, Ernst 46
happiness of people, as goal of government
        50–51, 58
Hardin, R. 159, 166
harm
    and causation 157
    and climate change 228
Hartig, Georg 55
Hausväterliteratur 58–59

Hayek, Friedrich 17, 137, 210–215, 225
  and Neurath 142–146
hazard 132
Hines, Gregory L. 95, 98–99, 102
Hirschman, Albert O. 94, 102–109
history
  of disaster science 116
  and Lisbon earthquake 122–128
  modern 128–132
  environmental 2–3, 6–7
  natural, of soil 73–82
  of political thought
    environmental 1–3, 10–12
    and environmental politics 19–20
    on fatalism 202–204
      Hayek 210–215, 225
      Tocqueville 204–209, 211–214, 218
  of rationality 185–186
  self-sacrifice in 226–227
  transitions in 107–108
History of Rome: The Punic Wars (Appian) 39
Hobbes, Thomas 17, 28
  on animals-humans divide 35–36
  on causation 195
  on fear of disasters 116–118
  on nature 31
  on science/scientific knowledge
    fear as stimulus for 119–120
    and politics 117–122
Horkheimer, Max 134–135, 146, 152, 154–155
  and Neurath 135–137, 147–152
humans
  and animal rights
    in Catholic scholastic law 33–34
    Hobbes on 35–36
    in natural law 32–33
  decentering of 9
  and disasters 128–129
  and nature 12
    Christian ideas on 33, 37–38, 222–223
    classic ideas on 24–25
    early modern political thought on 12–13, 23–25, 29, 36–42, 223–224
  well-being of, measurement of 138, 141–142
Hume, David 184
Hutt, William 98–100
Hutton, James 73–83, 91–92
  Williams' criticism of 82–84

identity, and individual action 177
idleness
  Machiavelli on 103–108

productiveness of 98
pseudo 99–100
of resources 15, 94–95
  as corruption/decadence 109–110
  economic value of 99–100
  environmental benefits of 95, 97–100, 110
  myth of 96–97
  see also slack
Illustrious controversies (Vázquez) 36–37
imperceptibility see negligibility
individual action
  on climate change 18–19, 160
  and harm principle 228
  and negligibility theory 18–19, 175, 177–178, 181–182, 188–189, 198–200
  rationality of 167–173, 190–191, 224
  and self-sacrifice ideal 227–228
  thresholds for 162–164
  and identity 177
  and negligibility theory 160, 182–183, 188–189
  political 160
  thresholds for 162–164
industrialism, environmental problems associated with 43
iniura 32–33, 35
instrumental rationality 161, 164, 168, 180, 182, 226
  and moral rationality 200–201
  and selfless behaviour 186–187
  in voting processes 164–165, 191
intergenerational decision-making 140
intergenerational justice 8–9
  early modern thought on 13
  and environmental issues 9–10
'Inventory of the Standard of Living' (Neurath) 138, 145–146
IPCC, on climate change 162–163
Ireland, Land League in 183
ius naturale 30

Jamieson, Dale 176
Joachim of Fiore 107–108, 110
Johnson, Fredrik Albritton 14–15
Jowett, William 84
Justi, Johann Heinrich von 53, 55, 61–62, 66
justice
  distributional 68
  intergenerational 8–9
    early modern thought on 13
    and environmental issues 9–10

Kagan, Shelly 174–175
Kant, Immanuel 122
Kapp, K. 141–142
Katrina hurricane, political implications of 118–119
Kermode, Frank 107
knowledge
    complete, illusion of 144–145
    local 144
        use in scientific forestry of 64–65
    see also science/scientific knowledge
Krutilla, John 99–100

land
    human ownership of 38–39
    use of, early modern thought on 63
Lane, Melissa 18–19, 180, 224, 226
    on instrumental rationality 182, 190–191
    on negligibility theory 187–189, 199–200
'The Latest Attack on Metaphysics' (Horkheimer) 147–148
Latour, B. 123–124
Lazarsfeld, Paul Felix 137
Leibniz, Gottfried Wilhelm 120
Lenin, V.I. 206
Leopold, Aldo 97–98
Leviathan (Hobbes) 35
Liebig, Justus von 45
The Limits to Growth (Club of Rome Report) 4–5
Linnaeus, Carolus 78
Lipsius, James 29
Lisbon earthquake (1755) 122–128
living, standard of 138
local knowledge 144
    use in scientific forestry of 64–65
Locke, John 37
logical empiricism 145, 148
London, Great Fire and Plague in (1660s) 118
Luhmann, Nikolas 131–132

McAdie, Alexander 124–125
Machiavelli, Niccolò
    on corruption 94–95, 103–104, 109
    on idleness 103–108
Macnab, Henry Grey 84–85
majoritarian politics 213–214, 216–217
Malthus, R.T. 53
Man and Society in Disaster (Disaster Research Group Report 1962) 128–131
mandate theory
    on climate change action 167–168
    on voting 165–166

Man's Responsibility for Nature (Passmore) 228
March, James G. 101–102
Marcuse, Herbert 146–147, 152
materialism 149
Medicus, Friedrich Casimir 62
Menand, Louis 208
mercantilism, political economic criticism of 60–61
Merchant, Carolyn 24, 41
Michaelis, Loralea 120–121
Mill, John Stuart 61, 194–195, 207–209, 228
Milligan, Spike 198
Mills, C. Wright 217–218
Mises, Ludwig von 139–140
Mitchell, Timothy 72
modernity
    early see Enlightenment/early modern science
    science/expert knowledge in 123–124
        disaster science 128–132
        distrust of 16, 216–217
    sustainability concerns in 43–44
Molina, Luis de 33–34, 39
Mont Pelerin Society 211–212
morality
    and rationality 200–201, 228
    of selfless behaviour 186–187
    see also ethics
More, Thomas 38
Moser, Wilhelm 55, 64
Muir, John 95–96, 222–223
'myth of idle resources' 96–97

The Natural History of the Mineral Kingdom (Williams) 82
natural law 30–33
    Catholic scholastic 33–34
    Notdurft (necessary use) concept in 52
nature
    agency of 9
    Hobbes on 31
    and humans 12
        Christian ideas on 33, 37–38, 222–223
        classic ideas on 24–25
        early modern political thought on 12–13, 23–25, 29, 223–224
        protection/conservation of 12, 110, 222–223
    and science 152
necessity
    of environmental politics 200, 229–230
    and rationality 194–197

negligibility theory 158–159, 161, 180–181, 186
  criticism of 159–160, 178–179, 187–189, 198
  and individual action 160, 182–183, 188–189
    climate change 18–19, 175, 177–178, 181–182, 188–189, 198–200
    voting 164–166, 188–189
Neurath, Otto 17–18, 133, 135, 138–142, 155
  and Hayek 142–146
  and Horkheimer 135–137, 147–152
Newcastle, coal reserves 85–86
NGOs, climate change action by 18
non-contingency principle 176
non-humans, agency of 9
Notdurft (necessary use) 52
nuclear war, studies on human behaviour in case of 128–129
Nussbaum, Martha 34, 125

obligations to posterity 67–68
Olson, Mancur 157–158, 182–183, 186, 199
O'Neill, John 17–18, 229
optimism
  about environmental issues 43
  of Hayek 210–215
  rationality of 212–213
optimistic fatalism 203–204, 206–207
  in environmental politics 217–218, 225–226
organizational slack 101–102
Our Common Future (UN Brundtland Commission Report) 5
overpopulation, early modern lack of concern about 53–54, 62

Pacala, Stephen 163
pain, experiencing of 181
Parfit, Derek 174–175, 181, 188–189
Paris Agreement on Climate Change 170
Park, Katherine 24, 119
Passmore, John 228
patria 40–41
patriarchal thought 28
Peel, Sir Robert 87–88
perfect competition models, rationality in 182–185
pessimism, and fatalism 202–203
Pettit, Philip 175–176
Petty, William 53, 61
Pfeiffer, Johann Friedrich von 48–51, 53–54, 61

Pfeil, Wilhelm 64–65
philosophy, and science 149–150
physicalism 133, 142–144
Pinchot, Gifford 96, 109–110
Pirillo, Diego 31
pivot theory 165, 188–189
  criticism of 189–190
plantations, forestry in style of 63
Plato 178
Pocock, J.G.A. 108–109
political action/activism 18–19, 160
political communities 39–41
political ecology 134, 155–156
  of Frankfurt School 133, 146–147, 152–154
  of Vienna Circle/physicalists 133
political economy
  and geology 93
  and mercantilism 60–61
political theory, environmental 7–10
political thought 19–20, 28
  environmental 1–3, 10–12
    on animals and human society 26–27, 30–36
    on government role 44, 47–52
    on nature and humans 12–13, 23–25, 29, 36–42, 223–224
    on sustainability 13–14, 44–45, 47, 52–54, 57–58, 65–69
  on fatalism 202–204
    Hayek 210–215
    Tocqueville 204–209, 211–214, 218
  on government role 44, 47–52, 67–68
politicality, of humans 26
politics
  American 206
  autocratic 218–219
  change/uncertainty in 166–167, 169
  deliberative 153–155
  environmental 3–4, 7–10, 169
    fatalism in 19, 202, 204, 209–210, 215–216, 220, 225
      anti-fatalism 210, 215–216, 218–220
      of climate change scepticism 17, 216–218
      optimistic fatalism 217–218, 225–226
    and fear 131–132
    and history of political thought 19–20
    necessity of 200, 229–230
    science scepticism and science dependency in 16–18, 154–156, 229

politics (cont.)
  and fatalism 202–203, 209, 211–212, 217–218
  of fear 116–122
  majoritarian 213–214, 216–217
  and science 15, 17–18, 123–124, 155–156
    Frankfurt School on 154
    Hobbes on 117–122
  technocratic 154–155
    criticism of 137, 147–148
  virtue in 58
Popper, Karl 145
Popplow, Marcus 59
populism 213–215
positivism 154–155
  criticism of 137, 147–148
posterity, obligations to 67–68
predictions
  of disasters 115–116, 123
  of environmental apocalypse 110
  of future, and scientific expertise 17
progress see technological progress
property 27–28
  and human relations with land 38–39
pseudo-idleness 99–100
pseudo-rationalism 141, 144–145
Putin, Vladimir 177

rational choice theory 139, 142, 145
  on individual climate change action 167–168, 171–173, 190–191, 198–199, 224
  on voting 164–171, 191–194, 197
The Rational Optimist (Ridley) 210–211, 213
rationality/reason 185–186
  consequentialist approaches to 173–177
  in economics 139, 142, 145, 194
    and cooperation 183–186
    and perfect competition models 182–185
  Frankfurt School on 134–135, 137, 151–153
  instrumental 161, 164–165, 168, 180, 182, 226
    and selfless behaviour 186–187
    in voting processes 164–165, 191
  moral 200–201, 228
  and natural disasters 126
  and necessity 194–197
  of optimism 212–213
  pseudo 141, 144–145
  super/Cartesian 143
  Weber on 139

'reason of state' discourse 28–29
reckless fatalism 206–207
redundant causation theory 168, 191–194
  on individual climate change action 169–171
  on voting 168–170, 192–194
religion
  and democratic fatalism 205–206
  and disaster science 123
  and environmentalism 110
  see also Christianity
renewal, and decadence 107–109
Republic (Plato) 178
resources
  exhaustion of 52–54, 82–86, 92
  idleness/non-use of 15, 94–95
    as decadence/corruption 109–110
    economic value of 99–100
    environmental benefits of 95, 97–100, 110
    myth of 96–97
    see also slack
  use of
    cameralist thought on 61–62
    and environmentalism 94
    political economists on 60–61
responsibility, environmental 228–229
  of states 11, 13
Ricardo, D. 60–61
Ridley, Matt 210–211, 213, 219
rights of animals 26–27
  in Catholic scholastic law 33–34
  Hobbes on 35–36
  in natural law 30–33
'ring of Gyges' story 178
Risk and Culture: An Essay on the Selection of Technological and Environmental Dangers (Douglas and Wildavsky) 131
risks/risk society 9, 131
Robertson, William 78
Robin, Corey 117–118
Rößig, Karl Gottlieb 66
Rousseau, Jean-Jacques 122, 178–179
Royal Society of Edinburgh 77–78
Rudwick, Martin 92
Runciman, David 19, 225–226

Salas, Juan de 34
Savonarola, Girolamo 108
Schaffer, Simon 118–119
Schultz, T.W. 100
Schumpeter, Joseph 111
science/scientific knowledge
  and alchemy 24

on climate change 162–163
of disasters
    history of 116, 122–128
    modern 128–132
    predictions of 115–116, 123
distrust of 16, 216–217
    and fatalism 216–217
economic planning based on 143
of Enlightenment/early modern period
        13–14, 44, 58–59, 64, 223–224
    on coal exhaustion 82–86, 92
    geological time conceptions 74–76,
        83–84, 91–93
    and security 121
    on soil fertility 73, 80–82, 91–92
and environmentalism 133–134
and fear 119–120, 124–127, 129–132
Frankfurt School criticism of 151–153
and nature 152
and philosophy 149–150
and politics 15–17, 123–124, 155–156
    environmental 16–18, 154–156,
        229
    Frankfurt School on 154
    Hobbes on 117–122
self-reflexivity of 148–150, 155
scientism, Hayek's criticism of 142–144
Scotland
    deforestation in 80
    Hutton's geological explorations of
        74–76
Scrope, George Poulett 87
Seckendorff, Ludwig Veit von 49, 52–53,
        55, 62
Second Treatise of Government (Locke)
        37
seismology, Lisbon earthquake as initiator
        of 122–128
self-preservation rights 30–31, 34
self-sacrifice 226–227
    in climate change action 227–228
selfless behaviour, and instrumental
        rationality 186–187
Shapin, Steven 118–119
Sidgwick, Henry 184–185
Silent Spring (Carson) 4
Sinnott-Armstrong, Walter 157
slack 15, 94, 100, 102–109
    economic 101
    environmentalist uses of 102, 109–111
    organizational 101–102
slaves, society/community membership of
        29–30
Smith, Adam 60, 83
    and Hutton 76–78, 80–81, 91–92

social sciences
    of disasters 128–132
    see also Frankfurt School
socialist economy 138–140
    calculation debates on 138–141
societies, human 26
    and animal rights 26–27, 30–36
    and slaves 29–30
soil fertility 45, 60
    Enlightenment conceptions of 73, 80–82,
        91–92
Sonnenfels, J. von 50–51
Sopwith, Thomas 70–72, 88–89, 92–93
Sorites paradox 163, 180–181, 189–190,
        193
Sorokin, Pitirim 130
sovereignty 29
Sprengel, Carl 45
standard of living, measurement of 138
Standish, Arthur 68
states
    environmental responsibilities of 11, 13
    legitimacy crises of, and
        environmentalism 5
    see also government
steam technology, coal needed for 73
Stockholm Conference on the Human
        Environment (United Nations) 4
Stoermer, Eugene 90
sustainability 5, 45–46
    early modern political thought on 13–14,
        44–45, 47, 52–54, 57–58, 65–69
    modern concerns about 43–44
    in pre-industrial age 43
    in wood supplies 55–56
symbiosis, human relations based on 27

technocratic politics 154–155
    criticism of 137, 147–148
technological progress
    belief in 207
    and environmental politics 210
The Theory of the Earth (Hutton) 74, 83
The Theory of Idle Resources (Hutt) 98
The Theory of Monopolistic Competition
        (Chamberlain) 185
Thompson, Charles Poulett 87
Thoreau, Henry David 6
thresholds
    for individual action 162–164
    unknowable 189–190
time
    deep 88
    double 110
    geological 73–76, 83–84, 91–93

Tocqueville, Alexis de 204–209, 211–214, 218
trade unionism, rationality of 183–184
A Treatise of Human Nature 184
Tribe, Keith 47
Tuck, Richard 18–19, 157–158, 224, 226, 228
  on instrumentality 164, 168, 180
  on politics 167
  on redundant causation theory 169–170
tyranny 36–37
  of the majority 213–214
  see also autocracy

Uebel, Thomas 17–18, 229
Ulpian 30
uncertainty, political 166–167, 169
unfairness
  and free riding problem 201
  and voluntary action 159
United Nations
  Brundtland Commission Report 5
  Paris Agreement on Climate Change 170
  Stockholm Conference on the Human Environment 4
United States
  agreement with China on climate change actions (2014) 169
  democracy/democratic beliefs in 204–206
  environmentalism in 95–97
urbs, and *civitas* 39–41
Utopia (More) 38

Vázquez de Menchaca, Fernando 36–37
Vend (Newcastle area coalmine owners) 85–86
Venice, concerns about wood supply in 56

Vienna Circle 135, 148
  and Frankfurt School 135–137
  political ecology of 133
  and technocratic politics 154–155
violations of rights, by humans against animals 32–33
virtue, in politics 58
voluntary action, and unfairness 159
voting
  negligibility theory applied to 164–166, 188–189
  rational choice theories on 164–171, 191–194, 197
  thresholds for 162

Wakefield, André 49
Waldron, Jeremy 197
Warde, Paul 13–14
Wars of the Romans (Gentili) 40–41
Watkins, J.W.N. 119–120
The Wealth of Nations (Smith) 80–81, 83
Weber, Max 139
well-being, measurement of 138, 141–142
Wildavsky, Aaron 131
wilderness, economic value of 98–99
Williams, John 82–86
Williamson, Timothy 189
Winstanley, Gerrard 38–39
Wither, George 37–38
Wolff, Christian 58
wood supplies 53–55, 80
  sustainable 55–56
Wrigley, E.A. 60
Wylam, William 89

Yeats, W.B. 107

Zalasiewicz, Jan 90